The Ultimate Ubuntu Handbook

A complete guide to Ubuntu 24.04, from installation
to advanced security and development

Ken VanDine

\<packt\>

The Ultimate Ubuntu Handbook

Portfolio Director: Kartikey Pandey
Relationship Lead: Reshma Raman
Project Manager: Sonam Pandey
Content Engineer: Arun Nadar
Technical Editor: Simran Ali
Copy Editor: Safis Editing
Indexer: Rekha Nair
Proofreader: Arun Nadar
Production Designer: Aparna Bhagat
Growth Lead: Shreyans Singh

First published: August 2025

Production reference: 1040725

Published by Packt Publishing Ltd.
Grosvenor House
11 St Paul's Square
Birmingham
B3 1RB, UK.

ISBN 978-1-83546-520-2

www.packtpub.com

This book is dedicated to two groups of people who have inspired and supported me throughout this journey.

Firstly, to the Ubuntu community – a vibrant and passionate group of individuals who embody the spirit of collaboration, sharing, and mutual support. Your dedication to creating a free and open source operating system that is accessible to all is a testament to the power of community and the human spirit. Your enthusiasm, expertise, and generosity have inspired me to share my knowledge and experience with others, and I am grateful to be a part of this community.

And finally, to my family – who have patiently endured the long hours, late nights, and countless moments of distraction as I worked on this book. Your love, support, and understanding have meant the world to me, and I am grateful for the sacrifices you have made to allow me to pursue my passion for open source and sharing my knowledge of Ubuntu. Thank you for being my rock, my motivation, and my inspiration. I hope that this book will make you proud and that it will be a small token of my appreciation for all that you do for me.

– Ken VanDine

Foreword

I've known Ken since our paths first crossed in the Ubuntu Community back in 2006, and we later worked together for nine years at Canonical. Throughout all those years, Ken has been an enthusiastic, professional, and fun expert to be around. Whether on calls with important partners, helping organize community events, or in fancy dress at an Ubuntu Developer Summit wrap party, Ken is the best sidekick you could ask for.

There are few people, inside or outside of Canonical, who know more about how to contribute to, configure, manage, and deploy Ubuntu than Ken. His expertise is both deep and broad, forged through Ubuntu's entire history, from the GNOME 2 desktop era, through the Unity years, and the evolution into the modern, popular developer desktop.

While Ken tells engaging stories over coffee or a beer, he excels at knuckling down and getting stuff done. The work he's put into this book is stellar. As an Ubuntu insider for coming on two decades, he is perfectly placed to convey every chapter with the confidence and expertise needed by software developers, DevOps engineers, hobbyists, and even technology veterans.

This book is anchored to Ubuntu 24.04, a **Long Term Support (LTS)** release, which makes it a solid and long-lasting investment. These releases are stable platforms for development and production workloads for years to come. The topics are well-explained, taking readers on a journey from the absolute basics to the perfect developer workstation setup and beyond. It's a real "zero-to-hero" publication.

The *Ultimate Ubuntu Handbook* is an essential resource for any Windows refugee or Apple refusenik, and for happy, willing converts, too! While the Linux desktop's market share may be small, the opportunity to spread Ken's wealth of knowledge to new users is immense.

As I experienced firsthand at Canonical, you can achieve great things with Ken's knowledge by your side. Readers will see immerse value in his expertise and the way he shares it with the world. I hope you enjoy reading this book as much as I have enjoyed working with Ken over the years.

-- *Alan Pope, Developer Advocate, and Ubuntu Community Member*

Contributors

About the author

Ken VanDine found his way into open source by following his innate curiosity about how things worked. Unable to inspect and modify the code of proprietary operating systems, Ken discovered Linux and open source via Slackware in 1993. Soon, he was responsible for **High-Performance Computing** (**HPC**) at a large pharmaceutical company, architecting a globally distributed Linux cluster and building purpose-built Linux systems, which led to future roles in open source, solving software distribution and optimization. Ken has over 30 years of experience building Linux distributions, with over 16 years working at Canonical on Ubuntu. During his career at Canonical, his focus has been on GNOME, Ubuntu Desktop, and Snap integration. When Ken is not working, he enjoys volunteering with Kramden Institute, a local non-profit that aims to bridge the digital divide, coaching youth baseball, and spending time with his family.

About the reviewers

Robert Ancell has been involved in the open source ecosystem for more than 20 years, both for his own interests and professionally as a developer for Canonical, the company behind Ubuntu. When not behind a screen, he enjoys cycling with his family in New Zealand.

Thijs van de Kamp is the Vice President of Network Connectivity Partnerships at Compudopt, a national nonprofit expanding technology access and education in under-resourced communities. He joined the organization in 2023 as Director of Technical Operations, where he improved internal systems and processes in collaboration with Canonical before being promoted to lead Compudopt's connectivity division. Since then, he has overseen the launch of broadband initiatives—including CBRS, **Fiber to the Home (FTTH)**, and 5G home internet. Thijs manages a national team under the COO and has led efforts in network design, device procurement, and system automation.

I'd like to sincerely thank Ken VanDine for his generous guidance and support across multiple projects. His willingness to share his insight and offer assistance whenever needed has been instrumental in my Linux education journey. Ken's passion for our mission shines through in everything he does, and his contributions have made a lasting impact.

Table of Contents

Part IV: Ubuntu, the Ultimate Development Platform   243

Preface

Welcome to the world of Ubuntu, a powerful and user-friendly operating system that has revolutionized the way we interact with our computers. As one of the most popular Linux distributions, Ubuntu has gained a reputation for its ease of use, flexibility, and commitment to community-driven development.

In this book, we will take you on a journey through the world of Ubuntu, exploring its features, capabilities, and applications. Whether you are a seasoned Linux user or just starting out, this book is designed to provide you with a comprehensive guide to getting the most out of your Ubuntu experience.

From installing and configuring your system to exploring the latest features and applications, we will cover it all. You will learn how to navigate the Ubuntu Desktop interface, manage your files and folders, and customize your desktop to suit your needs. We will also delve into the world of Ubuntu's software repositories, showing you how to find, install, and manage the thousands of free and open source applications available.

But Ubuntu is not just about technology – it's also about the community that drives it. In this book, we will introduce you to the Ubuntu philosophy and the values that underpin the project, including the importance of freedom, collaboration, and mutual support. You will learn how to get involved in the Ubuntu community, contribute to the project, and connect with other users and developers from around the world.

Throughout this book, we will use a combination of step-by-step tutorials, screenshots, and real-world examples to illustrate the concepts and techniques you need to know about to master Ubuntu. Whether you are a student, a professional, or simply a curious user, this book is designed to be your companion and guide as you explore the exciting world of Ubuntu.

So, let's get started on this journey together! With this book, you will be able to unlock the full potential of Ubuntu and discover a whole new world of computing possibilities.

Who this book is for

This book caters to a diverse audience, including software engineers (embedded, frontend, backend, full stack), machine learning/data science professionals, DevOps engineers, systems administrators, and technology enthusiasts (hobbyists). Whether you're eager to delve into Linux for the first time or seek to deepen your understanding of Ubuntu, this guide is designed to empower you. While a basic knowledge of operating systems is beneficial, no prior experience with Linux is required.

What this book covers

Chapter 1, Introduction to Ubuntu, explains what Ubuntu is, its history, and key concepts of Ubuntu and the open source ecosystem.

Chapter 2, What's New in Ubuntu 24.04?, walks you through changes in Ubuntu 24.04 since the previous LTS release, 22.04.

Chapter 3, Security and Transparency – The Advantages of Open Source Software, demonstrates the advantages of open source software.

Chapter 4, Getting Started with Ubuntu: A User's Guide, guides you through the installation process, ensuring you understand the necessary fundamentals.

Chapter 5, Using Your Ubuntu Desktop, takes you on a tour of the features found in Ubuntu.

Chapter 6, Software Discovery: Finding and Installing Applications, shows you how to find and install the software you want and need to get things done.

Chapter 7, Software Updates: Enhancing Security and Stability, demonstrates the importance of keeping your software updated.

Chapter 8, Getting Help: The Ubuntu Community and Beyond, introduces you to the amazing Ubuntu community as the most powerful resource when you need help and teaches you how to best engage with the community to become part of something bigger.

Chapter 9, Ubuntu in the Enterprise and at Scale, explains features commonly required for Ubuntu to be used in an enterprise environment.

Chapter 10, Command-Line Tricks and Shortcuts: Boosting Your Efficiency, demonstrates the powerful Linux command line and shows you that it's not something to be worried about; it's not just for power users but it can boost anyone's efficiency.

Chapter 11, Introduction to Network Security, explains key concepts of network security.

Chapter 12, Understanding Firewalls, delves deeper into network security, focusing on more advanced firewall usage.

Chapter 13, Safeguarding Information with Data Encryption, introduces concepts necessary for data privacy and how to leverage encryption to keep your data safe.

Chapter 14, Ubuntu for Developers, discusses the many ways Ubuntu can be used for development.

Chapter 15, Leveraging Containers for Development, explains key concepts necessary to understand Linux containers and how to use them to improve your development workflow.

Chapter 16, Cloud-Style VMs on Your Desktop, demonstrates how you can use virtual machines to simulate a cloud-style environment for development.

Chapter 17, Kubernetes Development on Your Desktop, shows how to set up your own Kubernetes cluster on your desktop.

Chapter 18, Building Your Data Science Toolkit, explains how to simplify setting up your data science environment on Ubuntu.

Chapter 19, Embracing the Spirit of Ubuntu, wraps up with more ways to not just use Ubuntu, but become part of the Ubuntu community.

To get the most out of this book

- **Start with the basics**: If you're new to Ubuntu, begin with the introductory chapters to get a solid understanding of the operating system and its core concepts.

- **Practice as you go**: Ubuntu is a hands-on operating system, and the best way to learn is by doing. Try out the commands, tools, and techniques described in each chapter to reinforce your understanding.

- **Experiment and explore**: Don't be afraid to try new things and explore the many features and tools that Ubuntu has to offer. From customizing your desktop to experimenting with new software, the more you explore, the more you'll learn and appreciate the power and flexibility of Ubuntu.

- **Take notes and review**: As you work through the book, take notes on key concepts, commands, and techniques. Reviewing these notes regularly will help solidify your understanding and make it easier to recall important information when needed.

- **Use the book as a reference**: This book is designed to be a comprehensive guide to Ubuntu, but it's not meant to be read cover to cover in one sitting. Use it as a reference, dipping in and out of chapters as needed, to help you solve problems, answer questions, and learn new skills.

- **Join the Ubuntu community**: The Ubuntu community is vast and active, with numerous online forums, social media groups, and local meetups. Joining the community will give you access to a wealth of knowledge, support, and resources to help you learn and grow with Ubuntu.

Conventions used

There are a number of text conventions used throughout this book.

CodeInText: Indicates code words in text, database table names, folder names, filenames, file extensions, pathnames, dummy URLs, user input, and Twitter handles. For example: "If you do not know the package name, don't fret! Simply running the ubuntu-bug command without any package name will give you a window to guide you through the process."

A block of code is set as follows:

```
import torch
torch.cuda.is_available()
```

Any command-line input or output is written as follows:

```
ken@monster:~$ sudo snap install authd-msentraid
ken@monster:~$ sudo mkdir -p /etc/authd/brokers.d/
ken@monster:~$ sudo cp /snap/authd-msentraid/current/conf/authd/msentraid.
conf /etc/authd/brokers.d/
```

Bold: Indicates a new term, an important word, or words that you see on the screen. For instance, words in menus or dialog boxes appear in the text like this. For example: "To ensure security updates are installed promptly, ensure **Download and install automatically** is selected in the dropdown next to **When there are security updates**."

> Warnings or important notes appear like this.

> Tips and tricks appear like this.

Get in touch

Feedback from our readers is always welcome.

General feedback: If you have questions about any aspect of this book or have any general feedback, please email us at customercare@packt.com and mention the book's title in the subject of your message.

Errata: Although we have taken every care to ensure the accuracy of our content, mistakes do happen. If you have found a mistake in this book, we would be grateful if you reported this to us. Please visit http://www.packt.com/submit-errata, click **Submit Errata**, and fill in the form.

Piracy: If you come across any illegal copies of our works in any form on the internet, we would be grateful if you would provide us with the location address or website name. Please contact us at copyright@packt.com with a link to the material.

If you are interested in becoming an author: If there is a topic that you have expertise in and you are interested in either writing or contributing to a book, please visit http://authors.packt.com/.

Share your thoughts

Once you've read *The Ultimate Ubuntu Handbook*, we'd love to hear your thoughts! Scan the QR code below to go straight to the Amazon review page for this book and share your feedback.

https://packt.link/r/183546520X

Your review is important to us and the tech community and will help us make sure we're delivering excellent quality content.

Stay Sharp in Cloud and DevOps – Join 44,000+ Subscribers of CloudPro

CloudPro is a weekly newsletter for cloud professionals who want to stay current on the fast-evolving world of cloud computing, DevOps, and infrastructure engineering.

Every issue delivers focused, high-signal content on topics like:

- AWS, GCP & multi-cloud architecture
- Containers, Kubernetes & orchestration
- Infrastructure as Code (IaC) with Terraform, Pulumi, etc.
- Platform engineering & automation workflows
- Observability, performance tuning, and reliability best practices

Whether you're a cloud engineer, SRE, DevOps practitioner, or platform lead, CloudPro helps you stay on top of what matters, without the noise.

Scan the QR code to join for free and get weekly insights straight to your inbox:

https://packt.link/cloudpro

Download a free PDF copy of this book

Thanks for purchasing this book!

Do you like to read on the go but are unable to carry your print books everywhere?

Is your eBook purchase not compatible with the device of your choice?

Don't worry, now with every Packt book you get a DRM-free PDF version of that book at no cost.

Read anywhere, any place, on any device. Search, copy, and paste code from your favorite technical books directly into your application.

The perks don't stop there, you can get exclusive access to discounts, newsletters, and great free content in your inbox daily.

Follow these simple steps to get the benefits:

1. Scan the QR code or visit the link below:

https://packt.link/free-ebook/9781835465202

2. Submit your proof of purchase.
3. That's it! We'll send your free PDF and other benefits to your email directly.

Part 1

Getting to Know Ubuntu

In this first part of the book, you will learn about the foundational aspects of Ubuntu, exploring its latest features and highlighting the advantages of open source software. From mastering Ubuntu Desktop usage to deciphering software support lifecycles, this part lays the groundwork for a comprehensive understanding of the Ubuntu ecosystem.

This part of the book includes the following chapters:

- *Chapter 1, Introduction to Ubuntu*
- *Chapter 2, What's New in Ubuntu 24.04?*
- *Chapter 3, Security and Transparency – The Advantages of Open Source Software*
- *Chapter 4, Getting Started with Ubuntu: A User's Guide*

1

Introduction to Ubuntu

Welcome to the world of **Ubuntu**! Whether you're a first-time Ubuntu user, a first-time Linux user, or a seasoned Linux veteran, this book will serve as a primer for getting the most out of your Ubuntu experience. We'll cover many key concepts, from what a Linux distribution is to the history of Ubuntu, all the way through setting up an optimal development or data science environment on Ubuntu.

We'll start with the most basic question: what is **Linux**? Just like Windows and macOS, Linux is an operating system. Linux is the most popular platform in the world today! Android is powered by Linux, as is most of the world's cloud and web infrastructure. An operating system provides software with access to your hardware. Actually, Linux is just the core part of the operating system (called a kernel) and is surrounded by other applications and services.

However, even though the Linux kernel provides the most critical part of the operating system, access to the hardware, more is necessary for the operating system to be useful. This is where the term **distribution** comes in, which is a collection of software required to boot and use the system effectively. The concept of a Linux distribution is actually what most people think of when they think of an operating system.

Many Linux distributions are available today, each with its mission, flavor, and value proposition. Essentially, each has its own curated collection of software that improves everything from hardware support to the user experience.

In this book, we'll focus on Ubuntu, which is widely known as the most popular and user-friendly distribution today. More specifically, this book is based on Ubuntu 24.04, the **Long-Term Support (LTS)** version of Ubuntu released in April 2024.

In this chapter, we're going to cover the following main topics:

- A brief history of Ubuntu
- The Ubuntu mission – free software for everyone
- Ubuntu releases – trust through stability
- The power of community – collaboration and support

A brief history of Ubuntu

Before we get to the history of Ubuntu, let me answer one of the most common questions I hear: how do you pronounce Ubuntu? Is it You-buntu or Oo-buntu? Ubuntu is pronounced Oo-buntu.

Ubuntu's story began in 2004, conceived by South African entrepreneur and developer Mark Shuttleworth, inspired by the ideals of the African philosophy of Ubuntu, which translates to *"humanity towards others."* The phrase *"I am what I am because of who we all are"* is commonly used to describe the term Ubuntu, which for me really sums up what Ubuntu is all about!

The first version of Ubuntu, codenamed Warty Warthog, was released on October 20, 2004. The version was 4.10, which marks the 10th month of 2004:

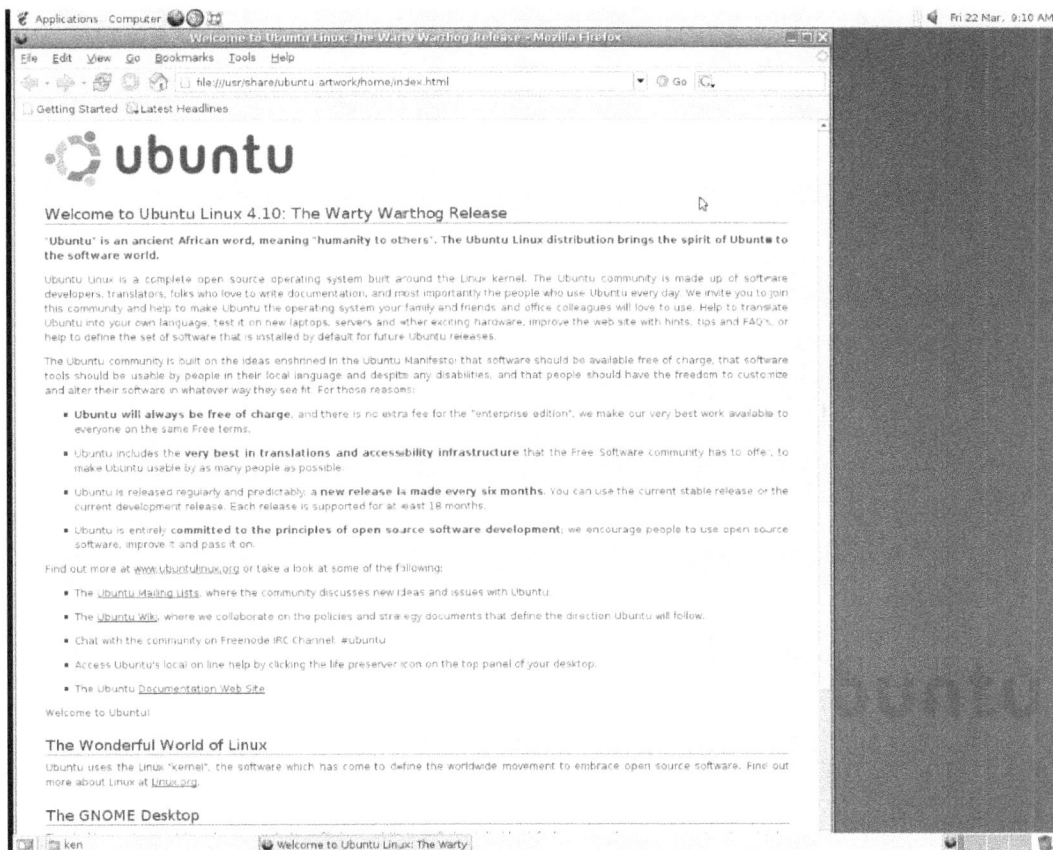

Figure 1.1 – Ubuntu Desktop Warty Warthog 4.10 user interface

A fun thing to know about Ubuntu releases is what's up with the code names. The Ubuntu code names comprise an adjective and an animal with the same first letter. Except for the first three releases, the code names are alphabetical by first letter, making them easy to distinguish. The adjective and animal chosen for the code name are based on a theme or goal for the release. You can imagine there was likely some symbolism with the Warty Warthog code name chosen for the first release as it was likely to have some warts.

Early versions of Ubuntu featured earthy brown colors throughout, and more recent releases feature a vibrant orange accent and beautiful eggplant colors.

Ubuntu has made huge strides in the past 20 years since the Warty Warthog release, with Ubuntu 24.04, Noble Numbat, the latest LTS released on April 25, 2024.

The Ubuntu mission – free software for everyone

Ubuntu's core mission revolves around the principle of free and open source software. It advocates for free access to software, along with the freedom to use, modify, and distribute. The philosophy aligns with the broader open source movement, emphasizing collaboration and community. You can learn more about the mission of Ubuntu at `https://ubuntu.com/community/ethos/mission`.

Ubuntu's values

As the Ubuntu community grows, it's important to never forget that Ubuntu embodies four key values:

- **Freedom**: Ubuntu celebrates freedom – freedom to choose, to change, to participate.
- **Reliable**: You can depend on Ubuntu. Like the people who make it, it is trustworthy and keeps its promises.
- **Precise**: Ubuntu is crisp and clean in engineering and attitude. There is beauty in the precision of the process and product.
- **Collaborative**: Working together is at the heart of Ubuntu. It is the essence of "*humanity towards others.*"

Let's drill down into these values a little more and highlight the important themes:

- **Freedom**: Freedom to do what you want with the software. People often use the term *free software*, which could mean *free as in beer* or *free as in speech*. While both are important within Ubuntu, the emphasis is on *free as in speech*. Ubuntu encourages everyone to use the software however they want, change it to suit their needs, and even distribute it to others.
- **Reliable**: For reliability, you need trust – a powerful noun here. It's important to be able to trust the software you use. That means trust in where it came from, who modified it, and the distribution channel it went through from when it was source code to the binaries you use on your system. There's another aspect of trust as well: when and how will you get critical security updates or new software versions? Ubuntu takes a great deal of pride in having a reliable release cadence, enabling users to predict when new versions will be available.

- **Precise**: Making strong, opinionated choices about what software will and will not be included in the default Ubuntu user experience. Providing the necessary user interface and tools to ensure the broadest audience can get the most out of their Ubuntu experience. This doesn't mean Ubuntu prevents you from installing other software or making different choices. Ubuntu drives users down the most probable road to success while providing flexibility and access to all the software that an advanced user might want.

- **Collaborative**: It's hard not to call out a favorite in this list of values because they are all incredibly important, but collaborative stands out here when you think back to the phrase "*I am what I am because of who we all are.*" We truly are stronger together, and the collaborative value is central to everything we do within Ubuntu. The saying "*It takes a village to raise a child*" may be a good analogy. Geographically separate teams of developers create and maintain the software found in Ubuntu – but there's more! These developers are not only geographically separate, but sometimes different companies also employ them, while some are students at different schools, and some aren't even coders. These teams of *developers* include translators, documentation authors, testers, and enthusiasts, all serving critical parts of the development process. And what's more amazing? Everyone is welcome to join in!

You can read more about the Ubuntu values at `https://design.ubuntu.com/brand`.

The Ubuntu logo is known as the *circle of friends*, three friends embracing in an unbreakable circle:

Figure 1.2 – Ubuntu logo as it appeared in Warty Warthog 4.10, October 2004

Here's a more recent version of the logo:

Figure 1.3 – Ubuntu logo as it appeared in Jammy Jellyfish 22.04, April 2022

As you can see, the *circle of friends* logo has evolved over the past two decades, but it still clearly emphasizes embracing each other.

Having learned about Ubuntu's origins, mission, values, and, most importantly, how to pronounce Ubuntu, we are ready to learn how vital Ubuntu releases are to those values.

Ubuntu releases – trust through stability

Ubuntu is trusted by millions of users worldwide due to its solid foundation, which has been built over the past two decades. It is trusted on all computing platforms, including desktops, laptops, servers, the cloud, the **Internet of Things** (**IoT**), manufacturing, and robotics.

All Ubuntu users should understand the anatomy of a Ubuntu release version. The version numbers consist of a two-digit year, a period, and a two-digit month.

Ubuntu 24.04 was released in April 2024 (see the explanation in *Figure 1.4*):

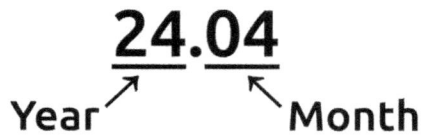

Figure 1.4 – The Ubuntu release version

Ubuntu releases occur every April and October. Releases in April of even years are LTS releases; more on that later in this chapter.

Different release channels

Ubuntu provides two release channels, more precisely, two cadences, depending on risk aversion and need:

- **LTS**: These releases focus on stability and receive security and bug fixes for five years, making them ideal for business-critical systems and users who prioritize a rock-solid system over the latest and greatest versions. For added confidence in security and compliance, Ubuntu Pro is offered as a subscription that provides support for up to 10 years.

- **Standard releases**: Released every six months, these versions offer the most recent software and support for the newest hardware. They balance stability and new features; however, their support span is shorter, lasting nine months.

As mentioned earlier, LTS releases occur on even years in April. These releases will get security and bug fixes for 5 years from release with optional support for up to 10 years with an Ubuntu Pro subscription. Between the LTS releases, there are standard releases every six months, often called **interim releases**. These releases are only supported for 9 months and are useful when you need the latest major releases of the software and don't require the trusted stability you get with the LTS release.

For example, as an LTS release, Ubuntu 24.04 will get standard support until April 2029, and with Ubuntu Pro, additional support through April 2034. However, as an interim release, Ubuntu 24.10 will get support through July 2025. For more information, see `https://ubuntu.com/about/release-cycle`.

Building trust through stability (and predictability)

There's that word *trust* again. Now that we all understand the Ubuntu release cadence and versioning scheme, let's discuss it again. Over the 20 years since the first release of Ubuntu, it's been well established that you can trust the reliability and stability of the software included in the release and the cadence to which you can expect to see new versions of Ubuntu. You can reliably predict when new major versions of Ubuntu will be released and effectively plan your journey.

Ubuntu's unwavering commitment to stability sets it apart in the ecosystem. Prioritizing a reliable and predictable foundation, Ubuntu has earned the trust of a broad and diverse user base. Focusing on stability empowers users and fosters a thriving ecosystem built around Ubuntu.

The power of community – collaboration and support

Ubuntu thrives on its strong and active community. This diverse group of users, developers, translators, and enthusiasts plays a crucial role in the operating system's success.

The community contributes via the following:

- **Development**: Programmers worldwide contribute code, fix bugs, and enhance features
- **Documentation**: Experienced users create guides, tutorials, and forum discussions to assist new users

- **Translations**: Ubuntu's broad international user base helps provide translations so that future users in their native tongues feel more welcome and can easily use their systems
- **Support**: Forums, chat services, email lists, and other means of community engagement provide a platform for users to seek help, share experiences, and learn from each other

This collaborative spirit fosters a welcoming and supportive environment for everyone interested in Ubuntu.

Summary

This chapter has provided a foundational understanding of Ubuntu's history and mission and the amazing community that powers its development. As you dive deeper into the world of Ubuntu, you'll discover a powerful, user-friendly operating system backed by a philosophy of openness and collaboration.

In *Chapter 2*, we'll get into what's new in Ubuntu 24.04. As it is an LTS, we'll cover new features since the previous 22.04 LTS.

Further reading

- **About Ubuntu**: https://ubuntu.com/about
- **Ubuntu's mission**: https://ubuntu.com/community/ethos/mission
- **Ubuntu's release cycle**: https://ubuntu.com/about/release-cycle

2

What's New in Ubuntu 24.04?

Ubuntu 24.04 is a release like no other, with significant changes ranging from a completely revamped installation to network security and data protection features necessary to make Ubuntu a viable operating system in more environments than ever.

Whether you're a veteran Ubuntu user or just starting to learn it, getting a glimpse of what to expect in the latest release is always helpful. Get ready to dive into a world of enhanced performance, security, and usability with a refreshed desktop environment, a streamlined installation process, and powerful new tools under the hood.

This chapter covers the following topics:

- A fresh look and feel – desktop environment enhancements
- Under-the-hood improvements
- Security focus – enhanced protection

A fresh look and feel – desktop environment enhancements

As a **Long-Term Support (LTS)** release, Ubuntu 24.04 is the culmination of two years of enhancements, refinements, and improvements. Of course, you can expect to see visible changes, some dramatic and many subtle. Let's take a tour through the visible changes and understand more about how these collectively come together to provide the experience you would expect from Ubuntu, and even open Ubuntu to many more audiences.

New installer

Everyone's journey with Ubuntu starts with the installation experience, which has been one of the most significant changes since 22.04. The Ubuntu desktop installer has been rewritten from the ground up since the previous LTS release, leveraging features of the **subiquity installer**. The subiquity installer has been used by Ubuntu Server since 18.04, providing a solid foundation to build a beautiful graphical installer:

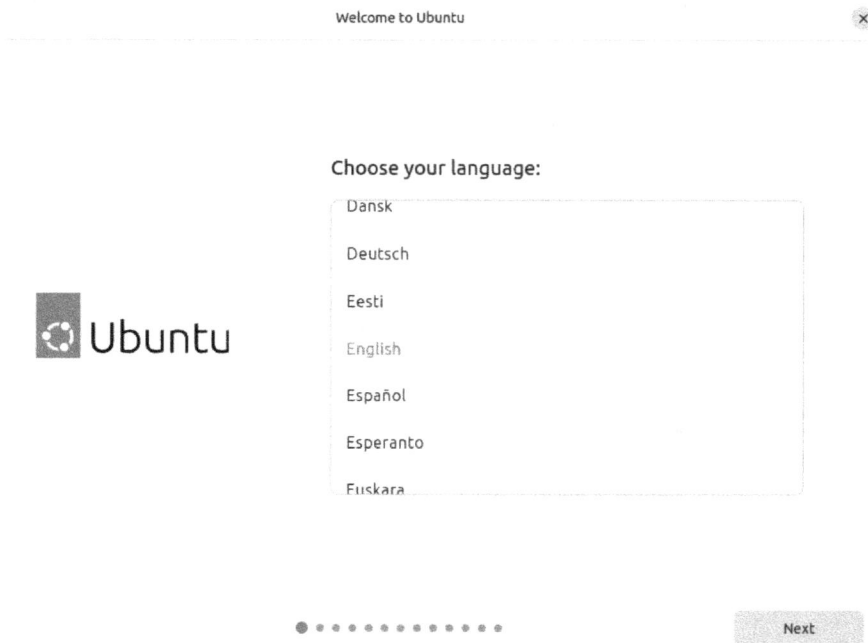

Welcome to Ubuntu   ✕

Choose your language:

Dansk

Deutsch

Eesti

English

Español

Esperanto

Euskara

● ● ● ● ● ● ● ● ● ● ● ● ●   Next

Figure 2.1 – Ubuntu Desktop installer

The new desktop installer is a graphical user interface that drives the trusted subiquity installer. This allows for more advanced installation features closely aligned with other Ubuntu products, such as Ubuntu Server and Ubuntu Core.

Highlights of the new installer

The new installer has improved accessibility options to ensure Ubuntu can be installed by anyone, regardless of ability. We can't say Ubuntu is as accessible as we would like. Still, it is an incredibly important topic within the Ubuntu community, and we will continue to strive to ensure Ubuntu is available and friendly to the broadest possible audience.

Additional **full-disk encryption** (**FDE**) options provide more options for protecting your data.

Advanced auto-installation features use a simple declarative text file (in **YAML** format) to define all aspects of the installation. This enables fully or partially automated installations, essential features for provisioning systems in a large-scale environment.

There is support for `cloud-init`, the industry-standard mechanism to initialize cloud providers and servers. A common example is automated installation with the configuration provided with `cloud-init`, further bolstering Ubuntu as a viable option for large-scale deployment.

New Ubuntu app center

An essential part of any operating system is discovering new applications necessary to get your job done on your computer and even finding applications to enhance your enjoyment. The new app center provides a beautiful, intuitive experience for discovering and installing apps you may enjoy. You can read about these apps, view screenshots and ratings, and rate software yourself:

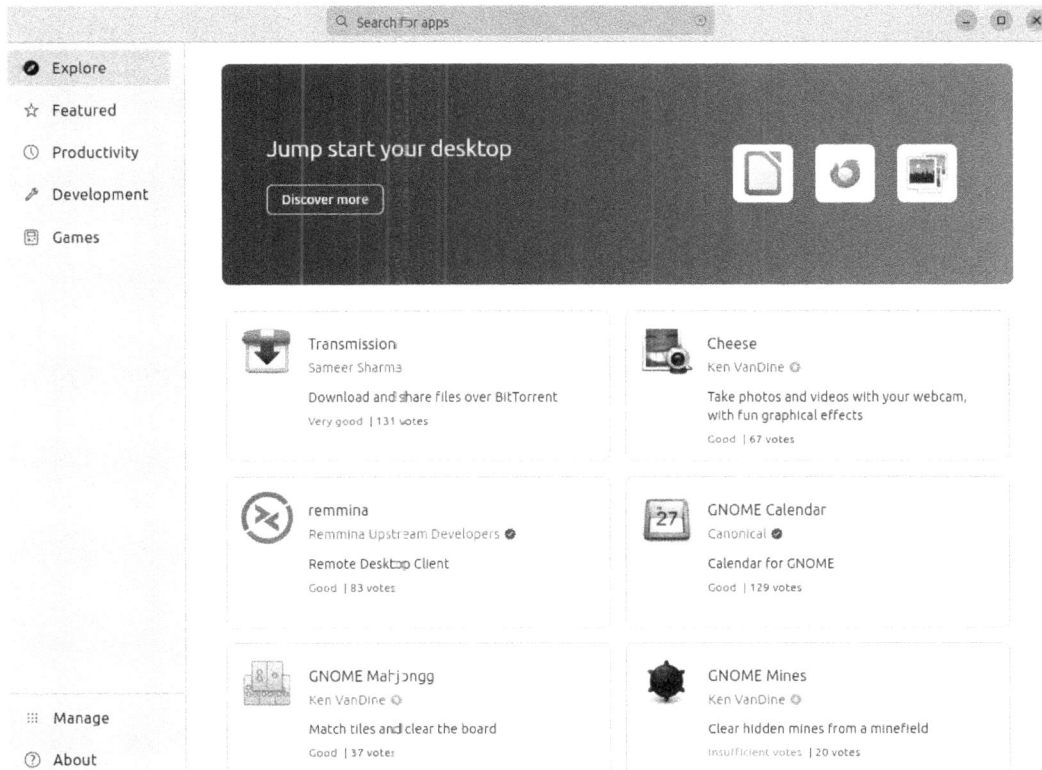

Figure 2.2 – App center

New firmware updater

Firmware is software embedded in a device that provides low-level functionality. It is essentially the instructions for a device to work as designed, independent of the operating system. BIOS, fingerprint readers, and wireless devices are common examples. On Linux, updates for device firmware often come from the **Linux Vendor Firmware Service (LVFS)**. The new Firmware Updater application included in Ubuntu 24.04 is a graphical tool to manage the firmware versions used by these devices, including the ability to upgrade, downgrade, and re-install firmware as necessary:

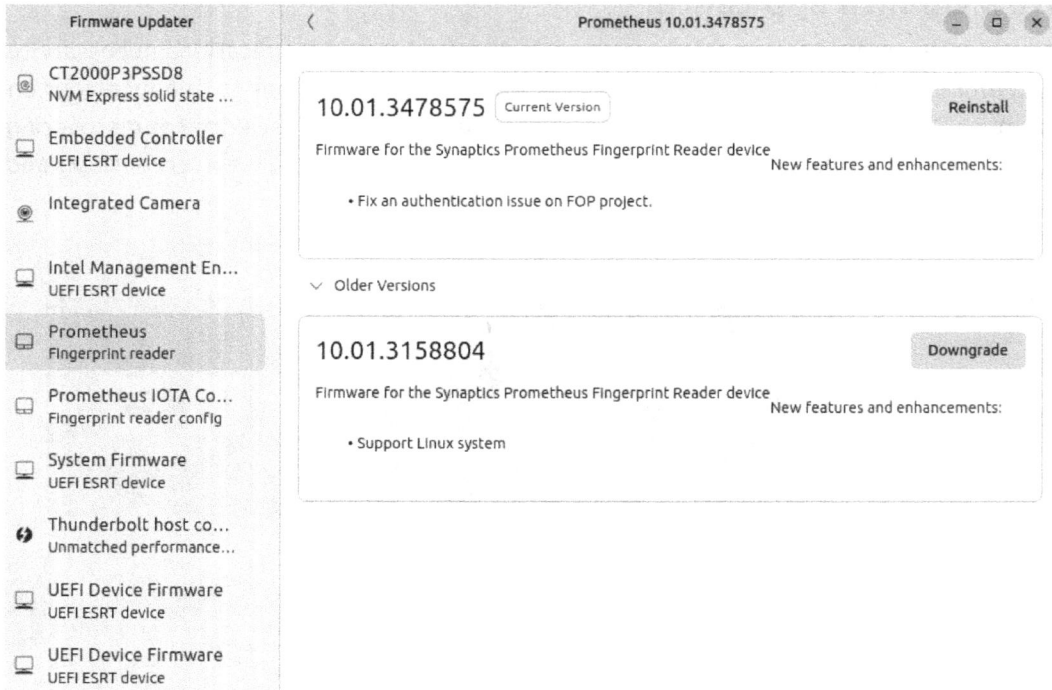

Figure 2.3 – Firmware Updater

Update to the Ubuntu font

The Ubuntu font family has been the default font used throughout the user interface since 2010, and it has seen very little change over those years. It is worth noting that this book uses the Ubuntu font throughout. For Ubuntu 24.04, the Ubuntu font has seen a nice refresh to align it more with modern typefaces. Most notable is the introduction of variable fonts and significantly improved support for non-Latin characters:

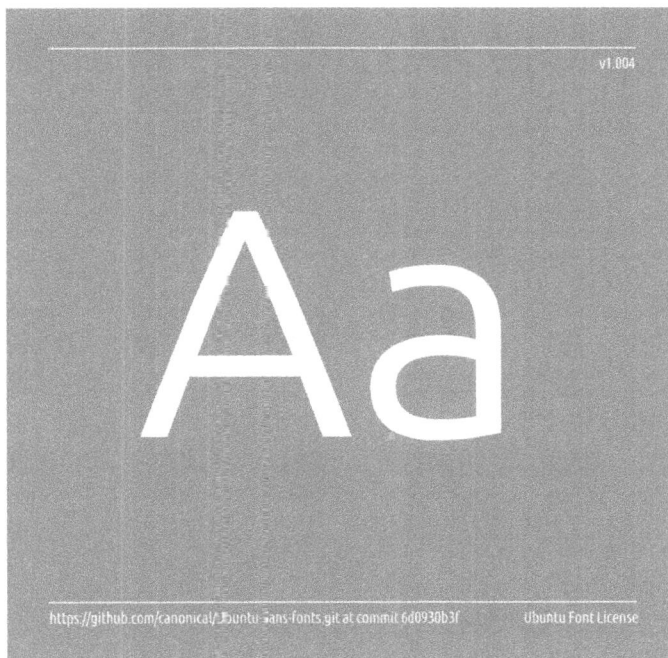

Figure 2.4 – Ubuntu font

GNOME 46

GNOME is Ubuntu's desktop environment, featuring a beautiful, intuitive, and easy-to-use desktop experience. Ubuntu 24.04 includes GNOME 46, the latest mjor milestone.

Files app

The Files app adds a new global search feature, activated by clicking the new search button or using the *Ctrl + Shift + F* keyboard shortcut and entering your search query. Search includes the ability to search the contents of files and filter by file type and modification date:

Figure 2.5 – Files: Global search

The new global search allows searching multiple locations simultaneously, and it is configurable in the Files app's newly refined **Search Locations** settings:

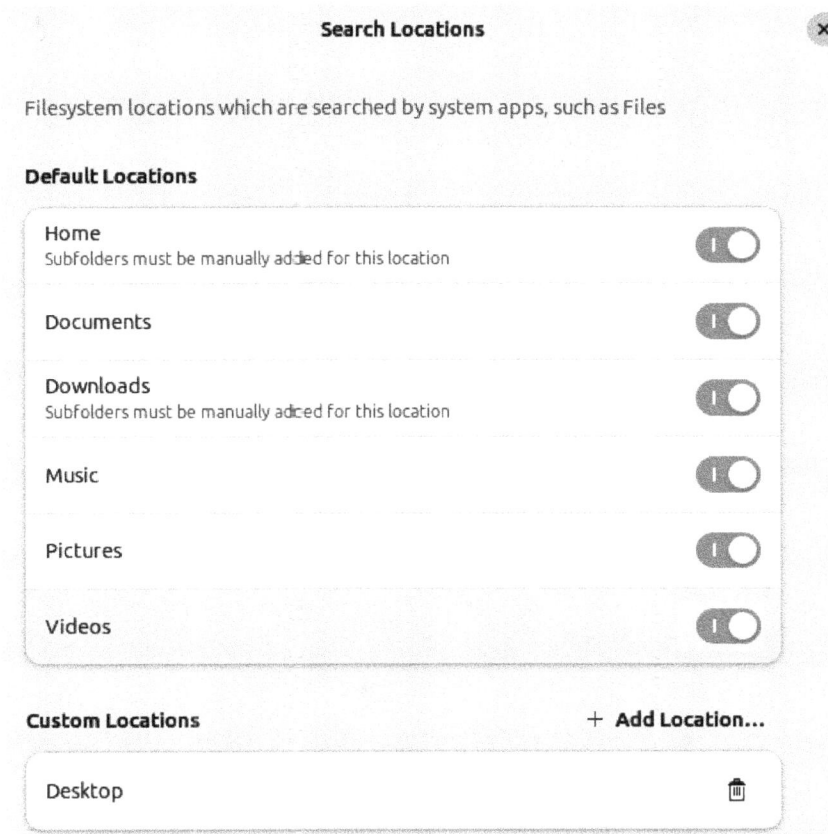

Figure 2.6 – Files: Global search preferences

Microsoft OneDrive

GNOME's **Online Accounts** includes the welcome addition of Microsoft 365 account support, available from the system settings. After successfully adding your Microsoft 365 account, OneDrive will appear in the sidebar of the Files app, allowing you to use and share files seamlessly as if they were local:

Q Settings ≡	Online Accounts — ☐ ✕
🖳 Ubuntu Desktop	Allow apps to access online services by connecting your cloud accounts

Connect an Account

G	Google	⟩
▦	Microsoft Personal	⟩
∞	Nextcloud	⟩
🗏	Microsoft Exchange	⟩
✉	Email IMAP and SMTP	⟩
🗓	Calendar, Contacts and Files WebDAV	⟩
🗝	Enterprise Login Kerberos	⟩

(Settings sidebar: ⠿ Apps, 🔔 Notifications, 🔍 Search, ☁ Online Accounts, ⦃ Sharing, 🖱 Mouse & Touchpad, ⌨ Keyboard, ◉ Color, 🖨 Printers)

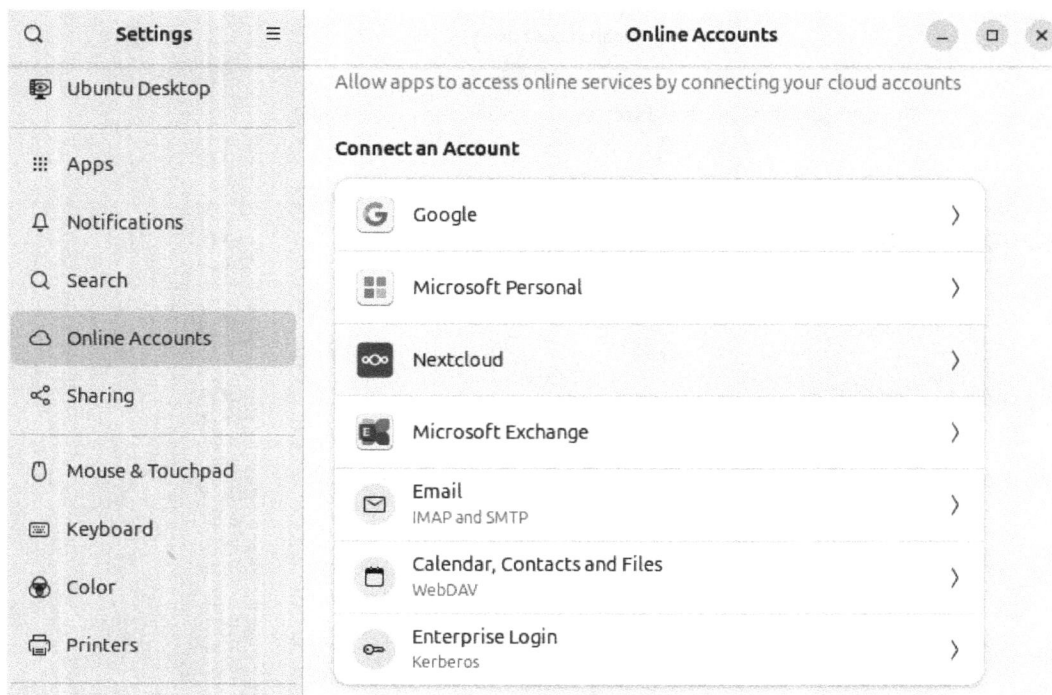

Figure 2.7 – Files: Global search preferences

Remote login with RDP

Remote Desktop Protocol (RDP) is an excellent option for remote login to a GNOME desktop. GNOME 46 significantly enhanced RDP support, allowing remote connection to a GNOME system that is not already in use, providing an improved experience for the remote user. This new remote login feature includes fully fledged remote access, which is helpful for remote workers, IT administrators, and more:

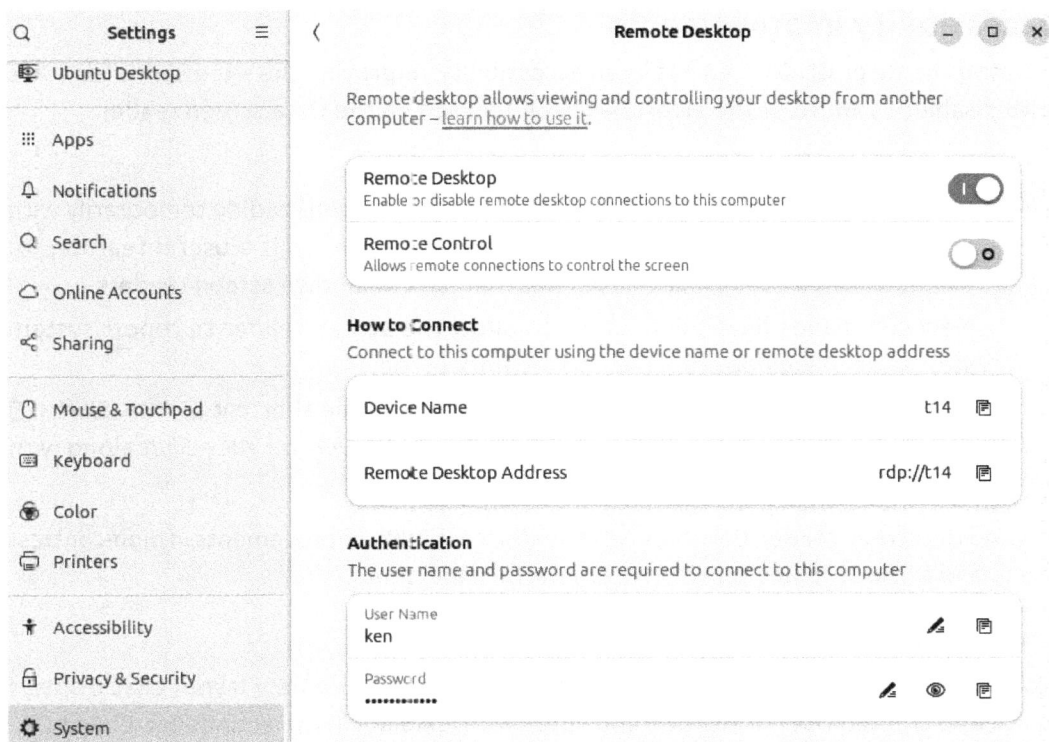

Figure 2.8 – GNOME Remote Desktop

Settings app

The System Settings app has seen a significant overhaul, including performance and navigational improvements.

Two new settings have been added to the touchpad settings. **Secondary Click** configures how secondary clicks (*right-clicks*) are performed with a touchpad, including options to use either two fingers or click in the touchpad's corner.

The other new setting allows the **Disable Touchpad While Typing** behavior to be turned off. This allows touchpad movement to be combined with keypresses, which is helpful for some apps and games.

Accessibility improvements

A strong theme of GNOME 46 has been accessibility, improving the experience for users with disabilities. Much of the effort has been focused on the Orca screen reader:

- Improved performance and reliability
- A new sleep mode feature allows users to disable screen reading temporarily with the *Ctrl + Alt + Shift + Q* keyboard shortcut. Sleep mode is a useful feature, for example, when using virtual machines that have their own screen readers.
- New commands have been added to allow the screen reader to report system status, including battery, CPU, and memory usage.
- Table navigation has been improved with a new toggle shortcut (*Orca + Shift + T*) and a command to jump directly to the last cell using *Orca + Alt + Shift* along with the arrow keys (←/→/↑/↓).

Beyond the screen reader, GNOME 46 has seen accessibility improvements in high-contrast mode and some switches shown in user interface elements.

Improved notifications

Notifications have seen a nice design refresh. This includes a new layout that displays which app created the notification and improved flexibility in the actions attached to it.

App window shortcuts

GNOME already had the ability to launch apps pinned to the dock with *Super + <Number>*. For example, *Super + 1* launches the first app pinned to the dock. With GNOME 46, you can launch a new window for running applications in a similar way. For example, *Super + Ctrl + 1* will launch a new window for the first app pinned to the dock.

On-screen keyboard

The on-screen keyboard has added automatic capitalization and new layouts for entering phone numbers, email addresses, and URLs.

Touch screen

Tap-to-click is now enabled by default, making the touch experience more intuitive.

Quarter-tiling window management

Quarter-tiling window management has been a long-desired feature, and it finally debuted in an Ubuntu LTS release for 24.04. Window management is how the desktop environment manages the placement of various windows on your screen. In the past, we were limited to being able to *snap* windows to either the left or right side of the screen to trigger resizing the window to fit exactly two windows side by side. With quarter tiling, you can now *snap* windows easily into quarters and sport some handy keyboard shortcuts to easily manage your window layout. We'll cover this in detail in *Chapter 5*.

Dynamic workspace indicator

GNOME's concept of multiple workspaces is underutilized. This feature has been around for decades on Linux and UNIX systems. Workspaces are a way to organize your open windows on separate virtual desktops; for example, windows related to a particular project could all be on one workspace. The dynamic workspaces allow you to create them automatically as needed by simply trying to move a window to another workspace; if it doesn't already exist, it'll be created. In GNOME 46, a handy workspace indicator in the top-left corner of your screen shows you how many workspaces you have, with an indicator of which is currently in focus:

Figure 2.9 – GNOME dynamic workspace indicator

We'll cover this in more detail in *Chapter 5*.

Wi-Fi credential sharing

GNOME 46 now includes a handy QR code generator for sharing Wi-Fi login credentials. Simply scan the QR code with your mobile device, and it will retrieve the Wi-Fi network name and password necessary to connect:

Figure 2.10 – GNOME Wi-Fi credential sharing

WireGuard VPN

WireGuard is a communication protocol built into the Linux kernel that can be used to create encrypted **Virtual Private Networks** (**VPNs**). WireGuard itself isn't new in Ubuntu 24.04, but it's now easier than ever for anyone to configure it and take advantage of the security benefits:

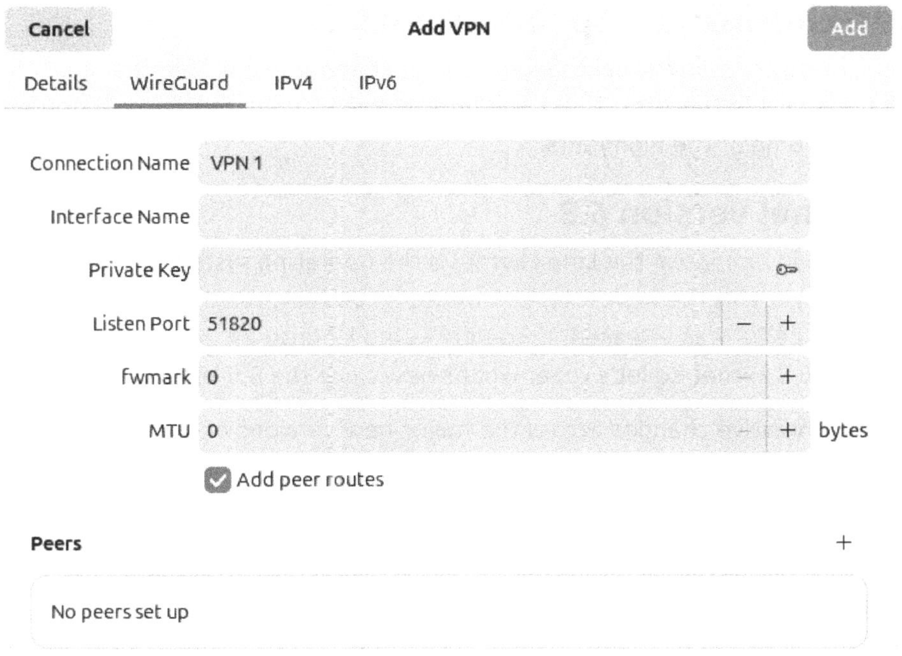

Figure 2.11 – WireGuard VPN configuration

We'll cover this in more detail in *Chapter 11*.

Firefox's native Wayland support

Wayland is the next-generation display server for Linux, which is the default on Ubuntu for most configurations. Thanks to Firefox's native Wayland support, you can expect smoother performance, especially with scrolling and animations. Wayland's architecture allows for more direct communication between the application and the graphics hardware, leading to a more responsive feeling. Additionally, Firefox on Wayland can take better advantage of your display's features, including sharper text on high-resolution screens and support for multi-touch gestures on touch-enabled devices. Overall, you can expect a noticeably better browsing experience.

As you can see, there have been considerable refinements throughout the desktop experience and some significant user experience changes, with the introduction of the new Ubuntu installer, new Firmware Updater, and quarter-tiling window management.

Under-the-hood improvements

Of course, there are many visual changes, but what about less visible changes? There are many far less visible features, fixes, and improvements that could easily go unnoticed. Let's go over some of the highlights.

Linux kernel version 6.8

As we covered in *Chapter 1*, the Linux kernel is the operating system's core that provides access to hardware at the lowest level. Ubuntu 24.04 features the 6.8 kernel, the latest release when 24.04 was released. If you are using Ubuntu 22.04 with all updates, you would have a 6.5 kernel, so let's cover what's new since the 6.5 kernel.

The list of cumulative changes across the major new versions of the Linux kernel is too long to cover here, so we'll focus on some select highlights.

The most exciting thing with every new kernel release is the added hardware enablement, supporting newer hardware that mightnot have worked with past releases.

A new scheduler, a key feature of the kernel that divides CPU time between processes, was introduced. The new schedule is more efficient, with less lag and reduced latency. Benchmarks show exciting performance boosts, particularly for gaming and other latency-sensitive workloads.

Significant improvements have taken place in z swap, which we'll cover in more detail in *Chapter 4*. This is a feature that's important for users with limited RAM.

The 6.8 kernel added support for Raspberry Pi 5, specifically enabling accelerated graphics. Raspberry Pi 5 is a nice advancement over past Pi devices, finally making it a compelling option for daily desktop use.

The 6.6, 6.7, and 6.8 releases each add support for additional game controllers, probably thanks to the work being done on the **Steam Deck** (handheld Linux gaming device by Valve).

PipeWire

The default sound server is now **PipeWire**. Ubuntu 22.04 included both PipeWire and **PulseAudio** but only used PipeWire for video. PipeWire is a nice upgrade over PulseAudio, providing performance improvements, improved hardware compatibility, and more robust Bluetooth support.

ZFS guided install

Ubuntu 24.04 reintroduced the ZFS-guided installation option. ZFS is a filesystem type that provides protection against data corruption and supports high storage capacity (256 ZiB), snapshots, copy-on-write clones, and continuous integrity checking. ZFS could be a great choice for dealing with large amounts of data; however, it can be complex to set up effectively. The Ubuntu 24.04 nstaller provides an optional guided install using ZFS, which will simplify use for most scenarios, if desired.

NetworkManager with Netplan

NetworkManager is common for handling network configuration, managing VPN access, and much more on desktop Linux systems. Providing an intuitive user interface for managing these essential tasks has been a staple of the experience for many years. With 24.04, NetworkManager will now integrate with **Netplan**, easing broader integration and managing large-scale deployments of Ubuntu systems. Netplan provides a consistent mechanism for storing and changing network settings without a user interface. The key here is that Netplan will allow large-scale deployments of Ubur tu systems in corporate environments that are manageable at scale without sacrificing the intuitive user interface of NetworkManager.

These have just been some of the highlights; however, countless others have accumulated since Ubuntu 22.04.

Security focus – enhanced protection

Ubuntu is breaking the mold for desktop Linux with 24.04, including must-have features required for critical environments such as enterprises, health care, and financial industries.

TPM-backed full disk encryption

Trusted Platform Module (TPM)-backed FDE, introduced in Ubuntu 23.10, will make an LTS debut in 24.04. Ubuntu has had passphrase-backed FDE for a very long time; however, being able to leverage the hardware TPM in modern computer hardware is a critical step in Ubuntu's widespread acceptance in many corporate environments. Not to mention, disk encryption is something everyone should at least consider. We'll talk more about disk encryption in *Chapter 13*.

Active Directory certificates auto-enrollment

In corporate environments often dominated by Windows PCs, **Active Directory** is leveraged for the login, policy, and management of systems. Ubuntu has Active Directory login and some Group Policy support, which has now been extended for 24.04 to include auto-enrollment to streamline connecting to secure corporate Wi-Fi networks and VPNs. This feature will greatly ease the adoption of Ubuntu by enabling more heterogeneous environments.

Summary

This chapter has covered many new features and improvements in Ubuntu 24.04 LTS. As discussed in *Chapter 1*, new releases of Ubuntu occur every six months. You can use and build on the knowledge you gained in this chapter by following the public release notes and development activity posted on Ubuntu's Discourse for future releases.

Further reading

- **Ubuntu 24.04 Noble Numbat**: https://discourse.ubuntu.com/t/noble-numbat-release-notes
- **Ubuntu Discourse**: https://discourse.ubuntu.com
- **GNOME 46 release**: https://release.gnome.org/46/

3

Security and Transparency – The Advantages of Open Source Software

In this chapter, we'll learn more about the numerous advantages of open source software, some of which you might not have expected. Many years ago, open source software was very niche, driven by a small group of enthusiastic individuals like myself clinging to these ideals and evangelizing freedom. We would tell anyone about the wonderful open source world with the patience to listen to us. Fast forward twenty years, and I am blown away by the fact that even people I meet who have never been interested in software or technology have heard of open source.

I like to believe that the culture around Ubuntu has impacted the adoption of open source software globally, but that could be my bias rooted in the Ubuntu community. However, nobody can argue the widespread adoption of open source within the more mainstream ecosystem is impressive. It's like a locomotive steaming ahead at full speed, driving innovation and building up speed with no end in sight. It's an impressive feeling, and I'm very excited to see where this takes us.

This chapter covers the following topics:

- I am who I am because of who we all are
- What is free software?
- Many people make light work – the power of open source
- Transparency builds trust – a foundation for secure computing

- How to make your mark on the world
- A showcase of open source projects

I am who I am because of who we all are

In chapter one, we learned about the South African word **Ubuntu** and its meaning. It loosely translates to *"I am who I am because of who we all are."* Unpacking that, I am proud to say how closely aligned the Ubuntu community culture is to this core value. We live by it every day within the Ubuntu community, and you, too, could be a valuable and welcome member. The idea is simple: *we are stronger together than alone*. The more we collaborate, the more we innovate, ensuring we build better software.

What is free software?

The term **free software** can confuse people, preventing them from seeing the real value of the free software movement. The Free Software Foundation defines it as *"the users have the freedom to run, copy, distribute, study, change and improve the software. Thus, free software is a matter of liberty, not price."* Historically, the free software community has used the analogy of *"free"* as in *"free speech,"* not *"free"* as in *"free beer."*

Of course, everyone likes to get something for free. We often want things we don't need if they're free. However, the freedom aspect of free software is often not understood as the true value of the concept. You are encouraged to not only use the software but also dissect it, learn how it works, enhance it to suit your own needs, and even redistribute it to others. As the software industry learned more about the freedom aspect of open source, the concept was harnessed and gained momentum, becoming something widely accepted and embraced as a way to innovate. There is no point in re-inventing the wheel when you can make the wheel better.

Many people make light work – the power of open source

As with most things, the more people contribute to an initiative, the more momentum we can build. This is valuable on multiple levels; the obvious is that the more people there are writing code, the more code gets written. But it's significantly more impactful than that. Imagine the following scenario.

A company creates software with a specific purpose and decides to release it under an open source license. They are often motivated to do that for a couple of reasons, but primarily with the hope that the users of that software will contribute feedback, bug reports, and potentially even bug fixes.

This, of course, equates to less work by the company, which has an economic impact. However, imagine a user of that software who does contribute back bug fixes, is later inspired to add new features to that software or make enhancements to the usability of the software. This benefits the original software creators and makes the software appealing to more users, solving additional needs and opening up the potential customer base.

As the number of users grows, the potential for additional feedback contributions, bug fixes, and feature enhancements grows. This is how real innovation happens: the software improves and meets the needs of a growing audience, and the cycle continues.

In that scenario, I mentioned a couple of ways people contributed to the software project, but there are many ways people and companies contribute. I'd encourage you to consider how you can help improve the software you use, becoming part of the driving force behind innovation.

Now that we've learned what free software is and how it is encompassed in Ubuntu's values, let's expand on that to demonstrate how these concepts correlate to security and trust.

Transparency builds trust – a foundation for secure computing

Another key value in open source/free software is transparency. Not only is the software's source code available, but the development processes are often visible to everyone. As a user of the software or perhaps the IT department looking to select some software to be used throughout your company, you can (and are encouraged to) view the source code, critique it, and audit it to ensure it's safe.

From a security perspective, this is a huge motivator for creating secure and reliable code. As the user or consumer of the software, you can read the code, understand the level of quality, and find security exploits or shortcuts the developers might have taken. These factors help you decide if you can trust the software for your use case. Still, the flip side is that this level of transparency encourages the developers to ensure quality code with a solid testing discipline. Developers, like anyone else, like to take pride in their craft. Working in a closed source, proprietary environment, they only worry about co-workers seeing their code. With the innate transparency of open source, much more care is put into writing quality code and ensuring thorough tests are included. This isn't something we can say about all open source software, but I do feel like you are much more likely to find these traits in open source software because nobody wants to be judged openly for the quality of their code.

These are traits that software consumers should take seriously. This is particularly important for companies relying on this software to help their business thrive. Doing this due diligence can go a long way to ensuring confidence.

If you are curious or have a genuine business need to evaluate choices in open source software, here is a brief list of things to assess.

Bug reports

Find the project's bug tracker and the type of bug reports filed. Be sure to look at closed issues as well as open issues. How timely were the replies to the issue? Was the issue adequately addressed? Was the issue ignored? Were the people involved in the issue polite and professional? These things should help you make a confident decision by considering, *"What if this was an issue I filed? How would I feel about this correspondence?".*

Tests

The number of tests in the code base gives a good sense of how much the project values testing. You can usually see how many of the tests are passing or regularly failing by looking at the project's code hosting infrastructure, which most likely hosts test runners and a dashboard that shows the current test status at a glance. These are all great indicators.

Documentation

Sadly, thorough documentation is not as common as we would like. However, having useful, thorough documentation signifies a mature project. Lack of documentation doesn't mean you shouldn't use the software; in fact, it could be a great way for you to get involved more by creating or improving documentation. Just consider whether there is enough documentation for you to get started effectively.

Code comments

You don't have to be a programmer by trade to read code comments. Code comments are sections of the source code that aren't code but documentation explaining what the code is meant to do and why, purely for the benefit of people reading the code to help them better understand what that particular section of code is used for. This is not only for other people reading it but also for the developer who wrote the code, who might come back to it years later and struggle to understand some of the rationales, so clearly documenting that as a code comment is valuable. Finding very little or no code comments in the project indicates that the developers might not be as experienced.

Does it build?

Most software projects include a README file or some variation that documents how to build or run it from source. By building from source, we mean compiling the source code into something the computer understands. This process uses a compiler to compile or build the software. Some large projects that have usually evolved over a long period can have a more complex build process than smaller projects. Regardless, the instructions should be easy to follow and produce something that can be used as described.

If you run into trouble compiling the source, it's a common sign that few newcomers to the project attempt to follow those instructions. If you encounter this situation, I encourage you to file a bug outlining your experience.

Code analyzers

There are tools for analyzing code and finding common problems. Access to the code means you can use any tool to analyze it to help make the best decision for you or your company.

If you were limited in choosing proprietary software, you could not evaluate any of these aspects. The ability to inspect the code yourself, see how the community engages with each other, and how active the project is, are powerful tools for making confident decisions.

A case study – XZ Utils backdoor

Let's review a real-world example of how many eyes on the code have found an actual exploit and prevented it from exposing systems to an attack on a massive scale.

XZ Utils is a set of command-line utilities widely used for compression. Commonly seen as compressed archives of files, like a Zip file on some other platforms, XZ offers excellent compression/performance. XZ is actually used by more than just some command-line utilities; it exposes the compression algorithm it uses in other applications and services. One of the services that leverage XZ is SSH, commonly used to remotely and securely log in to devices.

In 2022, an unknown contributor started submitting patches to the XZ project on GitHub. Through a series of legitimate contributions, this contributor eventually earned commit access to the project, which is a very trusted position. Two years later, after continued legitimate contributions to the project, they started to commit some changes, including assets (**binary blobs**) used in the test suite. This didn't actually raise any alarms; it was not uncommon, but the binary nature of the data in the test suite wasn't easily reviewable.

This was March 2024, and the changes to the test suite and the build system necessary to utilize the data made it into a public release of the software. With any new release of such commonly used software, Linux distribution packagers update packages to make it available to users. The malicious contributor even started emailing relevant lists for these distributions, encouraging them to update to the new version, which is also not uncommon.

This change started to make its way into several distributions that moved quickly. Shortly after, it started to make its way into the Ubuntu development release, which would later be released as Ubuntu 24.04 and was discovered. This vulnerability never made it into the Ubuntu release and, therefore, never into real Ubuntu users' systems.

The discovery was made in late March, just two weeks after it was released, by a software engineer at Microsoft who had noticed an anomaly in their automated tests of **Postgres**, a prominent open source database server. The anomaly was timing-related; some tests started taking a little longer than normal, which caught his attention. He started to dig into what was happening, profiling the processes and uncovering the exploit, even discovering how the vulnerability could be used in SSH to allow remote code execution without authentication.

This vulnerability was discovered and fixed within a couple of weeks. It never reached the point where an attacker could use it. This was thanks to the transparency provided by open source. Developers worldwide, working for many different companies, are constantly leveraging open source software in their own environments for their own software, providing the necessary coverage to prevent this level of attack. I can't say malicious code never makes it into open source code bases; it might, and it might even go unnoticed. But there's more opportunity to discover it early with the transparency provided by the open source ecosystem.

So far, we've learned about free software and its value to innovation, security, and trust. Let's discuss why you may want to get involved and present a path to get started.

How to make your mark on the world

Getting involved in open source can be very rewarding, and I can say from my own experience that it is a great way to build lifelong friendships. I've been involved for over 30 years and have met my closest friends by engaging in the community. Engaging in the community makes the world smaller; you'll learn the people involved are geographically separated worldwide, making this an excellent opportunity to build diverse relationships. The free software culture is the most open and accepting community you'll ever find.

Generally, the most challenging thing about getting involved is taking that leap and deciding to join the community. These free software communities won't come to you, directly inviting you with inspirational words of wisdom on where to start. You have to take that initiative, find a place to engage, and just do it.

Find a community around the software you are interested in. For example, the Ubuntu community is enormous and broad, including software targeting desktop users to server, cloud, and web technologies. You name it, and there is a way to find a subset of the Ubuntu community with similar interests. However, you can look at the upstream projects directly as well. When I say *upstream*, this means the software projects developing the software included in Ubuntu. For example, Ubuntu includes the **GNU Network Object Model Environment** (**GNOME**) desktop. The Ubuntu community includes people with an interest in GNOME on Ubuntu. However, consider joining the GNOME community and finding ways to contribute directly within GNOME, which ultimately trickles down into future Ubuntu releases.

Start with the Ubuntu community and work back into the upstream you are interested in. Ubuntu is broad enough; finding like-minded people is easy and can be a valuable resource when finding the best way to engage.

There are many ways to get involved in free software. Some common ways to get involved are discussed ahead.

Feedback/bug reports

This is the more common entry point for people to get involved. You use the software and find a bug, or at least it doesn't do something you expect it to do in the way you expected it. Filing a bug report against the project outlining your expected behavior versus the resulting behavior is usually easy. This is valuable to all software projects. Often, this is the first report of an actual bug, and the developers are generally very happy to see these reports and happily fix them. Even if it is not a bug, it's valuable feedback showing the developers, designers, and product managers what your expectation was, helping to shape future work done on the project.

Documentation

Many open source projects start as just one individual or a couple of developers loosely organized with a common goal. Documentation is often neglected in that situation, so as a new user of the software, creating or improving existing documentation is a great way to get started contributing to the project. Particularly when you are new to the software, your perspective is still untainted compared to that of the more well-established project members. This is an excellent opportunity to improve the documentation. Documentation contributions are often the most welcome as the project developers often struggle to make time for documentation.

Translations

The world has gotten smaller, enabling such a broad user base for the software to be spread worldwide, speaking any number of languages. Developers working on the project will likely speak one or two languages. Still, of course, the software should work as expected in the native language of users worldwide. Handling translations in software is a well-established process and is generally very accessible for people with little or no programming experience. This is also a fantastic way to get involved in a project; providing translated strings for text used throughout the software is usually really easy, and the barrier to getting the translation accepted by the project maintainers will be much lower than writing code.

Community engagement

All of the previously listed ways to contribute could be considered community engagement, but let's cover them here more specifically as ways to engage with the broader community of the specific software. This could include helping others when posting on support forums, posting bug reports, asking questions on an email list, or even a community chat system such as **Matrix**, **Mattermost**, **Slack**, or **Discord**.

Code

Of course, all software projects require people to write code to fix bugs or enhance features. Code contributions have a higher barrier of entry than other ways of contributing, but they are immensely valuable and come with a natural sense of accomplishment.

Now that you understand why you may want to engage with an open source project and how you might do it, let's highlight a few popular open source projects and showcase the value they bring to the free software ecosystem.

A showcase of open source projects

As mentioned before, Ubuntu comprises software from many open source projects. Let's take a look at some large, successful open source projects.

GNOME

Starting in 1997, **GNOME** was originally an acronym for the **GNU Network Object Model Environment**, but that isn't applicable these days, and it has simply become GNOME.

GNOME is the desktop environment in the default Ubuntu Desktop release. Like Ubuntu, GNOME is broad. GNOME provides the desktop shell, which is how you interact with your computer graphically. Window management, finding and launching applications, and seeing status notifications when an application needs attention are just a few of the critical things GNOME provides. GNOME is commonly considered simple and intuitive, by not providing overly complex settings.

But the GNOME project is much more than that. It includes many system libraries and desktop services necessary for applications to behave consistently. For example, what should a notification of an unseen message look like? GNOME provides the infrastructure for any messaging app to display that notification consistently.

GTK (which originally stood for **GIMP ToolKit** but is no longer used), part of the GNOME project, is the graphical toolkit used in many Linux apps today. GTK provides widgets used as **user interface** (**UI**) elements in applications, ensuring a consistent user experience across all apps.

Many applications included in Ubuntu are also part of the GNOME project. These include photo management, email, calendaring, calculators, messaging apps, image and document viewers, and systems settings.

GNOME provides governance and has a foundation responsible for ensuring the project has the resources necessary to achieve its goals.

The **GNOME Users and Developers European Conference** (**GUADEC**) is an annual conference held in July. Historically, it has been held in Europe; however, it has also been hosted in Mexico and the United States recently.

GNOME is a fantastic example of a thriving, open, and welcoming community. To get involved in the GNOME project, visit https://welcome.gnome.org/ to discover how to get involved. You'll find links to the GNOME Matrix servers for chat-based communications, developer discourse forums, developer documentation, and source code.

KDE

Starting in 1996, KDE was originally a play on the **Common Desktop Environment (CDE)**, commonly used on most Unix systems. The K in KDE originally was thought to stand for Kool, so **KDE** was the **Kool Desktop Environment**. It has since been referred to as the **K Desktop Environment**, losing the Kool adjective.

Similar to GNOME, KDE is primarily a desktop environment. It provides all the necessary window management capabilities, a desktop shell to find files and applications, and a launcher for applications.

While KDE isn't part of the Ubuntu Desktop experience, it is featured in the official Ubuntu flavor, **Kubuntu**. Kubuntu provides a beautiful, polished KDE experience in Ubuntu.

As a full-featured desktop environment, KDE also provides system libraries, a graphical toolkit, and desktop infrastructure necessary to provide a common user experience. The KDE project isn't responsible for the graphical toolkit but does leverage the Qt Toolkit for consistency.

The KDE project also hosts many applications designed with the KDE user experience in mind.

Unlike GNOME, KDE is commonly known for providing more advanced user interfaces and settings, allowing maximum flexibility to tweak things to your liking. This could be ideally suited for users who enjoy tweaking things heavily rather than relying on designers to provide them.

Akademy, the KDE world summit, is an annual summer event in Europe that brings together developers and users to celebrate the community's accomplishments, collaborate, and plan. To get involved in the KDE project, visit `https://kde.org`.

Mozilla

Founded in 1998, **Mozilla** is a free software community spawned out of the then-commercial **Netscape** browser. Originally intended to be responsible for an open source platform used in Netscape's commercial products, Mozilla has survived far longer than Netscape.

Mozilla is most well known for **Firefox**, a popular web browser featured in the default Ubuntu Desktop install. However, Mozilla is also responsible for an extensive portfolio of software focused on open standards and interoperability:

- **Bugzilla**, a popular bug-tracking solution
- **Pocket**, a read-it-later online service

- **Thunderbird**, a popular email client
- The **Gecko** layout engine used in both Firefox and Thunderbird, amongst many other open source projects

Mozilla is an immensely important open source project with a very important mission: to make the internet a better place. The importance of open standards on the internet can't be emphasized enough, and Mozilla is the real champion of this cause. Without a project like Mozilla, we would see more websites that only work on specific browsers or, worse, do not work as expected on different operating systems. Mozilla fights the good fight to keep the internet free and open while emphasizing the importance of privacy features.

To get involved in the Mozilla project, visit https://www.mozilla.org/contribute/.

Summary

In this chapter, we've learned critical concepts about open source and the ecosystem it provides. In particular, we've learned about the free software culture and the difference between *free* as in *free speech* and *free* as in *free beer*.

While the freedom we are afforded by leveraging open source software is the most critical takeaway, we can't ignore the security benefits.

The level of transparency involved in developing and distributing open source software is key to trusting your software supply chain.

Understanding these aspects of open source shows us the movement's importance and helps us see how we can not only benefit directly from it but also become part of it.

Further reading

- Public disclosure for the XZ Utils vulnerability: https://ubuntu.com/security/CVE-2024-3094

Join the CloudPro Newsletter with 44000+ Subscribers

Want to know what's happening in cloud computing, DevOps, IT administration, networking, and more? Scan the QR code to subscribe to **CloudPro**, our weekly newsletter for 44,000+ tech professionals who want to stay informed and ahead of the curve.

https://packt.link/cloudpro

4

Getting Started with Ubuntu: A User's Guide

We've learned more about **Ubuntu**, its origins, Ubuntu's versioning and release cadence, and the value of open source. In this chapter, we'll cover helpful information about planning your installation, advanced installation topics, and getting the most out of Ubuntu. If this is your first time installing **Linux**, don't worry; it's actually remarkably easy compared to other **Operating Systems (OSs)**. We will cover the super-straightforward guided installation process and expand on more advanced scenarios to ensure you can be confident in your installation.

The chapter covers the following topics:

- Booting up – your first steps with Ubuntu
- Installation made easy – a guided process
- Ubuntu welcome
- Essential hardware – installing necessary drivers

Booting up – your first steps with Ubuntu

For most users, the guided installation is the best choice and a breeze for anyone. However, let's consider some scenarios that may require decisions before you begin your installation. This chapter will ensure you understand what decisions must be made to properly prepare your device for installation and equip you to make those decisions.

Decisions

During the installation process, you will have the opportunity to answer some questions to ensure you get the features you want or need. Let's quickly touch on the concepts that might be useful to understand before you start the installation process. Don't worry, there are no wrong answers. In fact, if you just choose the default options through most of the installation screens, you will get a very usable system:

- **Dual-boot**: Does your computer already have an OS installed that you want to preserve? If so, do you have enough free disk space? How do you resize to ensure you have enough space for multiple OS installations?

- **Encryption**: Do you want to store the encryption key using the **Trusted Platform Module (TPM)**? Do you want to enter a passphrase to boot your encrypted device? Or is encryption not necessary for your use case? For more information on drive encryption, see *Chapter 13*.

- **Automated installation**: Do you want an automated installation to ensure your system is configured to match a predefined standard?

- **Proprietary drivers**: Do you have hardware that requires third-party proprietary drivers, such as NVIDIA graphics or Realtek Wi-Fi? We love hardware with open source drivers in the Linux kernel, but that's not always possible. If you have hardware requiring proprietary drivers, you must enable proprietary driver support during installation.

- **Storage configuration**: Do you need the flexibility to customize your disk partitions or filesystem? Do you have a preferred filesystem type, or would you benefit from later adding additional storage and growing a logical filesystem seamlessly?

- **Enterprise login**: Do you need to enroll your system in an existing corporate network, such as **Active Directory**?

Please familiarize yourself with these before installing to ensure you make the best decisions for your use case. Once you feel ready to take that leap and join the wonderful world of Ubuntu, we'll need to proceed with downloading, creating an installer, and installing Ubuntu.

Downloading and preparing the USB installer

The first step is to download Ubuntu's installation media. Visit `https://ubuntu.com/download` and select the version of Ubuntu you want.

You can choose from the following:

- **Desktop**: The most popular desktop Linux distribution on the planet!
- **Server**: Suitable for server deployments or the base for crafting more minimal systems, installing just the packages you want.
- **Flavors**: These are alternative versions of Ubuntu that provide unique experiences. Some examples are Kubuntu, Lubuntu, Ubuntu Budgie, and Ubuntu Mate. More information can be found at https://wiki.ubuntu.com/UbuntuFlavors.
- **Cloud**: Images used for public cloud deployments.
- **Core**: A strictly confined immutable system optimized for embedded devices, **Internet of Things (IoT)**, and purpose-built appliances

We'll focus on the Desktop installation for this book. Download the .iso file at https://ubuntu.com/download, a read-only bootable image on a single file. The ISO file is designed to be written to a USB stick. Once you've downloaded the file, create a bootable USB stick with the installer. The process for doing this will vary depending on what OS you are currently running.

Ubuntu

If you are already on an Ubuntu system, I recommend **Startup Disk Creator**, which is installed by default. It's very intuitive; simply select the Ubuntu Desktop ISO file you downloaded, insert your USB stick, and select it. Then, click **Make Startup Disk**:

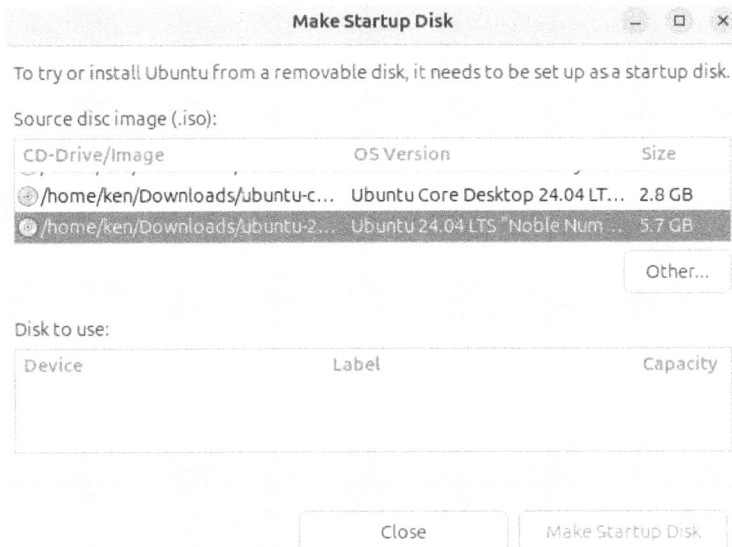

Figure 4.1 – Startup Disk Creator

Other Linux systems, Windows, or Mac

balenaEtcher is a very nice, intuitive tool for working with disk images. It works on most Linux distributions and Windows and Mac systems. To download it, and for instructions for its use, see `https://etcher.balena.io/`.

Regardless of which tool you used to create your USB stick, you should now have everything you need to begin installing Ubuntu.

Installation made easy – a guided process

The Ubuntu installer provides a guided installation process, which leads you through the installation in a very intuitive way. In this chapter, we'll walk you through that guided installation process, explaining important concepts along the way.

Boot installation media

Now that you've prepared your USB stick with Ubuntu installation media, it's time to boot your computer! Insert the USB stick in a USB port on your computer, preferably USB3, to ensure maximum performance. USB ports with visible blue inside the port are USB3. With the USB stick connected, you must boot your system from USB rather than from the hard drive. You must either interrupt the boot with a keypress or change the boot order in your system's BIOS to boot from USB media before the hard drive. The process for this will vary depending on your specific computer. For example, on my laptop, pressing the *F12* key when seeing the manufacturer's logo will prompt me to choose a one-time boot device on some systems, and the *F1* key pressed at the same point in the boot process will take me into the BIOS configuration. Since the process of doing this varies, we can't cover it in this book. Check your system user manual or search the internet for specific system procedures.

With your system booted from the USB device, you will see the Ubuntu installer window within a functional Ubuntu live session.

The following table briefly summarizes the pages included in the guided installation process. You can choose the default values on each page, but we'll walk you through each page to ensure you understand what's happening:

Pages	Purpose
Locale	Select the interface language
Accessibility	Configure accessibility options
Try or Install	Choose between trying Ubuntu in a live session or installing Ubuntu

Pages	Purpose
Keyboard	Set keyboard layout
Network	Connect to network
Refresh Installer	Update the installer to the latest version
Software Selection	Choose an installation set, default applications, or an expanded set of pre-installed applications
Proprietary software	Allow installation of proprietary media codecs and drivers
Storage	Configure target disk
Identity	Create a first user account
Confirm	Confirm selections and begin installation
Finished	Confirm installation is complete and initiate a reboot

Table 4.1 – Installation steps

If you require more advanced installation choices, we'll explore some of the more advanced features of the relevant pages later in this chapter.

Language

This first screen is intuitive; select your preferred language and click the **Next** button:

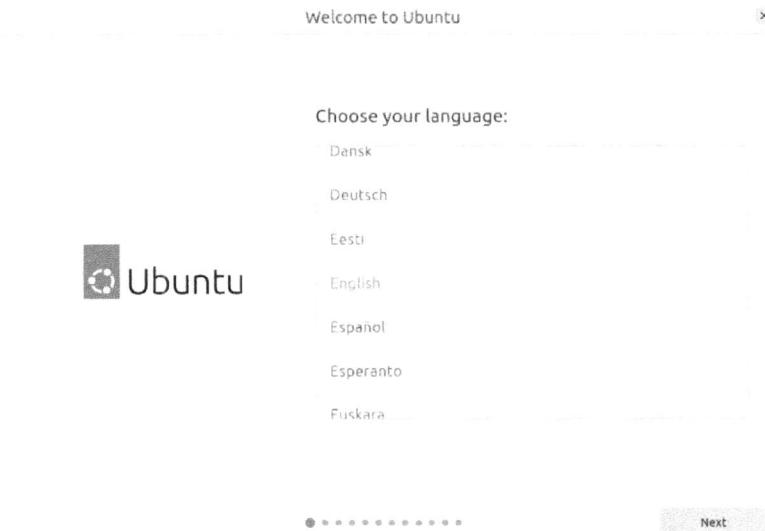

Welcome to Ubuntu ×

Choose your language:

Dansk

Deutsch

Eesti

English

Español

Esperanto

Euskara

Ubuntu

Next

Figure 4.2 – Language selection

Accessibility

Accessibility options are critical for users with accessibility needs, such as those who are sight- or hearing-impaired. On the next page of the installer, you will be able to enable any of these accessibility features; however, please note that some of them are also available at any time with a keyboard shortcut. For example, an *Alt* + *Super* + *S* keyboard combination will enable or disable the screen reader, which reads the text to a visually impaired user at any time.

Important note

Throughout this chapter, we'll reference keyboard shortcuts, including the *Super* key. The *Super* key is also known as the *Windows* key, commonly represented by the Microsoft Windows logo on the key. It is often between the *Ctrl* and *Alt* keys on the bottom left of the keyboard.

Getting to this point to enable the screen reader can be challenging for a visually impaired user. A helpful hint is that you will hear an audio cue when the system is booted and the installer screen is ready. Once you've heard this, you can utilize the *Alt* + *Super* + *S* keyboard combination to enable the screen reader, making it possible to continue through the installation process or use the Ubuntu live session:

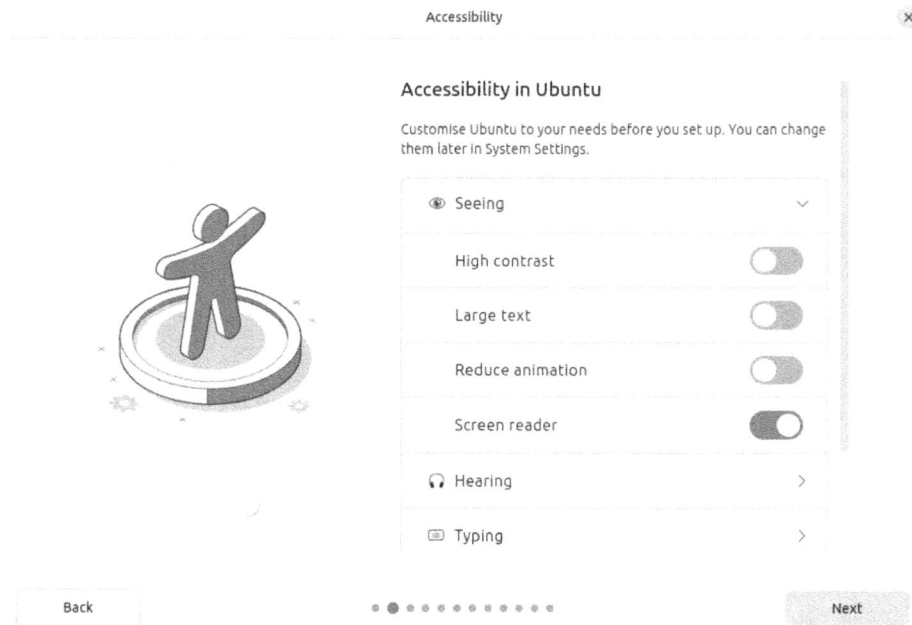

Figure 4.3 – Accessibility in Ubuntu

Keyboard layout

Keyboard layout is important. Many countries use different layouts, and if you choose the wrong one, some keys on your keyboard won't work as expected. In most cases, the installer will detect the appropriate layout. You can also test your keyboard layout selection by typing in the provided text field. Ensure this looks reasonable for your device and proceed:

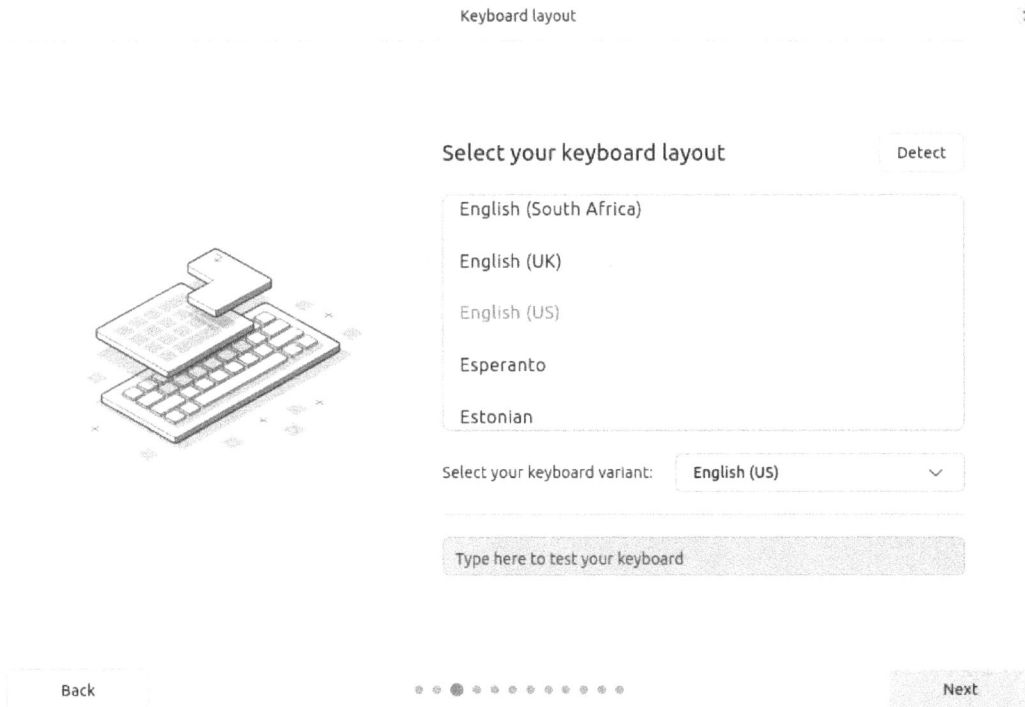

Figure 4.4 – Keyboard layout

Network

Network configuration isn't required for completing installation, but there are some nice conveniences if you are connected while installing:

- Option to update the installer to the latest version, potentially fixing bugs
- Download updates during installation
- Automatically install necessary driver packages online

Here's the **Internet connection** page:

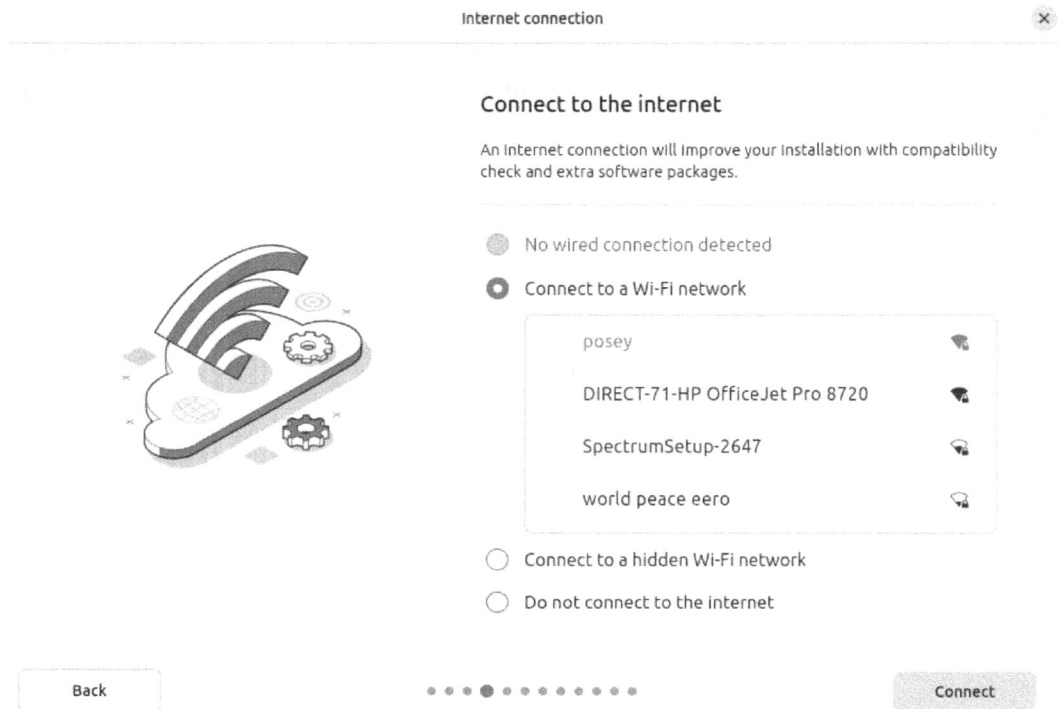

Internet connection   ✕

Connect to the internet

An Internet connection will improve your installation with compatibility check and extra software packages.

⊙ No wired connection detected

◉ Connect to a Wi-Fi network

posey	
DIRECT-71-HP OfficeJet Pro 8720	
SpectrumSetup-2647	
world peace eero	

○ Connect to a hidden Wi-Fi network

○ Do not connect to the internet

Back   ● ● ● ◉ ● ● ● ● ● ● ●   Connect

Figure 4.5 – Network connection

Update installer

If an update is available for the installer itself and you are online, you will see this page, allowing you to update the installer to the latest version. This isn't required, and I'd suggest only doing this if you suspect there might be a bug fixed in the installer that is necessary for your configuration. You can choose **Update now** or simply **Skip** to proceed:

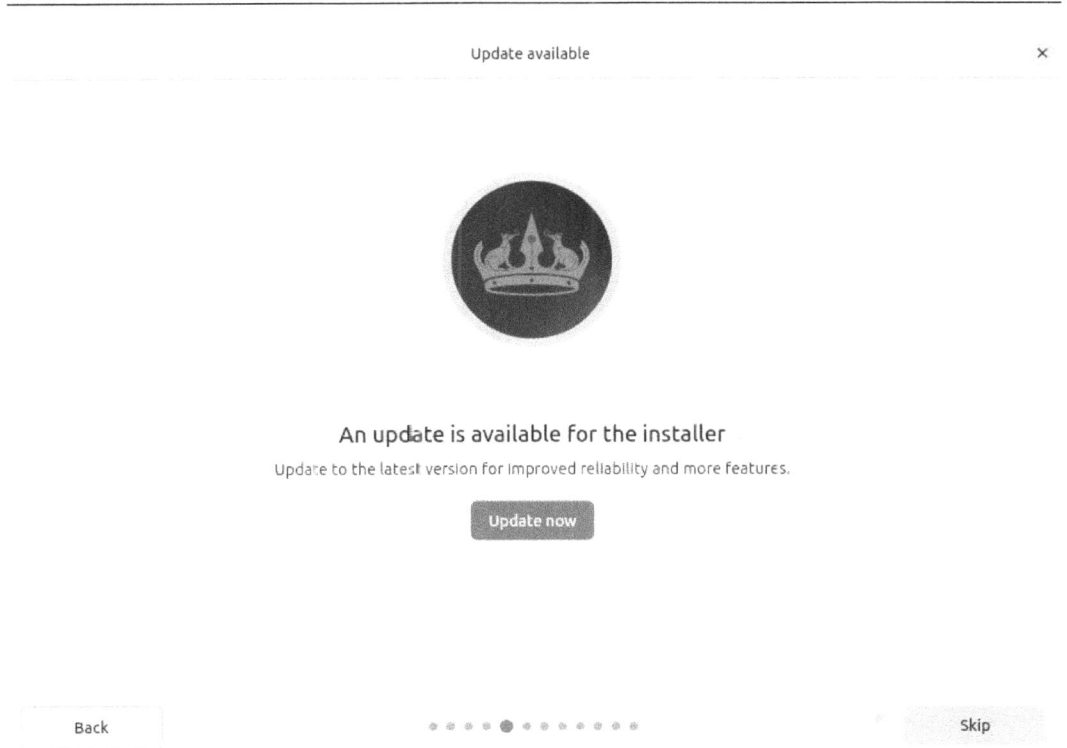

Update available   ×

An update is available for the installer

Update to the latest version for improved reliability and more features.

Update now

Back   • • • • ● • • • • • •   Skip

Figure 4.6 – Update installer

Try Ubuntu and Install Ubuntu

The Ubuntu installation media includes a full live Ubuntu system, allowing you to try Ubuntu before installation without altering your existing system. This is particularly useful for verifying that your hardware works as expected. Just note that proprietary drivers will not be used in the live session. To use the live session, select **Try Ubuntu**:

What do you want to do with Ubuntu?

○ **Install Ubuntu**
Install Ubuntu alongside (or instead of) your current
operating system. This shouldn't take too long.

◉ **Try Ubuntu**
You can try Ubuntu without making any changes to
your computer.

Back   • • • • ● • • • • • •   Close

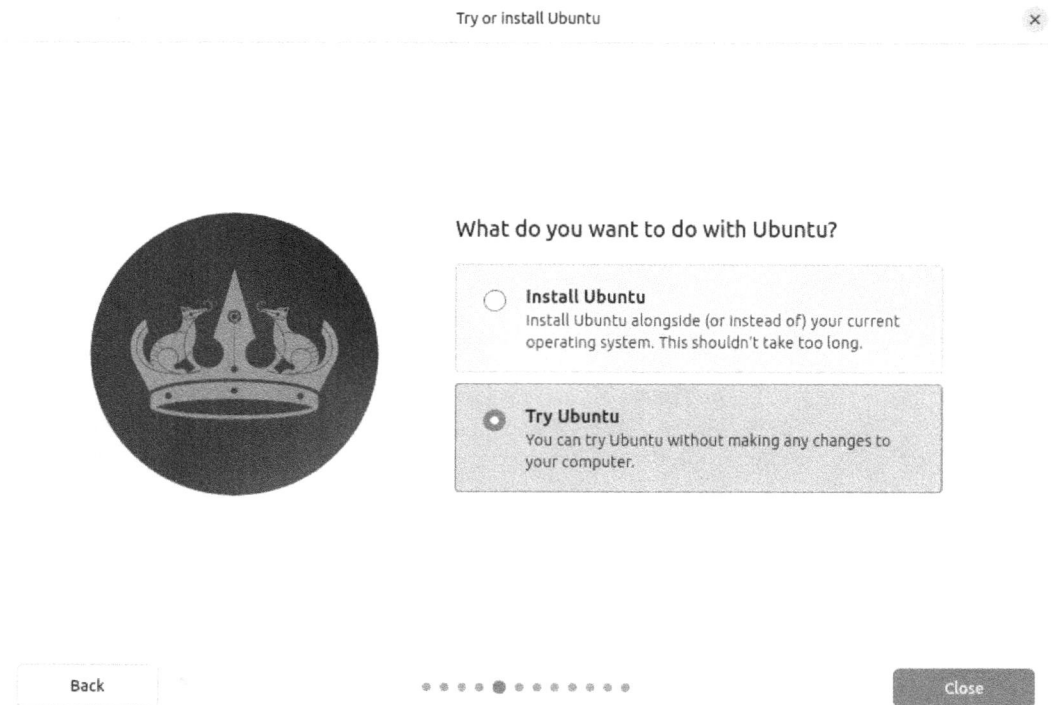

Figure 4.7 – Try Ubuntu

As mentioned, the live session is a full Ubuntu Desktop experience. This means you can use most of the included apps as if you have already installed your system without modifying it. This can be useful for evaluating Ubuntu before deciding to install it, perhaps verifying that your hardware all works with Ubuntu or just seeing whether it's something you want to commit to installing on your system.

The live session is also useful for various system rescue cases. If your system doesn't boot for some reason, you can boot to the live system to attempt to recover data or repair your installation.

To install Ubuntu, we'll choose **Install Ubuntu** and proceed:

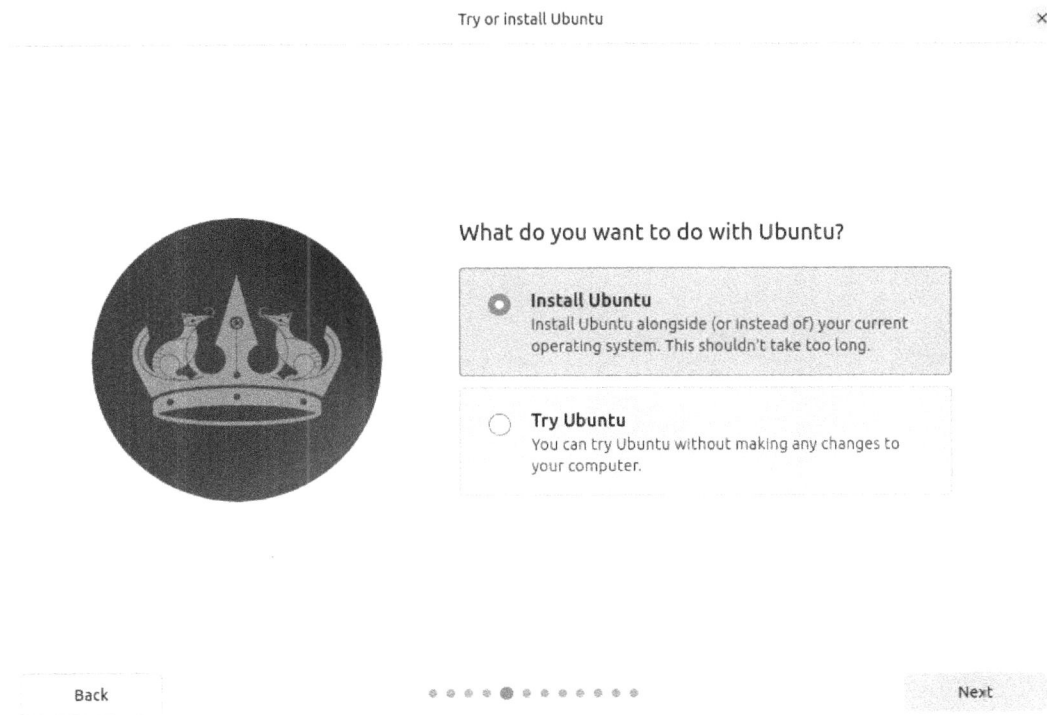

Figure 4.8 – Install Ubuntu

Interactive installation

Generally, you would want to choose the interactive installation, which allows you to navigate the installation one page at a time and configure your system to your liking:

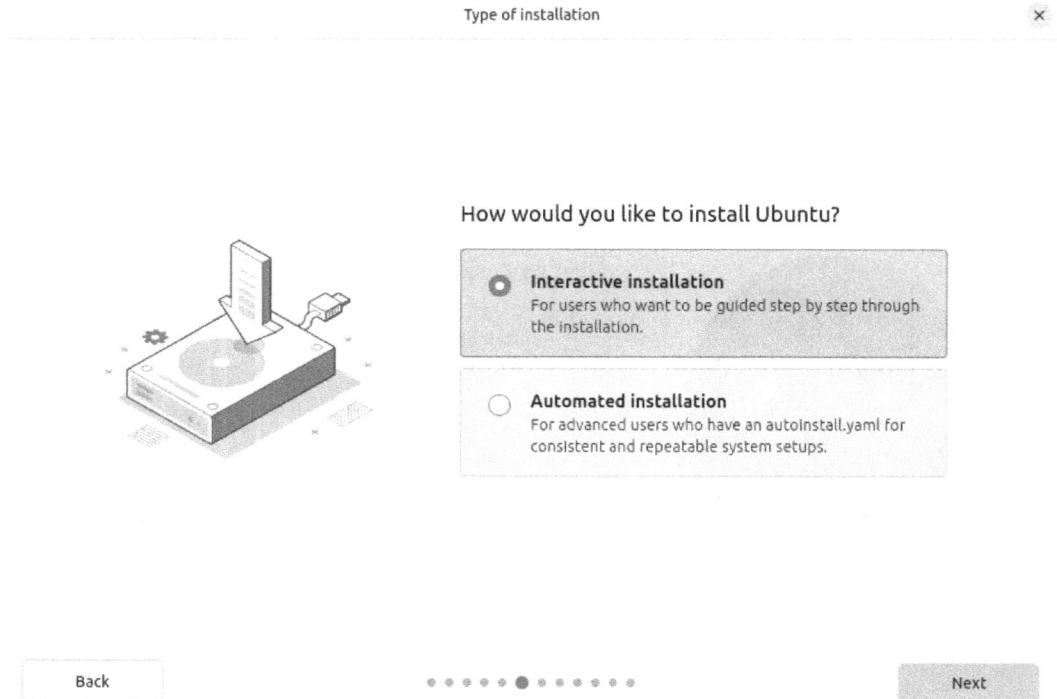

Figure 4.9 – Interactive installation

Automated installation

For some environments, such as an IT-managed system, it's desirable to ensure that many systems are installed and configured in a predictable and maintainable manner. In this case, you can craft an `autoinstall.yaml` file containing all the configuration information necessary to partially or completely automate the installation process:

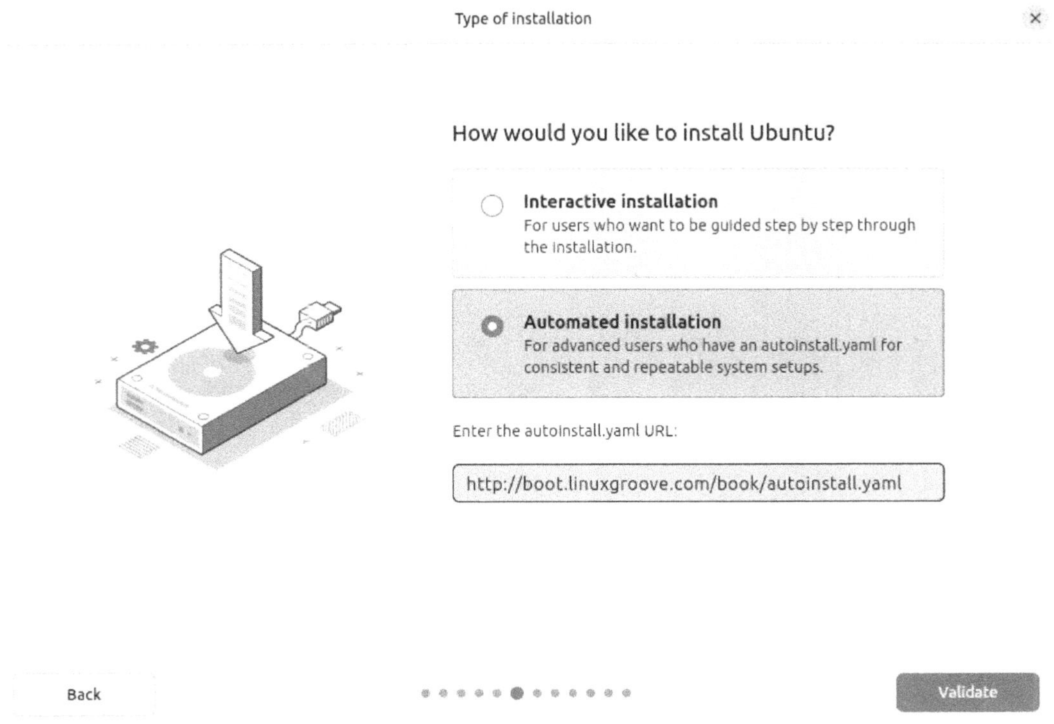

Figure 4.10 – Automated installation

More details can be found at `https://canonical-subiquity.readthedocs-hosted.com/en/latest/intro-to-autoinstall.html`.

Applications

The default Ubuntu installation includes quite a few useful applications, such as a calculator, a video player, and, of course, a web browser. This default software selection is designed to provide the apps most users need right after installation without requiring internet access to get the user started.

However, additional applications not included in the default selection may be necessary for your use case. Applications such as Thunderbird and LibreOffice are included on the USB installation media as part of the extended selection. These can be installed directly from the USB installer without internet access:

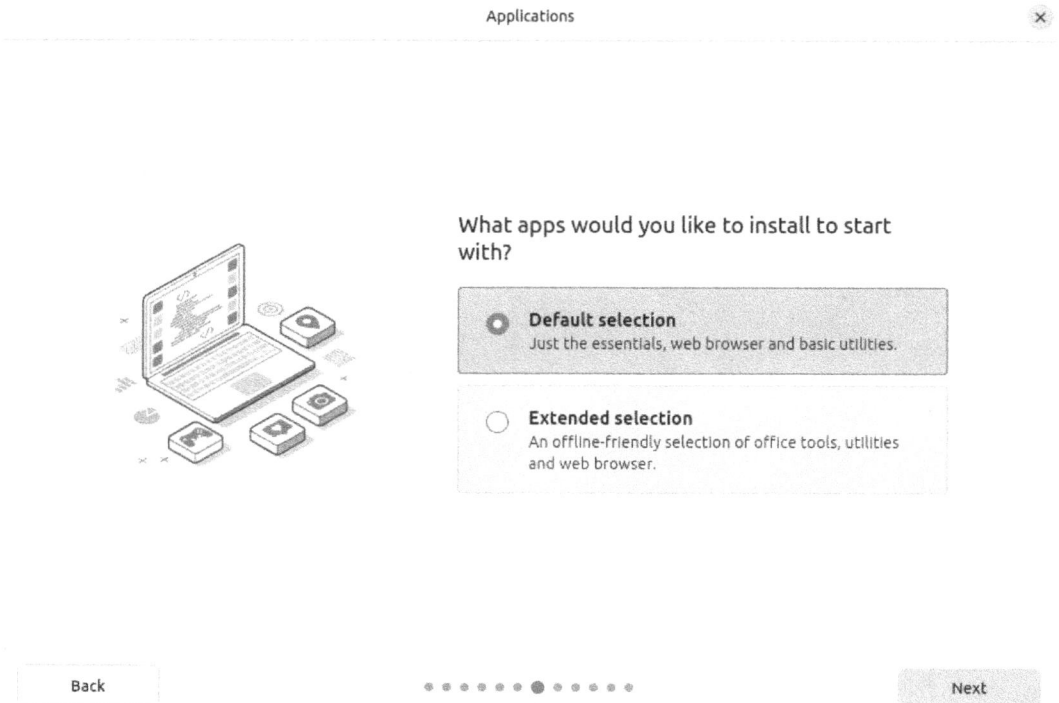

Figure 4.11 – Application selection

Proprietary drivers and codecs

Ubuntu doesn't install proprietary drivers or codecs by default. Proprietary drivers may be necessary to ensure your system functions as expected. For example, an open source driver is available if you have an NVIDIA graphics card; however, it isn't as complete as the proprietary driver. You need to check the third-party software option to get that proprietary driver.

Common audio and video formats are compressed, meaning smaller file sizes and reduced streaming bandwidth requirements. For playback, you need to be able to decode these compressed media formats. To do this, you need the proper codecs installed. Some popular codecs are open, but many popular formats, such as MP4, require patented codecs.

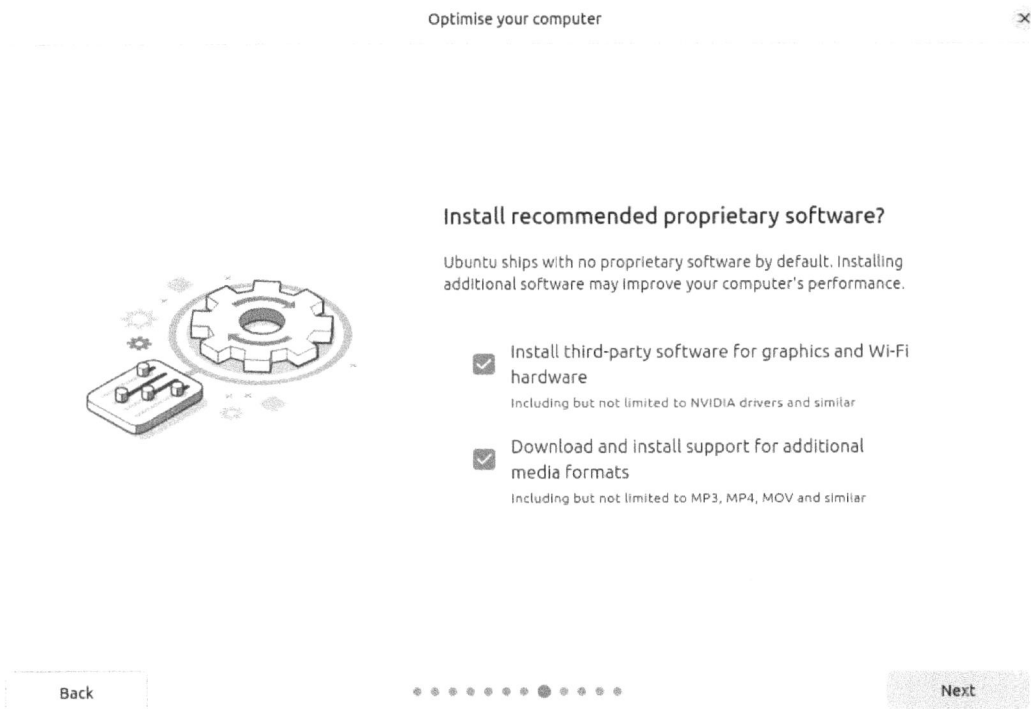

Figure 4.12 – Proprietary drivers and codecs

Disk setup

For most situations, choose the default on the **Disk Setup** page, which allows the installation to use the entire disk. However, if you already know you want more control over this, choose other filesystem options, multi-disk systems, or dual-boot scenarios:

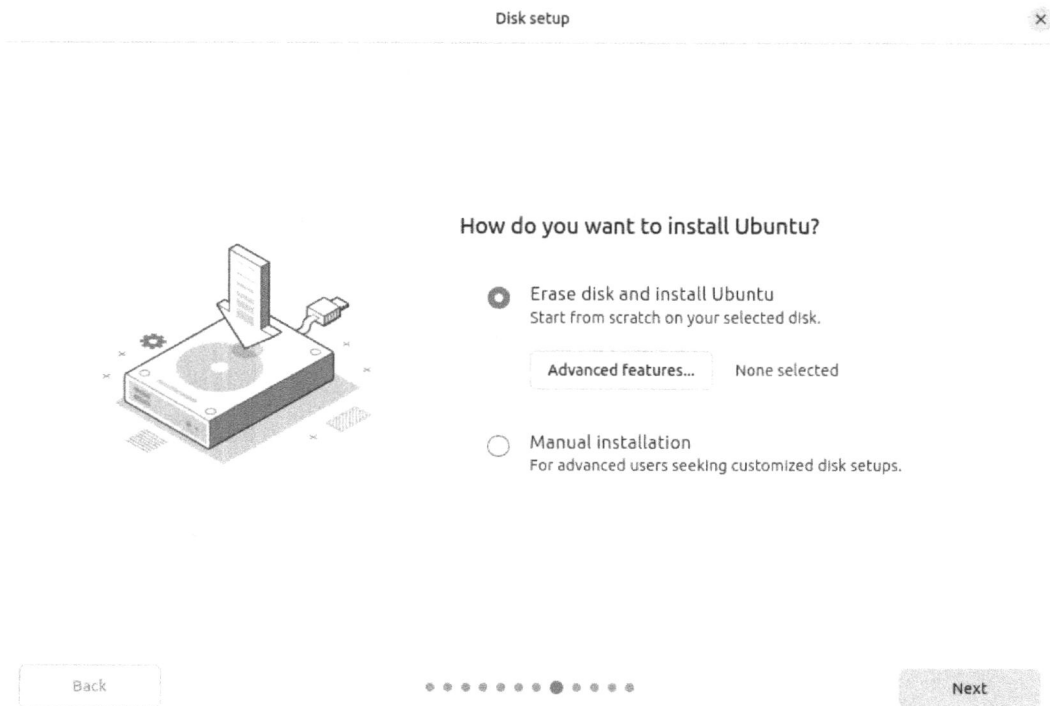

Figure 4.13 – Disk setup

Installation options

On this page, the installer will detect previously installed OSs and allow you to install Ubuntu alongside other OSs. For example, if you have Windows installed, you can keep Windows and install Ubuntu, keeping your Windows installation intact.

If an existing OS is detected and you choose to install Ubuntu alongside it, you'll be guided through resizing the disk partition where the existing OS is installed, allowing room for Ubuntu.

You can also choose to erase the disk and install Ubuntu, automatically creating the disk partitions and filesystems suitable for most use cases.

You can also choose manual installation, which gives you total control over configuring your disk. I recommend this option only if you have very specific needs you are already familiar with.

Advanced features

You can enable some advanced features on the same page, including encryption, which I highly recommend. We'll cover encryption in more detail in *Chapter 13*.

If you want or need to encrypt your drive to protect your data, there are three options: **Logical Volume Manager (LVM)** with encryption, **Zettabyte File System (ZFS)** with encryption, and hardware-backed encryption. Of these, the ZFS and hardware-backed options are still considered experimental. Read more about them in *Chapter 13* before deciding to utilize them here. If you want encryption, I recommend using LVM with encryption. With this option, you will be prompted to enter a passphrase very early in the boot process, which is used to decrypt the disk:

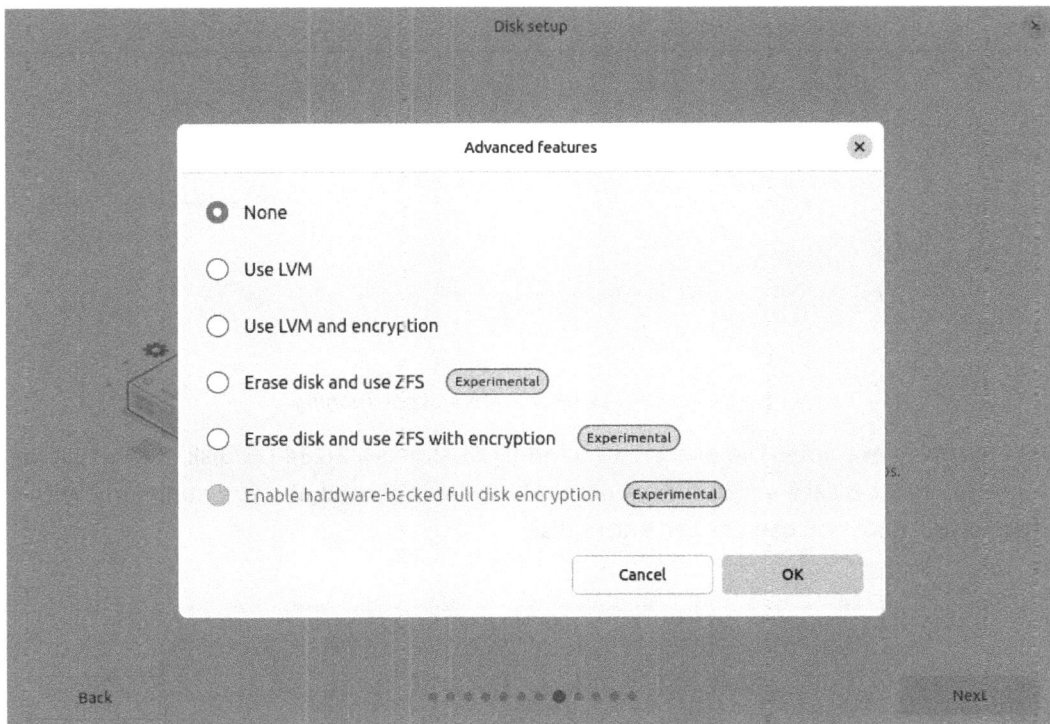

Figure 4.14 – Disk setup – Advanced features

Manual installation

If you choose the manual installation option, you'll be guided through creating and formatting disk partitions. I don't recommend this unless you have a very specific configuration in mind, and if that's the case, you have probably done this before:

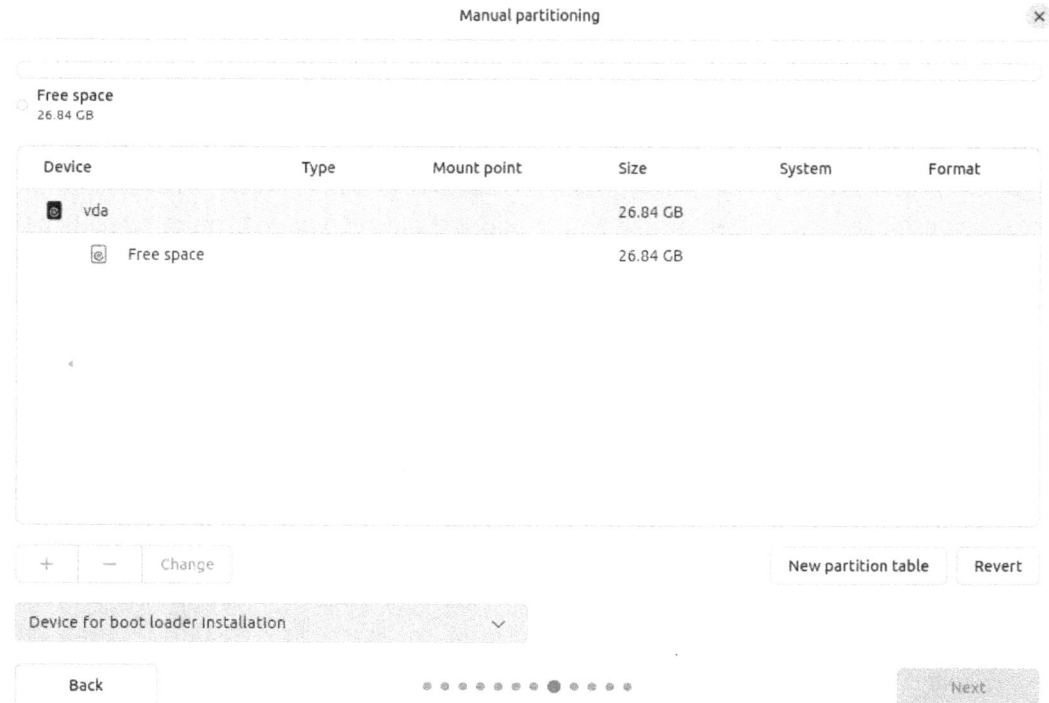

Figure 4.15 – Disk setup – Manual partitioning

Here's a basic example. The preceding screenshot shows a 26.84 GB disk in a virtual machine. You must create a root filesystem that will be mounted at / at a minimum. With a small virtual disk, you can use the entire disk:

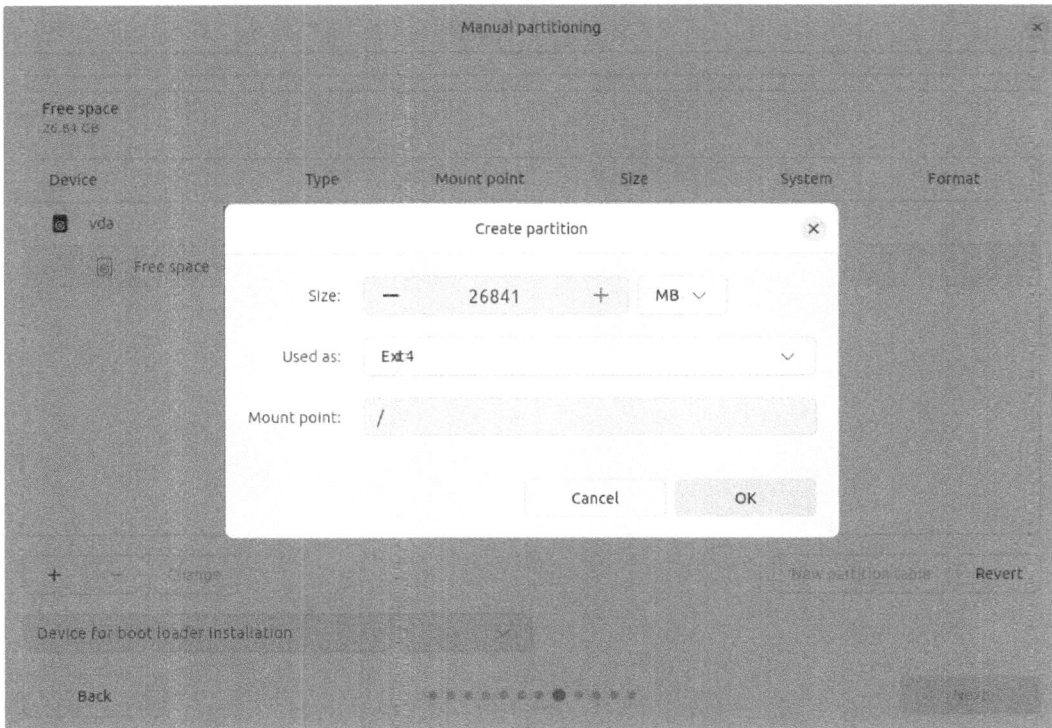

Figure 4.16 – Disk setup – New partition

A more practical example would be a much larger disk partitioned to keep user data separate from the root filesystem. This can be useful for later re-installing the OS without erasing the user data or home partitions. In this scenario, you would create a root filesystem on a partition mounted as / and a separate partition mounted at /home, where user home directories are generally located.

If you manually partition your drive, you can also create a swap partition. Swap is a partition or file that extends the memory available to the system. On modern systems, most people have enough **Random Access Memory** (**RAM**) not to worry much about swap space. However, it's still suggested that you create swap space on your computer to prevent out-of-memory situations, which can cause severe stability issues. If you don't create swap when partitioning the drive, the installer will create swap as a file stored on the root filesystem, but you may choose to create swap as a partition yourself:

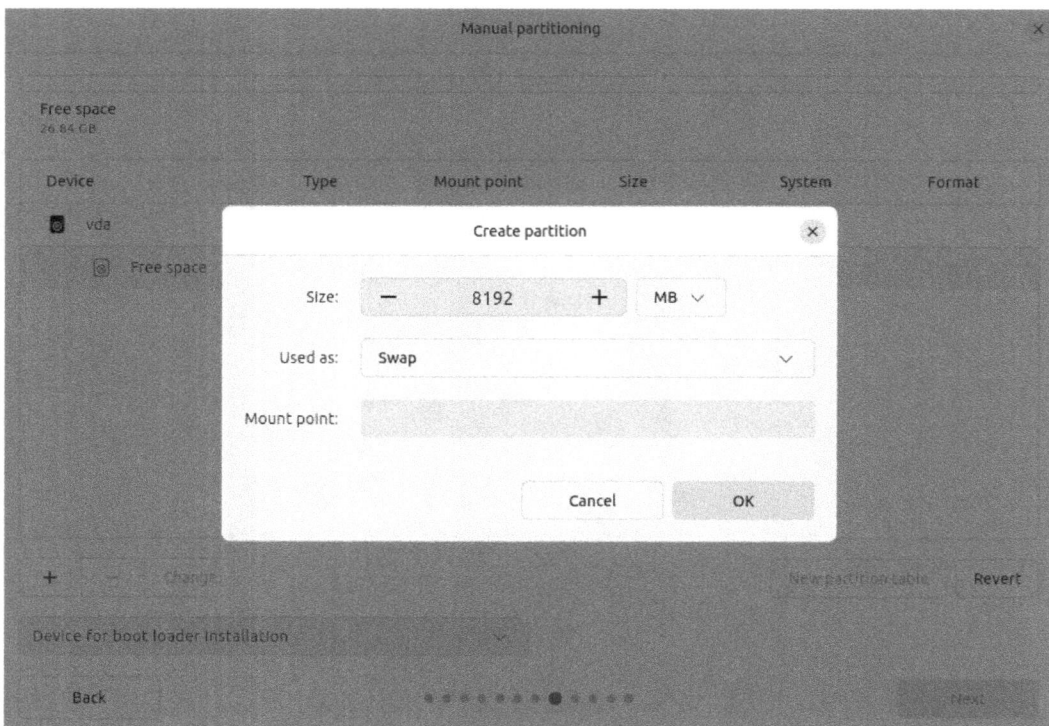

Figure 4.17 – Disk setup – Swap partition

Account creation

Creating a user account for your system is very self-explanatory. Your name, computer name, and password are likely all you'll need.

Optionally, you can uncheck the **Require my password to log in** option, which will auto-login your user when the system boots:

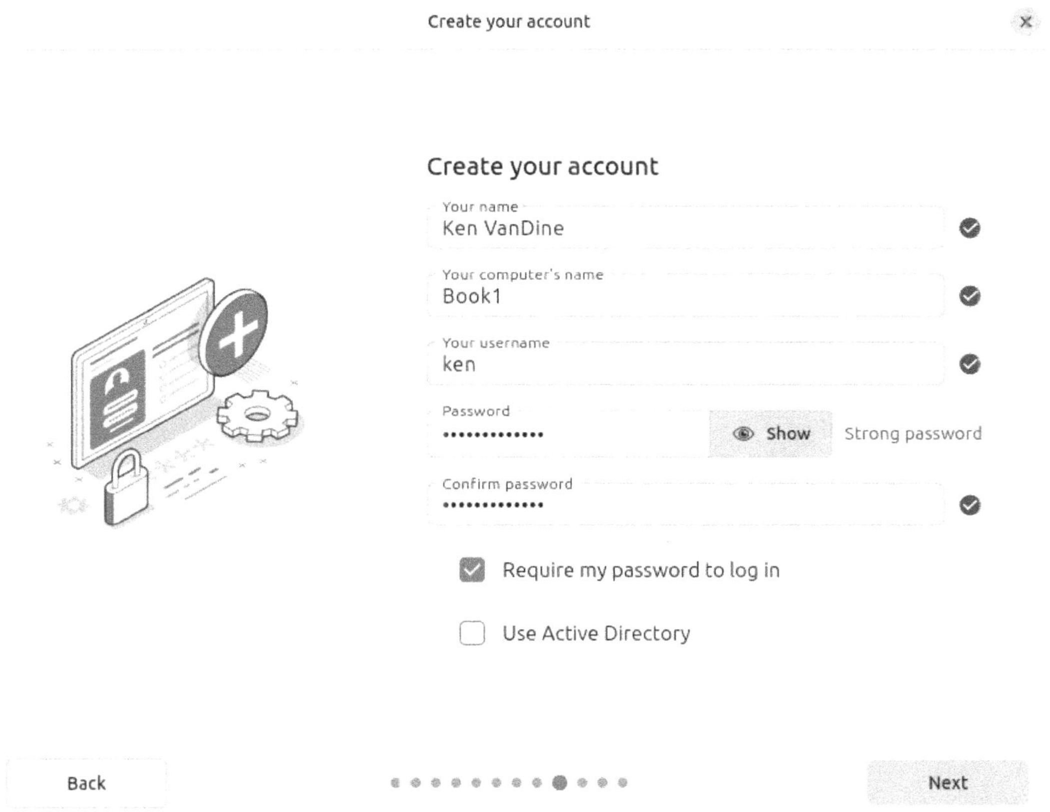

Create your account   ✕

Create your account

Your name
Ken VanDine ✓

Your computer's name
Book1 ✓

Your username
ken ✓

Password
●●●●●●●●●●●● 👁 Show   Strong password

Confirm password
●●●●●●●●●●●● ✓

☑ Require my password to log in

☐ Use Active Directory

Back   ● ○ ○ ○ ○ ○ ○ ○ ● ○ ○ ○   Next

Figure 4.18 – Create your account

Active Directory

In a corporate environment, you may need to enable Active Directory support by ticking the checkbox next to **Use Active Directory**, allowing you to join the computer to a domain and authenticate from Active Directory:

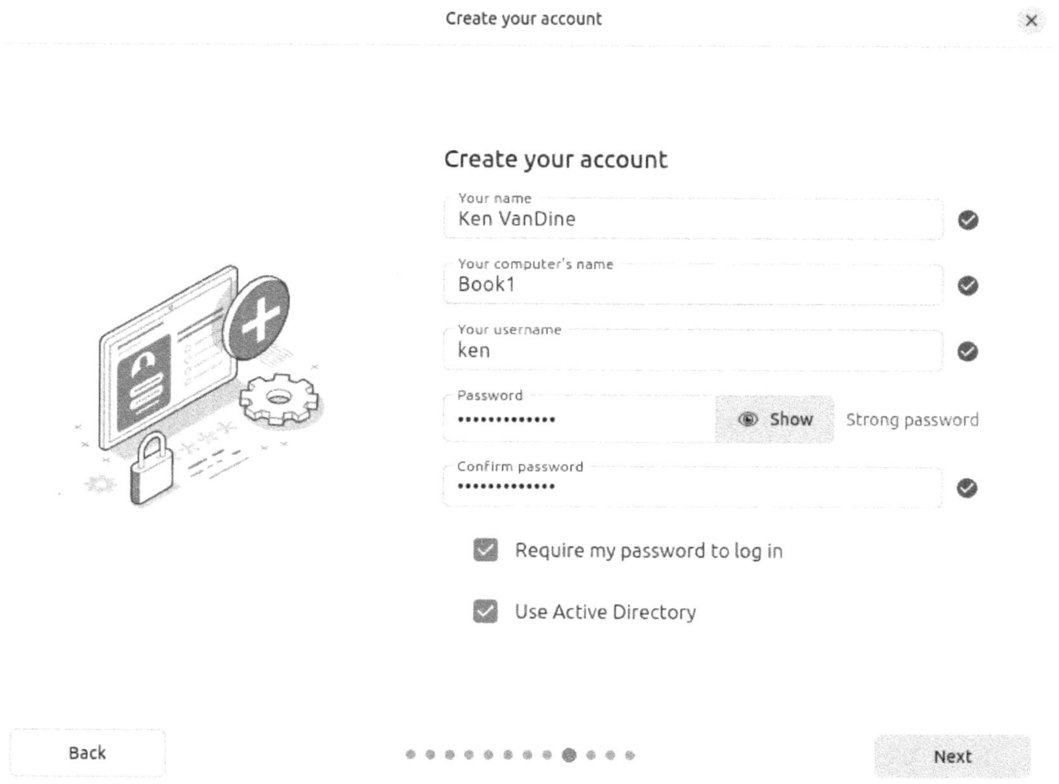

Figure 4.19 – Use Active Directory

Most corporate environments require computers to be part of an Active Directory domain, which allows authentication from a remote directory and policy-driven device administration. Ubuntu Desktop integrates well in an environment that is often dominated by Windows devices. Just note that this step needs to be completed by a user with domain-join privileges, often your IT department:

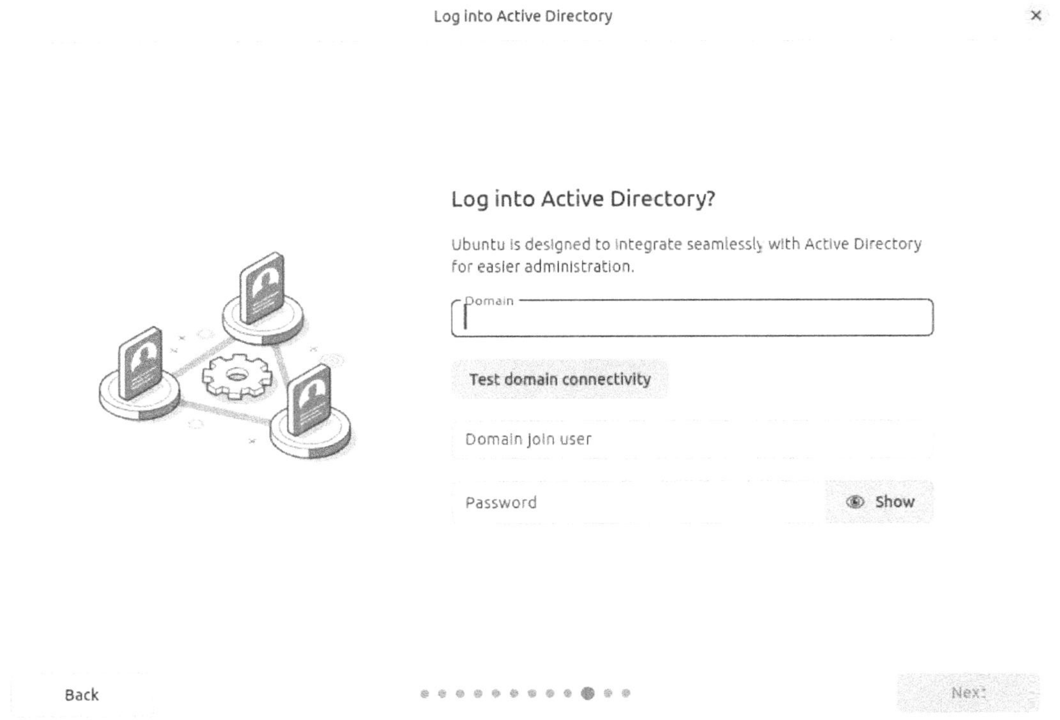

Figure 4.20 – Log into Active Directory?

Time zone

Choose your location on the world map, or type your location to search for a city near you:

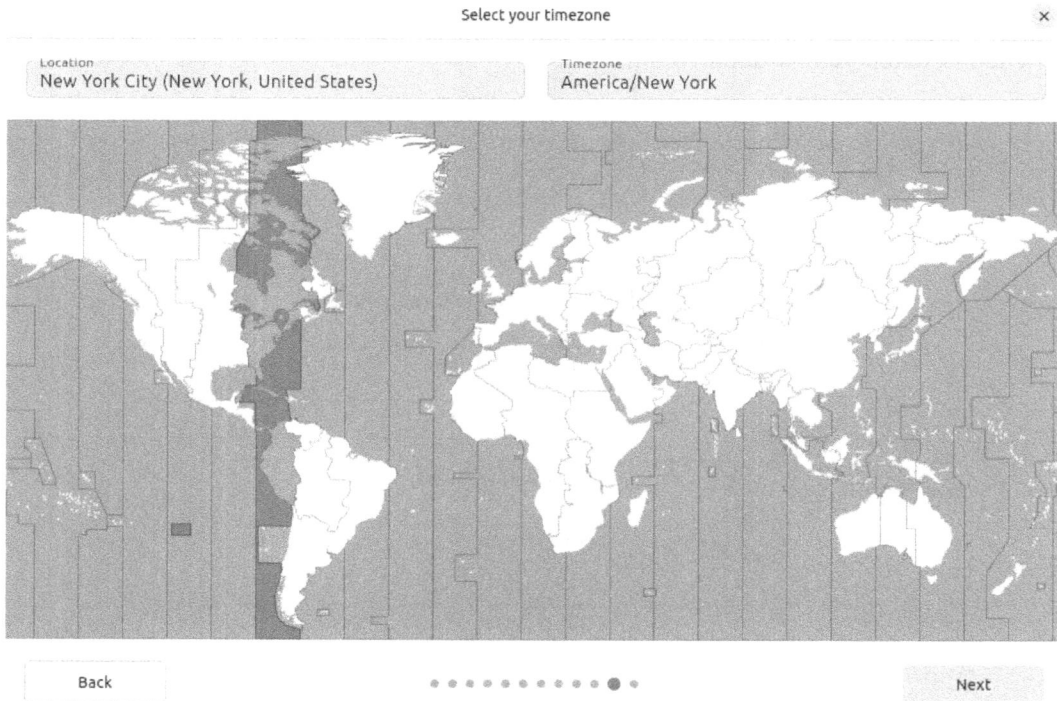

Figure 4.21 – Select location/time zone

Confirmation

The final page allows you to review your choices before altering your system. Installing an OS on your computer is destructive and will wipe out data. Review your choices carefully before proceeding:

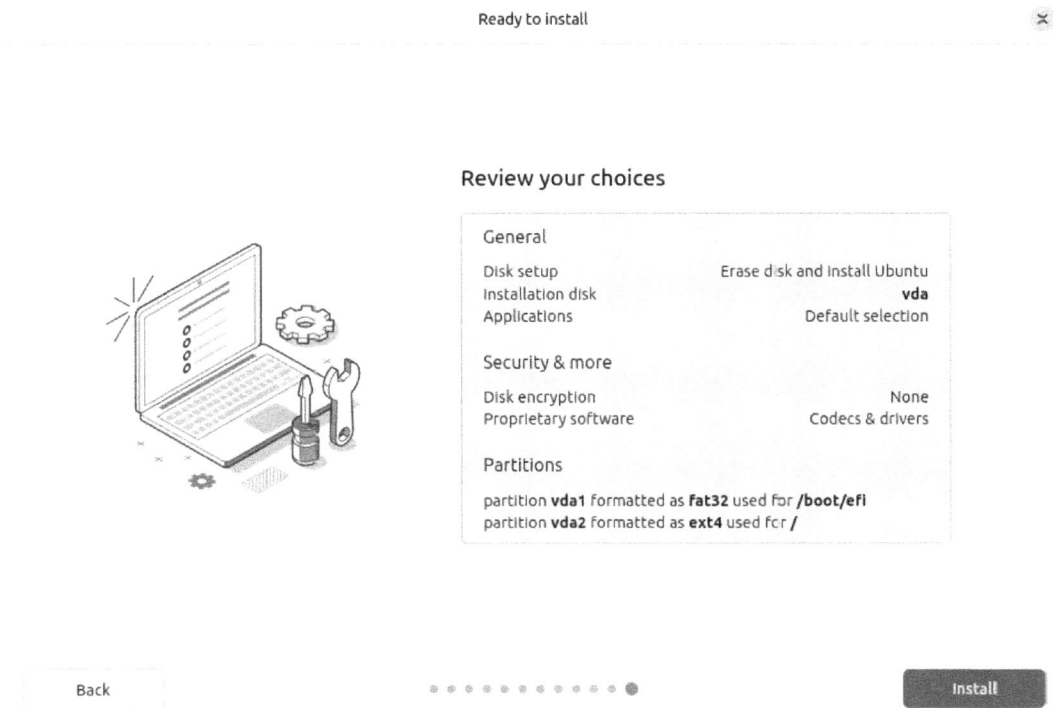

Figure 4.22 – Confirm and install

Slideshow

While the installation is in process, you can view a slideshow with useful information and the installation progress at the bottom of the screen. These slides change automatically, but you can also navigate to the previous or next slides and pause the slideshow:

Fast, free and full of new features

The latest version makes computing easier than ever.

Whether you're a developer, creator, gamer or administrator you'll find new tools to improve your productivity and enhance your experience in this release.

Copying files...

Figure 4.23 – Install progress slideshow

Debugging

It's always possible that you might encounter an error during installation. In the case of an installation error, the installer will display a dialog describing the error. However, seeing more verbose progress can also be useful, including following the installation debug log right in the installer interface. At the bottom right of the page, next to the installation progress indicator, there's a small icon that looks like a terminal or command prompt icon. Clicking this expands a terminal view inside the installer, showing the debug output produced by the installer:

Ubuntu 24.04 LTS

```
Jun 30 15:00:43 ubuntu subiquity_log.3249[5158]: Running command ['mount', '--make-private', '/tmp/
tmpjowwmvpe/mount/dev'] with allowed return codes [0] (capture=False)
Jun 30 15:00:43 ubuntu subiquity_log.3249[5158]: Running command ['umount', '/tmp/tmpjowwmvpe/mount/
dev'] with allowed return codes [0] (capture=False)
Jun 30 15:00:43 ubuntu subiquity_log.3249[5158]: finish: cmd-in-target: SUCCESS: curtin command in-
target
Jun 30 15:00:43 ubuntu subiquity_event.3249[3249]:  curtin command in-target
Jun 30 15:00:43 ubuntu subiquity_event.3249[3249]: configuring apt
Jun 30 15:00:43 ubuntu subiquity_event.3249[3249]: installing system
Jun 30 15:00:43 ubuntu subiquity_event.3249[3249]:  executing curtin install initial step
Jun 30 15:00:43 ubuntu subiquity_log.3249[5522]: /usr/bin/ubuntu-drivers
Jun 30 15:00:43 ubuntu subiquity_log.3249[5523]: /usr/bin/ubuntu-drivers
Jun 30 15:00:44 ubuntu subiquity_log.3249[5515]: start: cmd-install: curtin command install
Jun 30 15:00:44 ubuntu subiquity_log.3249[5515]: curtin: Installation started. (24.0.0-3-gc66faffee)
Jun 30 15:00:44 ubuntu subiquity_log.3249[5515]: LANG=en_US.UTF-8
Jun 30 15:00:44 ubuntu subiquity_log.3249[5515]: 'reporter' not found in config file.
Jun 30 15:00:44 ubuntu subiquity_log.3249[5515]: curtin: Installation started. (24.0.0-3-gc66faffee)
Jun 30 15:00:44 ubuntu subiquity_log.3249[5515]: Exporting resume data to /tmp/tmpv2gld4xq/resume-
data.json so that further stages can be executed in a later invocation.
Jun 30 15:00:44 ubuntu subiquity_log.3249[5515]: {'WORKING_DIR': '/tmp/tmpxefuhnh0/scratch',
'OUTPUT_FSTAB': '/tmp/tmpxefuhnh0/state/fstab', 'OUTPUT_INTERFACES': '/tmp/tmpxefuhnh0/state/
interfaces', 'OUTPUT_NETWORK_CONFIG': '/tmp/tmpxefuhnh0/state/network_config', 'OUTPUT_NETWORK_STATE':
'/tmp/tmpxefuhnh0/state/network_state', 'TARGET_MOUNT_POINT': '/target', 'CONFIG': '/tmp/tmpxefuhnh0/
state/config'}
Jun 30 15:00:44 ubuntu subiquity_log.3249[5515]: curtin: Installation finished.
Jun 30 15:00:44 ubuntu subiquity_log.3249[5515]: Skipping unmount: config disabled target unmounting
Jun 30 15:00:44 ubuntu subiquity_log.3249[5515]: TIMED INSTALL_COMMAND: 0.002
Jun 30 15:00:44 ubuntu subiquity_log.3249[5515]: finish: cmd-install: SUCCESS: curtin command install
Jun 30 15:00:44 ubuntu subiquity_event.3249[3249]:  executing curtin install initial step
Jun 30 15:00:44 ubuntu subiquity_event.3249[3249]:  executing curtin install partitioning step
```

‹   ❚❚   ›   installing the system…

Figure 4.24 – Installation debug output

Installation complete

You will be prompted with **Continue testing** or **Restart now** when the installation is complete. **Continue testing** will close the installer and allow you to continue to use the live session.

Choosing **Restart now** will reboot the system into your new installation. Enjoy Ubuntu!

Figure 4.25 – Installation complete

Now that your installation is complete and you've restarted your computer, let's examine the out-of-the-box experience after logging in for the first time. You will be greeted with a graphical wizard for additional steps.

Ubuntu Welcome

After logging in for the first time, the Ubuntu Welcome wizard will guide you through some more steps, including an introduction to Ubuntu Pro and an opportunity to help Ubuntu by sharing some basic system information.

Ubuntu Pro

Ubuntu Pro is a comprehensive subscription service for open source software security. Before I discuss this subscription service, let me mention that it is actually free for up to five devices. With Ubuntu Pro, you get access to the following:

- **Expanded Security Maintenance (ESM)**: ESM gives you access to security fixes for over 25,000 packages for 10 years, significantly extending the support for your LTS installation

- **Livepatch kernel update service**: Kernel Livepatch provides kernel security fixes without requiring reboots
- **Compliance and hardening**: Tools are provided to support complex compliance requirements

For personal use, everyone can get Ubuntu Pro for up to five devices for free, and official Ubuntu Community members get Ubuntu Pro for up to 50 devices! For more information, see https://ubuntu.com/pro:

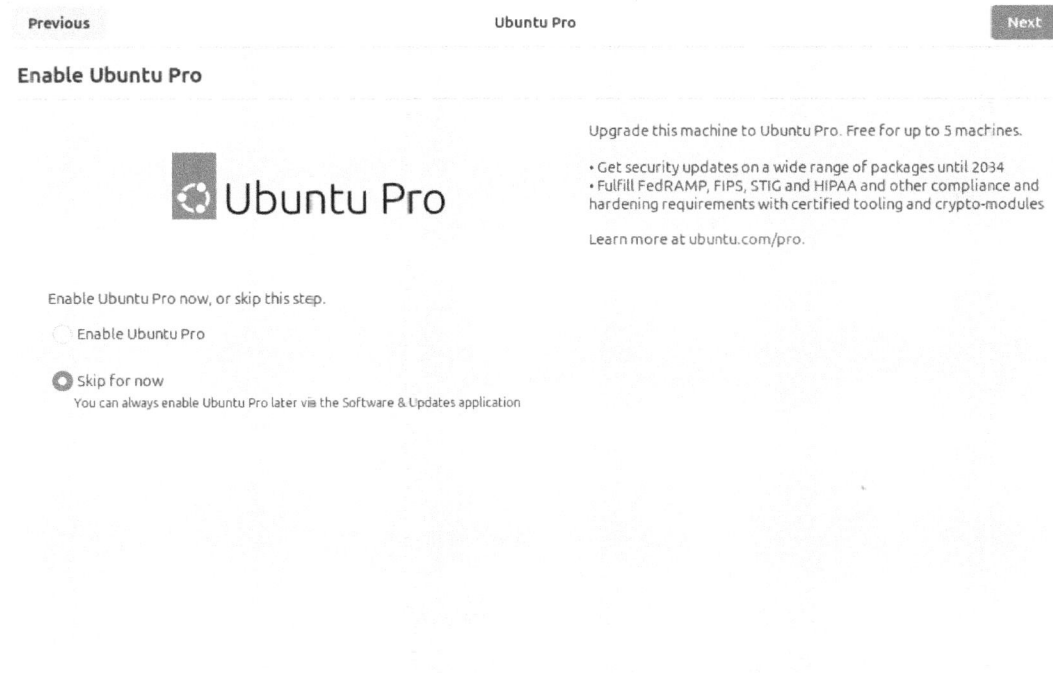

Figure 4.26 – Ubuntu Welcome – Enable Ubuntu Pro

Ubuntu report

Understanding the types of hardware users have is very useful for improving Ubuntu. This page in Ubuntu Welcome lets you opt out of submitting a report to the Ubuntu report service. All data sent to this service is anonymized and in no way associated with your identity or your computer:

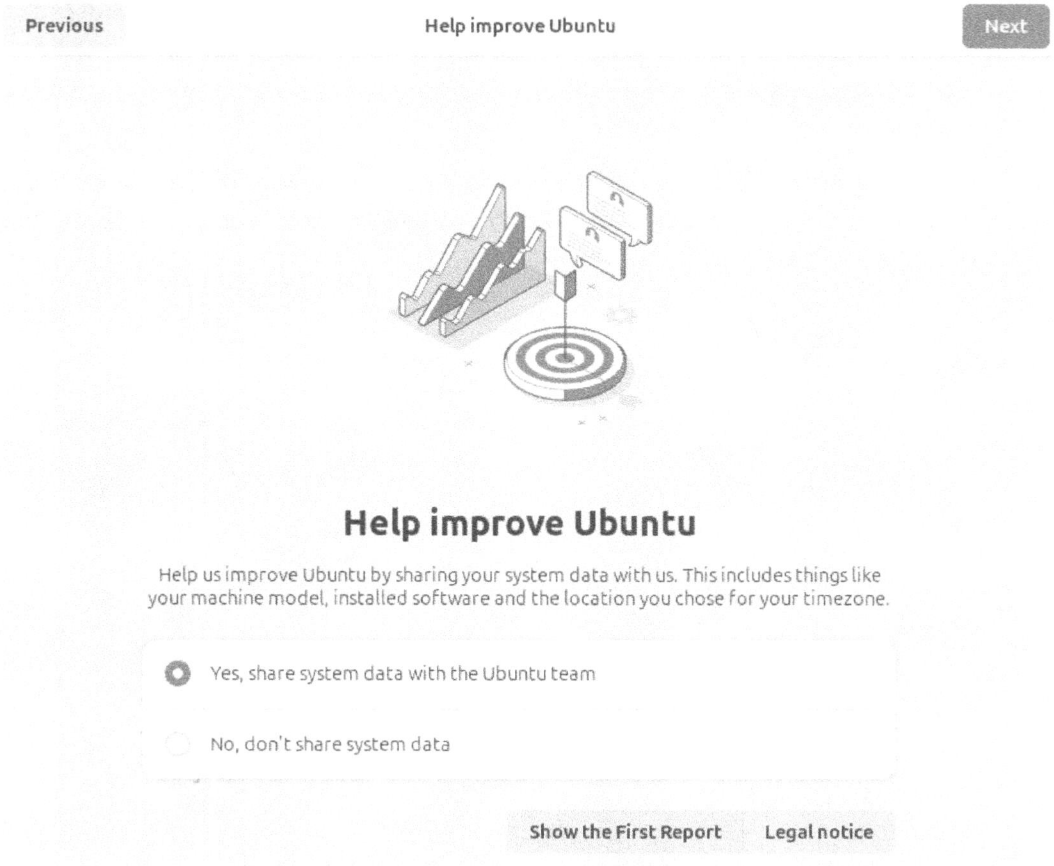

Help improve Ubuntu

Help us improve Ubuntu by sharing your system data with us. This includes things like your machine model, installed software and the location you chose for your timezone.

◉ Yes, share system data with the Ubuntu team

○ No, don't share system data

Show the First Report   Legal notice

Figure 4.27 – Ubuntu Welcome – Ubuntu report

Here are examples of some of the information that's sent:

- Manufacturer
- **Central Processing Unit (CPU)**
- **Graphics Processing Unit (GPU)**
- RAM
- Screen resolution

After completing the Ubuntu Welcome wizard, your Ubuntu Desktop is ready for use!

Essential hardware – installing necessary drivers

Drivers are the necessary packages necessary to allow you to use your hardware. For example, for wireless networking to work, there needs to be a driver that supports the Wi-Fi device on your computer. Usually, these are included in Ubuntu and require no additional steps for you to install or enable them.

You may have hardware that doesn't have an open source driver, which may require some extra steps to install. A common example of this is an NVIDIA graphics card. During the installation process, there was an **Optimize Your Computer** screen; if you checked the box to allow installation of proprietary software and you have an NVIDIA graphics card, the installer would have automatically installed the appropriate driver. However, if not, or you want to switch which version of the driver you are using, you can use the **Additional Drivers** tool:

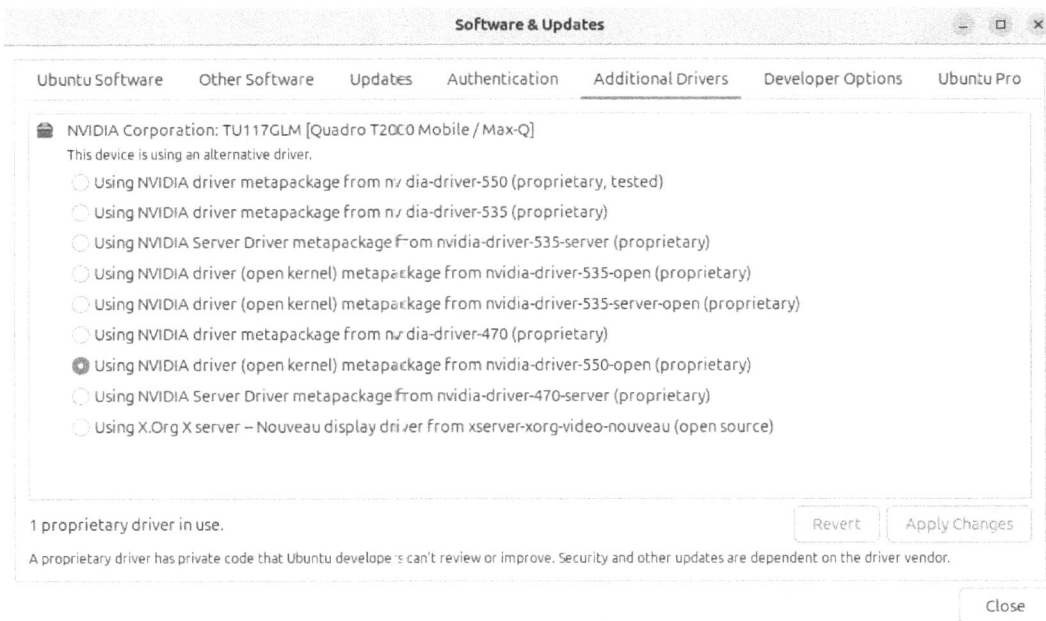

Figure 4.28 – Additional Drivers

The **Additional Drivers** tool will list hardware devices detected that require proprietary drivers. You can see in the preceding example that I have an NVIDIA Quadro T2000 and I'm currently using version 550 of the driver. If you would like to switch to a different version of the driver, or even to the open source nouveau driver, you can simply select the driver you want and select **Apply Changes**. Once the new driver is installed, you will need to reboot to use it.

Summary

In this chapter, we've covered important considerations before beginning installation, proceeded through a guided installation process, and dove into more advanced installation scenarios such as encryption, Active Directory enrollment, and manual disk partitioning.

In *Chapter 5*, we will explore how to effectively use your **Ubuntu Desktop**, starting with covering the basic usage and expanding into more powerful features, such as dynamic workspaces and tiling window management.

Further reading

- Ubuntu Desktop Installation Documentation: `https://ubuntu.com/tutorials/install-ubuntu-desktop`

Part 2

Getting the Most Out of Your Ubuntu System

In this part of the book, you will learn more about using Ubuntu Desktop, finding and installing the applications you need, and the importance of keeping your system up to date. We'll explore the amazing Ubuntu community and learn how to best engage with the community to get the help you need. We'll jump into some more advanced topics such as using Ubuntu in an enterprise environment as well as boosting your efficiency with the command line.

This part of the book includes the following chapters:

- *Chapter 5, Using Your Ubuntu Desktop*
- *Chapter 6, Software Discovery: Finding and Installing Applications*
- *Chapter 7, Software Updates: Enhancing Security and Stability*
- *Chapter 8, Getting Help: The Ubuntu Community and Beyond*
- *Chapter 9, Ubuntu in the Enterprise and at Scale*
- *Chapter 10, Command-Line Tricks and Shortcuts: Boosting Your Efficiency*

5

Using Your Ubuntu Desktop

Now that we've taken the leap and installed **Ubuntu Desktop**, it's time to learn more about the desktop experience Ubuntu provides. What does that even mean? What exactly is the desktop? These are all great questions, and we'll dig into them as we progress through this chapter.

The chapter covers the following topics:

- Mastering the desktop: your gateway to applications
- Unveiling the power of workspaces: multitasking made easy
- Introducing tiling window management
- Capturing screenshots and screen recording
- Controlling your desktop like a pro with keyboard shortcuts
- Working with files and folders: the power of file management
- The power of customization: tailoring your Ubuntu experience
- A tour of essential applications

Mastering the desktop – your gateway to applications

When we say *desktop*, we're referring to the graphical interface you see after logging in to your computer. At the most basic level, it's how you launch and interact with your applications. You can also consider tasks such as finding your applications, launching the application, managing your applications' windows, changing focus, minimizing, maximizing, and closing applications.

Applications

The primary way to find your installed applications is through the **application grid**, often referred to as the **app grid**. To raise the app grid, click on the Ubuntu logo at the bottom left of your screen. You can raise the app grid using the *Super + A* keyboard shortcut:

Figure 5.1 – Finding the application grid

Note

Throughout this chapter, we'll reference keyboard shortcuts, including the *Super* key. The *Super* key is also known as the *Windows* key, commonly represented by the Microsoft Windows logo on the key. It is often between the *Ctrl* and *Alt* keys at the bottom left of the keyboard.

With the app grid shown, you can navigate to the icon for the application you want to launch or type in some search criteria to filter down the app grid list of apps. Clicking the icon for any application will open that app:

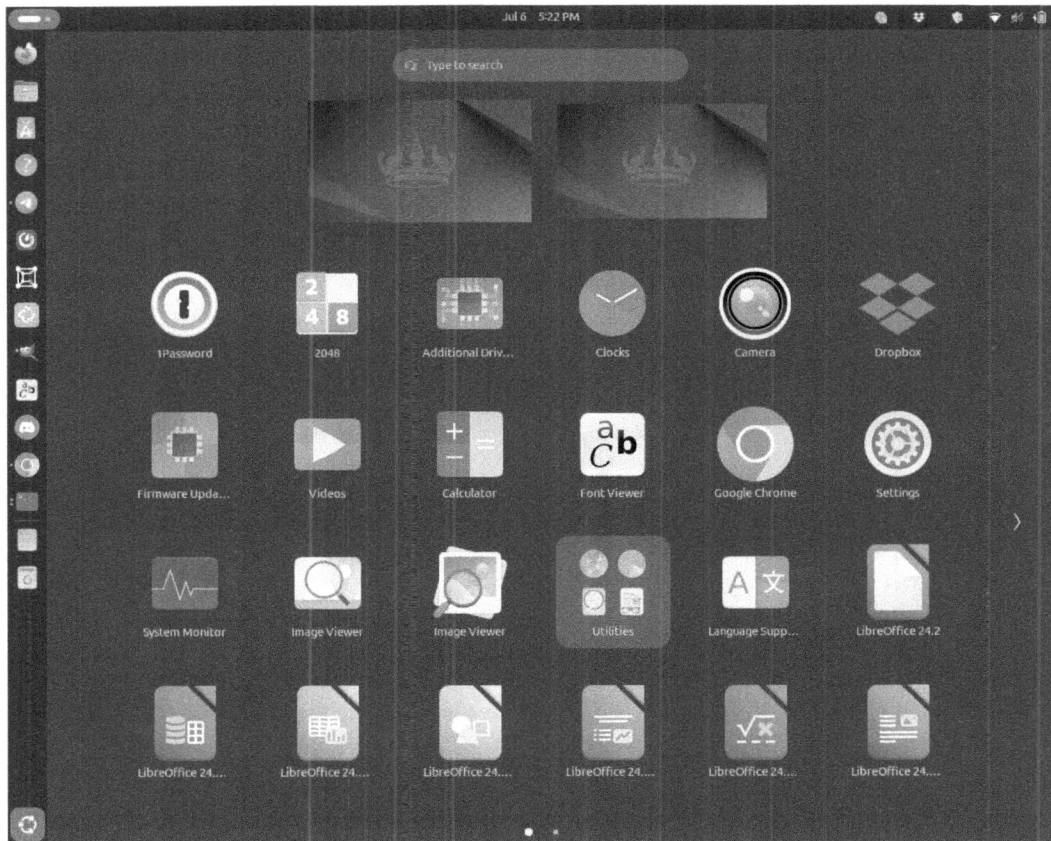

Figure 5.2 – The application grid

The application grid looks pretty simple, right? Well, it is, but it's also very flexible. Notice in the preceding figure that four icons appear to be grouped with the label **Utilities**. This is a folder of applications. To add more icons to the **Utilities** folder, simply drag the icon you want to move and drop it in **Utilities**.

What if you want to create additional folders to organize your applications yourself? Drag one icon and drop it on another icon you wish to group; this creates a new folder! The new folder will have the label **Unnamed Folder**. Select the new folder, and you'll see an *edit* icon at the top right, which changes to edit mode. In edit mode, you can type over the name with a name of your choice.

On systems with dual graphics cards, the application icons will provide an option to launch with the discrete graphics card. This isn't all that common, but some laptops, in particular, are sold with both integrated graphics and discrete graphics. The discrete graphics card is a higher-performance option that is more suitable for gaming and data science use. Some apps, such as **Steam**, have built-in logic to ensure discrete graphics are used if available. However, in GNOME (the desktop environment), you have the ability to specify whether you want to run any app using the discrete graphics card. This isn't the default because discrete graphics use more power and generate more heat, which is not ideal on a laptop:

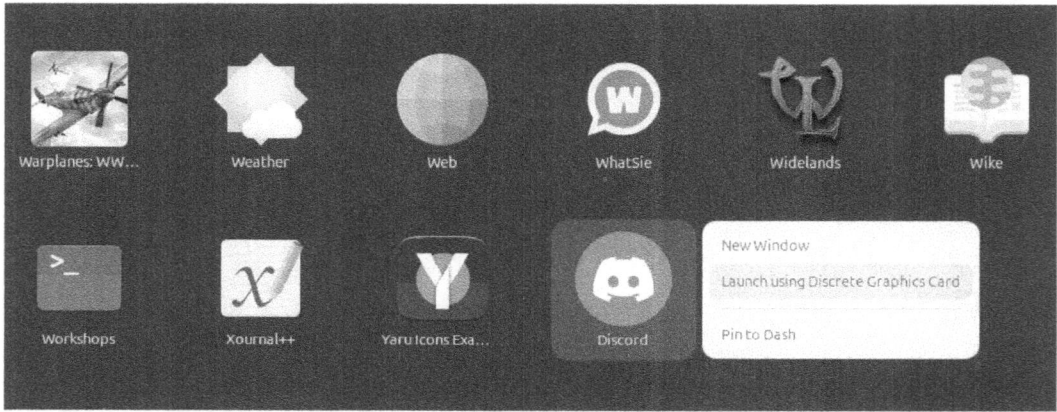

Figure 5.3 – Launching with discrete graphics

Figure 5.3 shows the right-click menu for the **Discord** application launcher on a laptop with integrated and discrete graphics. Selecting **Launch using Discrete Graphics Card** will start Discord and ensure it runs on the discrete graphics card rather than the default behavior or using the more power-efficient integrated graphics. This option will not be shown if your system doesn't have multiple graphics cards.

Dock

The **Ubuntu Dock** is located on the left-hand side of the screen and provides icons for all your favorite and running applications. Some application icons, such as the Firefox browser, are pinned to the dock by default. When you pin an application to the dock, it adds it as a favorite. To add new favorites, right-click an application icon in the app grid and click **Pin to Dash**, as shown in *Figure 5.3*. For an application already running, you can right-click on the icon in the dock and click **Pin to Dash**. To remove an application from your favorites, right-click on the icon in the dock and click **Unpin**.

You can distinguish which apps are currently running by the small dot next to the icon. Each dot represents a window, so if three Firefox windows are open, you'll see three dots next to the Firefox icon.

Applications can also embed information along with their icons. For example, a messaging app could display a small emblem showing the number of unread messages.

A right-click on an application icon will also give you some quick shortcuts to application-specific actions such as **New Window**, **New Incognito Window**, **New Message**, and so on. The right-click on the app icon will also let you preview all windows for the application and raise focus for the window you choose. You can do this by right-clicking and selecting **All Windows**, which will embed a small graphical preview of each window currently open for the application. Click on the preview to focus on the selected window:

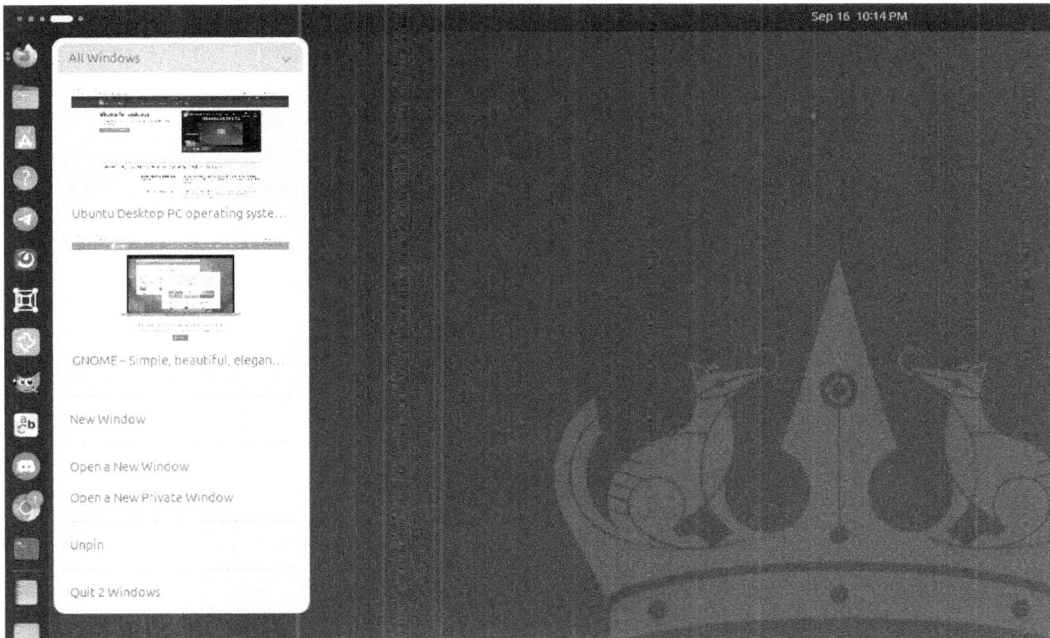

Figure 5.4 – Ubuntu Dock: Right-click

As mentioned earlier, the Ubuntu Dock has an Ubuntu logo at the bottom that shows the application grid.

Customization

Some settings can be customized for the Ubuntu Dock, and they are found in the **Ubuntu Desktop** panel in the system settings:

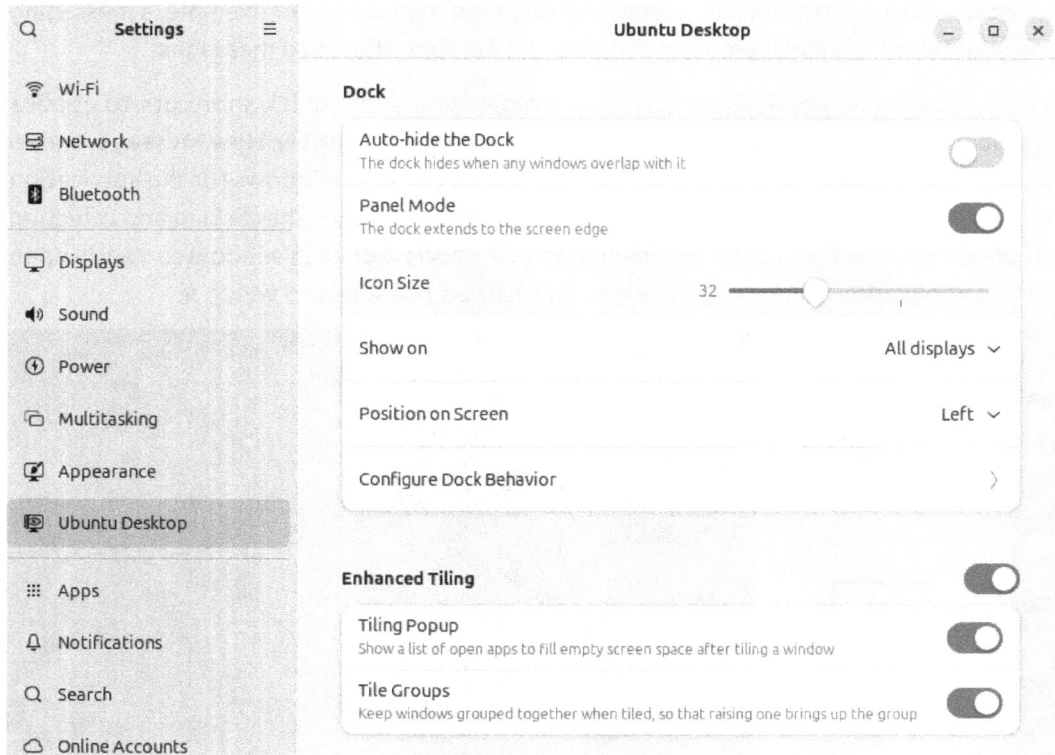

Figure 5.5 – Ubuntu Dock Settings

Let us run through these:

- **Auto-hide the Dock**: When enabled, the dock hides when any windows overlap with it.

- **Panel Mode**: The dock extends to the screen edge. When enabled, the panel will be the full length of the screen; when disabled, the panel will dynamically resize based on the number of icons displayed.

- **Icon Size**: The size to display the icons. The dock's width will grow/shrink to match the icon size. The smaller the icon size, the more icons can be displayed.

- **Show on**: For multiple displays, such as a laptop with an external monitor, you can configure the dock to be displayed on all displays or specific displays.

- **Position on Screen**: This allows you to change where the dock is located on the screen: on the left, right, or bottom. By default, it's on the left.
- **Configure Dock Behavior**: Enable or disable showing icons for network-mounted storage, removable storage devices, and trash.

Panel

The small top panel provides a space to display important system and application information and some quick actions for various desktop tasks.

Date/time and notifications

The current date and time are centered on the top panel, as shown in *Figure 5.6*:

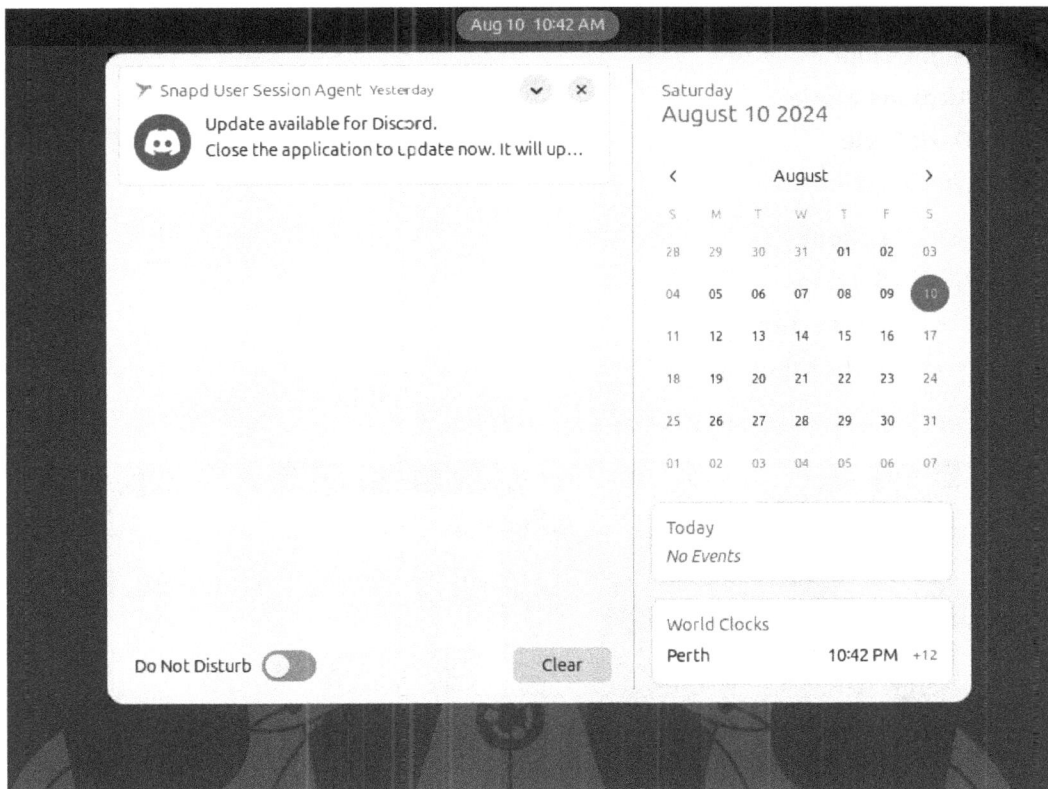

Figure 5.6 – Notification area

Clicking on this area of the panel displays an overlay that includes a calendar, event notifications, and system and application notifications. A toggle also enables/disables the **Do Not Disturb** mode, which quiets notifications when enabled.

Indicators

Indicators provide a quick way to see status. This can be thought of as system status, such as battery life or Wi-Fi connection, or application status such as unseen messages.

System indicators

These include the following:

- **Power**
- **Volume Control**
- **Brightness Control**
- **Network**
- **Bluetooth**
- **Night Light**
- **Airplane Mode**
- **Dark Style**
- **Quick Actions**:
    - **Logout**
    - **Settings**
    - **Lock screen**
    - **Screenshot**

The system indicators are intuitive, as seen in *Figure 5.7*:

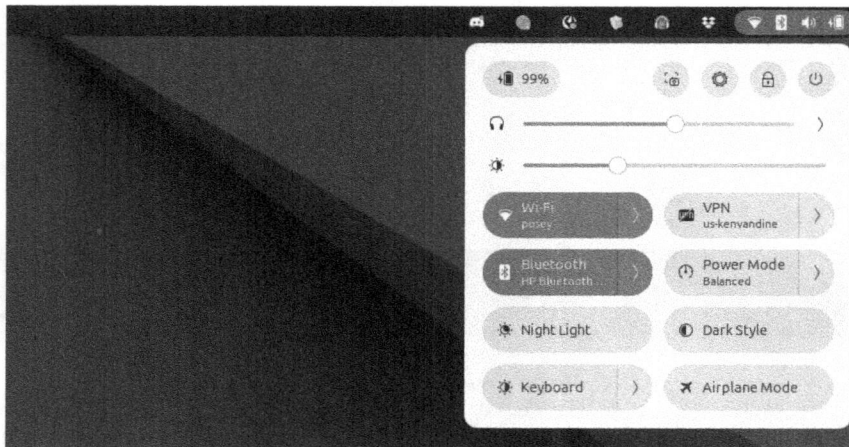

Figure 5.7 – System indicators

Note the quick access to both volume and brightness sliders. A microphone control will also be present if the device is actively used. *Figure 5.7* also shows quick access to Wi-Fi, Bluetooth, and so on. Bluetooth and Wi-Fi are enabled, reflected by the state of the quick control, which is orange. Clicking the control will disable or enable it depending on the current state. Clicking the arrow on the right edge of the control will expand for further options. The controls can also show additional information, such as the Wi-Fi network's name or connected Bluetooth devices.

Application indicators

Running applications can embed a status notifier in the application indicator. For example, **Telegram** displays an indicator showing the number of unread messages and provides a quick menu to access Telegram features. *Figure 5.7* shows application indicators for some running apps. Notice that the Discord and Telegram icons in the panel have emblems, indicating unread messages in those applications. Once all messages are seen, the application will remove the emblem.

Many popular applications take advantage of this area, most notably, messaging apps such as Telegram, WhatsApp, Discord, and so on.

Dropbox, a popular file sync service, provides an indicator that displays the status of your file sync, usage information, and quick menu items.

The **Canonical Livepatch** service, included in Ubuntu Pro, displays the kernel Livepatch status on your system.

1password, a popular password storage application, uses an application indicator to provide quick access to your passwords and other private information stored by the service.

Workspace indicator

There is a small indicator at the top left with controls for managing your workspaces, which we'll cover in more detail in the next section.

So far, we've discussed the basic desktop experience, including interacting with your applications, window focus, application indicators, and notifications. Next, we'll go into more advanced desktop usage with workspaces.

Unveiling the power of workspaces – multitasking made easy

It's very common to deal with multiple windows of individual applications and switching between different running applications. Workspaces are a way to group windows for running applications in logical ways. For example, perhaps you are a developer and want to separate your development work from administrative work such as email. You can put your VS Code and Terminal windows in the same workspace, and your browser can open your email and calendar in a different workspace.

This nicely groups your most relevant windows, allowing easy, quick navigation without distractions. Workspaces are organized horizontally; you can imagine them as separate desktops, such as monitors. The difference is they don't take up any more physical space on your desk!

To manage and navigate your workspaces, click on the far left of the top panel. The item used to access your workspaces is also an indicator showing you how many workspaces you currently have and which one you are currently focused on.

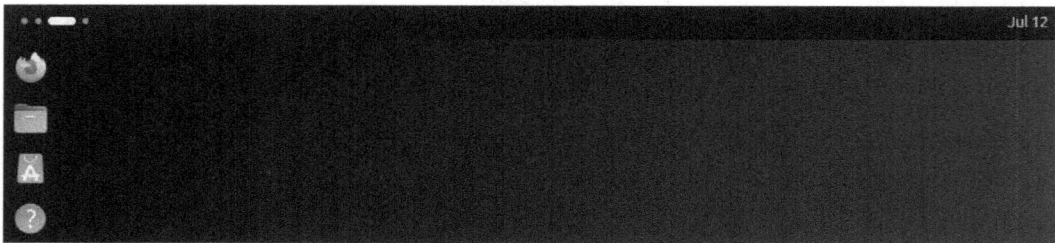

Figure 5.8 – Workspace indicator

In the preceding example, there are four workspaces, with the third workspace focused.

Notice, in *Figure 5.9*, that you can see four screen previews just below the search input box:

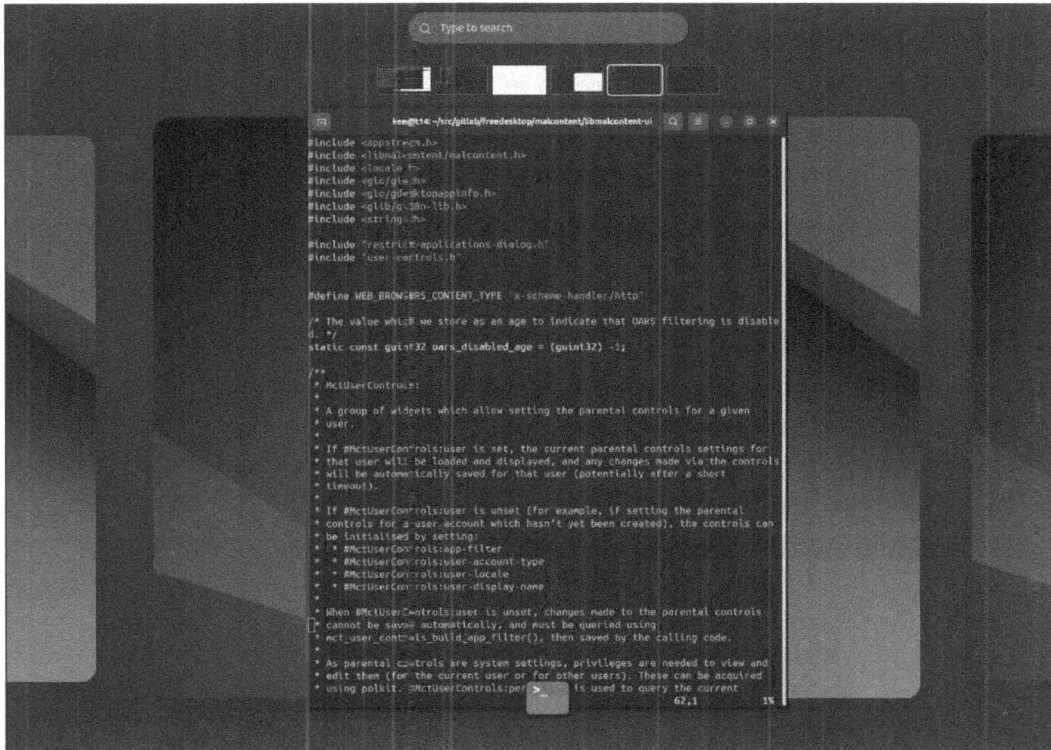

Figure 5.9 – Workspace selector

These previews show you what's on each workspace screen. You can select windows in those previews and drag them to other workspaces by dropping them on the preview of the workspace you would like that window. You can also click on the preview of the work-space you are interested in, which will reposition the larger view of the workspace to the workspace selected. If you drag a window preview to the workspace on the far right, it'll dynamically add an additional workspace. In my case, in the preceding screenshot, I have four workspaces. By default, you start with just one workspace, but when you try to use a second one, it gets created for you.

You can also change your workspace view with a keyboard shortcut: *Ctrl + Alt + Left* or *Ctrl + Alt + Right*, which switches focus left or right accordingly. You can also focus a window and move it to other workspaces by focusing the window you want to move and pressing *Ctrl + Alt + Shift + Left* or *Ctrl + Alt + Shift + Right*. This changes your workspace view and drags the focused window to the same workspace.

When changing workspaces using the keyboard shortcut, if the workspace you stop on has multiple windows, you'll notice the focused window has an animation, making it appear to pop. This is so you know which window is currently focused before you start typing, which could prevent you from typing something sensitive into a window you shouldn't.

You can see how new workspaces are created dynamically as needed and removed dynamically. Closing the last window on a workspace automatically removes it.

Workspaces are a great way to organize your workflow and enhance your ability to focus on the task at hand.

Introducing tiling window management

Traditionally, **window management** uses a stacking approach, meaning that application windows could cover other windows or be covered by other application windows. Clicking on any of the windows in *Figure 5.10* will bring it to the front and focus it to accept input, whether by mouse, touch, or keyboard:

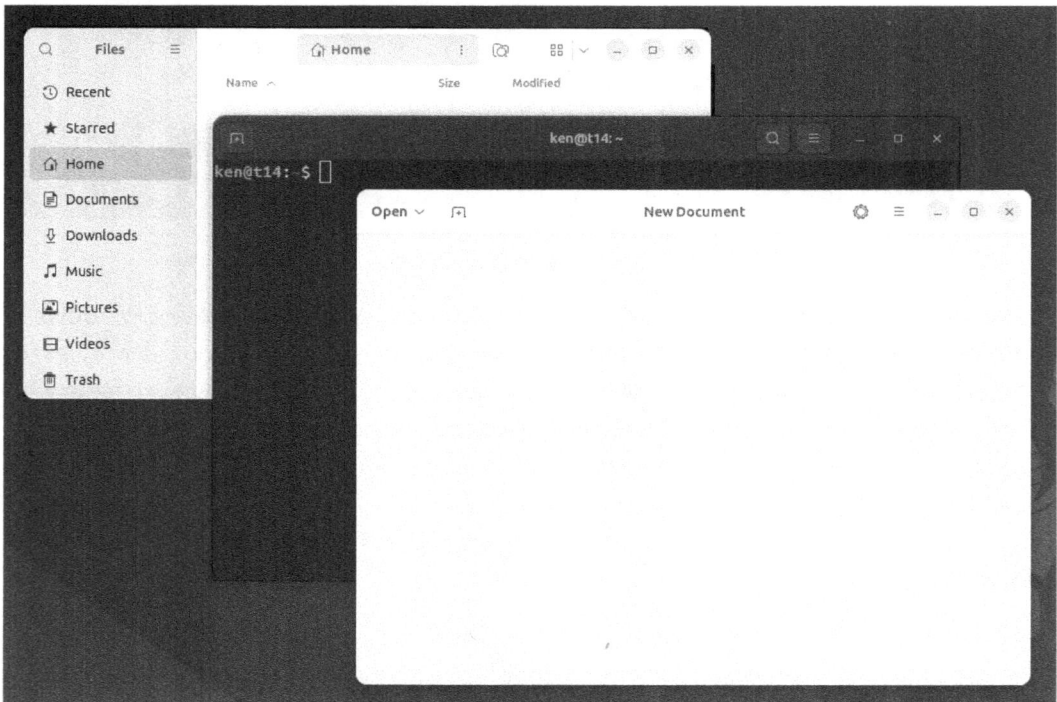

Figure 5.10 – Window stacking

Ubuntu does allow window stacking, which is familiar to anyone who has used most desktop operating systems. Additionally, Ubuntu provides quarter-tiling window management.

Tiling window management is a concept that has been around for many years, but it is often only utilized by power users who have spent significant time setting up their environment. Environments with tiling window management often lack many things most people are already accustomed to.

Ubuntu brings tiling window management features to the masses without compromising users' expectations.

So, what are tiling windows? You can probably guess that they are tiled windows that do not cover each other:

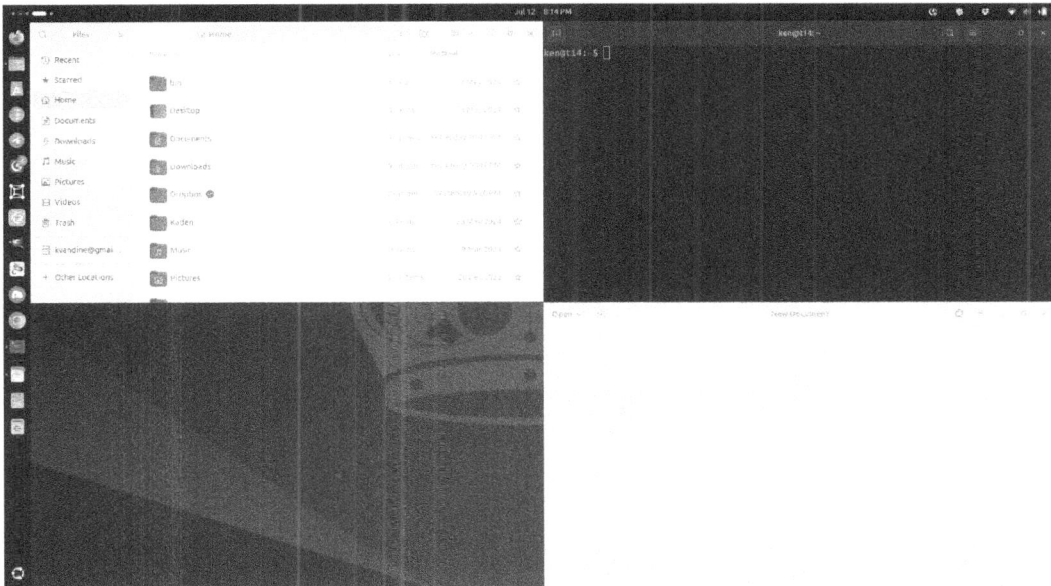

Figure 5.11 – Window tiling

As you can see in *Figure 5.11*, there are three neatly tiled windows with a fourth empty tile, allowing room for another app. The windows are not covered, making it easy to see what's happening in each one.

I described this feature as **quarter-tiling window management**, which is limited to four equally distributed tiled windows on a screen or workspace. However, it doesn't have to be four windows. It could be one, two, or three as well! The preceding figure shows three windows, all equal in size, but the window on the left could also be tiled at full height:

Figure 5.12 – Three window regions

The screen is divided into regions, and each region can be filled with an application window. Rather than being sized arbitrarily, application windows are *snapped* into a region. *Figure 5.12* shows the screen divided into three regions rather than the four regions shown in *Figure 5.11*.

Figure 5.13 shows the screen divided into two regions, separated vertically. This could just as easily be divided horizontally; you get the idea:

Figure 5.13 – Two window regions

To organize your windows this way, simply click on the title bar of the application you would like to tile and drag it to where you want to put it. When your cursor hits the edge of the screen, you'll see an outline on your screen as a placeholder for the region the window will *snap* to when released. For example, when you drag it to the right edge of the screen, you'll see an outline appear, indicating the window will snap to half the size of your screen horizontally. If you release it, that's where your window will stay. However, if you move the cursor until it hits the top right of your screen, the outline will change to only the top-right quarter.

Hint

Holding the *Super* key lets you grab the window by clicking anywhere, not just the title bar. You can also control window tiling with handy keyboard shortcuts. *Super + Left* and *Super + Right* will tile the current window to either the left or right, respectively.

Figure 5.14 shows the window tiling settings:

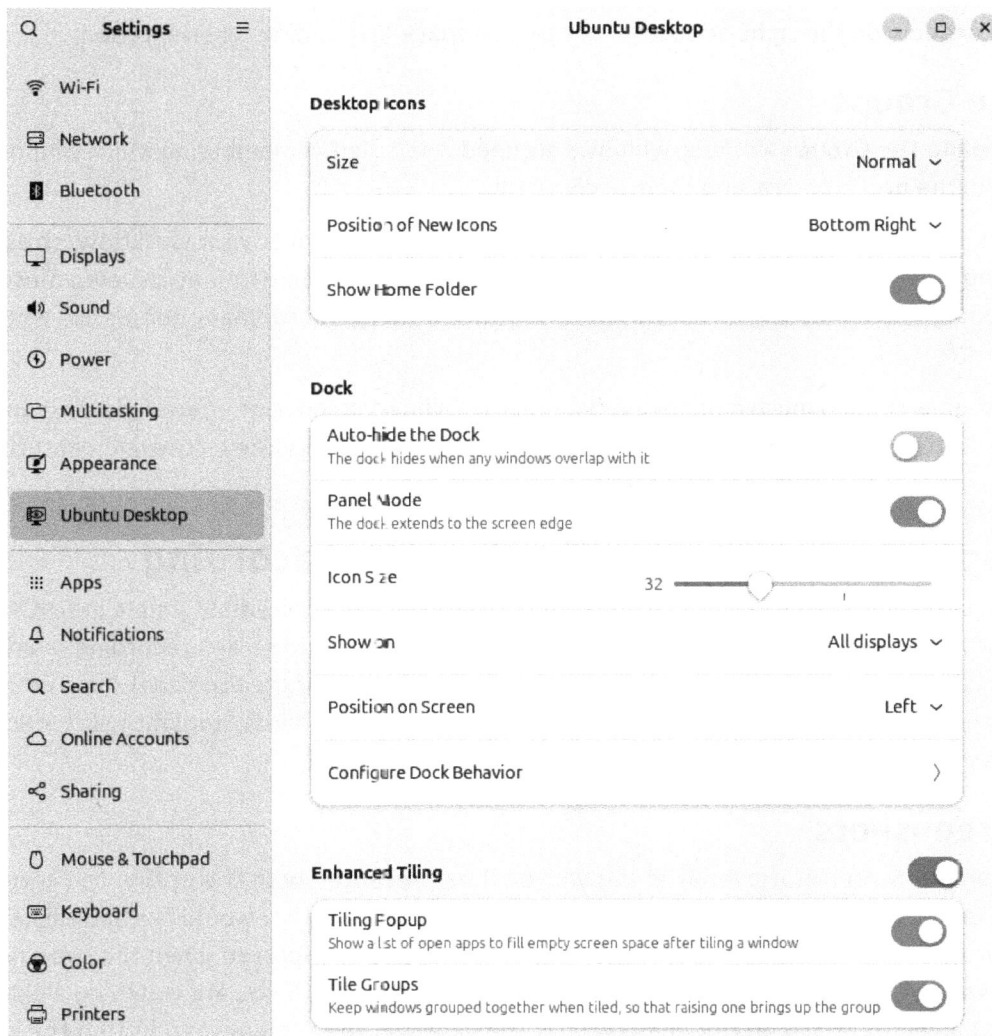

Figure 5.14 – Enhanced Tiling settings

To access these settings, open the **Settings** app, navigate to the **Ubuntu Desktop** page, and look for the **Enhanced Tiling** section near the bottom.

Tiling Popup

With **Tiling Popup** enabled, when tiling a window, a popup is shown with a list of apps and windows open in the current workspace, including window previews. Selecting any of these apps or windows will snap that window into the available space and tile it nicely. Holding the *Shift* key when selecting an app or window will tile the window on the left or top of the free space, depending on orientation. Alternatively, holding the *Alt* key will tile the window on the right or bottom of the free space, depending on orientation.

Tile Groups

Enabling **Tile Groups** will keep windows grouped when tiled, remembering which windows are in the group and raising them accordingly.

Tiling your windows is a great way to have ultimate control over your workflow, streamlining how you interact with your applications. It does take some time to develop muscle memory while adapting to the workflow of window tiling, but for many people, it's worth the effort.

Of course, there is much more to everyday use than how you manage your windows, launch applications, and disable Bluetooth. We'll continue on our journey, covering capturing screenshots and keyboard shortcuts.

Capturing screenshots and screen recording

Capturing screenshots and performing screen recordings is incredibly simple in GNOME, which has an integrated, intuitive overlay. The screenshot and screen recording overlay can be accessed from the system indicator on the right side of the top panel. Even better, it is easily accessed with the *Print Screen* key; on some keyboards, it might just be *Print*, *PrtScr*, or *prt sc*.

Screenshots

When the Screenshot overlay is shown, you'll be presented with the option to capture the entire screen, a single window, or a region. Choose which you would like and click the Capture button. Note that the contents of the display are captured when the overlay is shown, not when the capture button is clicked. For example, if you are watching a video and hit the *Print Screen* key, the frame of the video on the screen when hitting the key will be captured.

When the screenshot is captured, it's saved in **Screenshots** under your Pictures folder. It's also stored on your clipboard, where you can easily paste it into any application capable of pasting images, such as a **LibreOffice** document.

Screencasts

The Screenshot overlay also includes a toggle to switch between capturing an image or video. If toggled to **Video**, select a region on your screen to record and press the Record button. When recording starts, the overlay is closed, and you can use your computer with the region you selected being recorded. While recording, there will be a small red recording indicator in the top panel showing the elapsed time of your screen recording. Clicking on that indicator will stop the screen recording, and your video will be saved in **Screencasts** under your Videos folder.

Controlling your desktop like a pro with keyboard shortcuts

We already discussed using keyboard shortcuts for tiling window management, but there are handy shortcuts for nearly everything. *Table 5.1* provides a reference of keyboard shortcuts for interacting with the desktop:

Super	**Switch between the Activities** overview and **Desktop**. In the overview, start typing to instantly search your applications, contacts, and documents.
Alt + F2	**Pop up a command window (for quickly running commands).** **Use the arrow keys to quickly access previously run commands.**
Super + Tab	**Quickly switch between windows. Hold down** *Shift* for reverse order.
Super + `	**Switch between windows from the same application or from the selected application after** *Super + Tab*. This shortcut uses ` on US keyboards, where the ` key is above *Tab*. On all other keyboards, the shortcut is *Super +* the key above *Tab*.
Alt + Esc	**Switch between windows in the current workspace. Hold down** *Shift* for reverse order.

Ctrl + Alt + Tab	**Give keyboard focus to the top bar. In the Activities** overview, switch keyboard focus between the top bar, dash, windows overview, applications list, and search field. Use the arrow keys to navigate.
Super + A	**Show the list of applications.**
Super + Page Up and *Super + Page Down*	**Switch between workspaces.**
Shift + Super + Page Up and *Shift + Super + Page Down*	**Move the current window to a different workspace.**
Shift + Super + ←	**Move the current window one monitor to the left.**
Shift + Super + →	**Move the current window one monitor to the right.**
Super + Left	**Tile the current window to the left.**
Super + Right	**Tile the current window to the right.**
Super + ↑	**Maximize the current window.**
Super + ↓	**Unmaximize the current window.**
Ctrl + Alt + Delete	**Show the Log Off** dialog.
Super + L	**Lock the screen.**
Super + V	**Show the notification list. Press** *Super + V* again or *Esc* to close.
Ctrl + Alt + T	**Launch the Terminal.**

Table 5.1 – Getting around the desktop

Ubuntu has a very powerful built-in screenshot tool, accessible with very simple keyboard shortcuts:

Print	Launch the screenshot tool. On some keyboards, this might be *PrtScr*.
Alt + Print	Take a screenshot of the currently focused window.
Shift + Print	Take a screenshot of the entire screen.
Shift + Ctrl + Alt + R	Start and stop screencast recording.

Table 5.2 – Capturing from the screen

Most applications provide some common functionality using well-known keyboard shortcuts:

Ctrl + A	Select all text or items in a list.
Ctrl + X	Cut (remove) selected text or items and place them on the clipboard.
Ctrl + C	Copy the selected text or items to the clipboard.
Ctrl + V	Paste the content of the clipboard.
Ctrl + Z	Undo the last action.
Ctrl + Shift + C	Copy the highlighted text or commands to the clipboard in the Terminal.
Ctrl + Shift + V	Paste the contents of the clipboard in the Terminal.

Table 5 3 – Common editing shortcuts

More information on keyboard shortcuts can be found at `https://help.ubuntu.com/stable/ubuntu-help/shell-keyboard-shortcuts.html.en`.

Having mastered the art of keyboard shortcuts, you can consider yourself a power user! There are many keyboard shortcuts, and they will take time to remember. But wait... to be a true power user, we need to be able to find and use files and folders.

Working with files and folders – the power of file management

Ubuntu includes the GNOME **Files** app for easy access and management of your files:

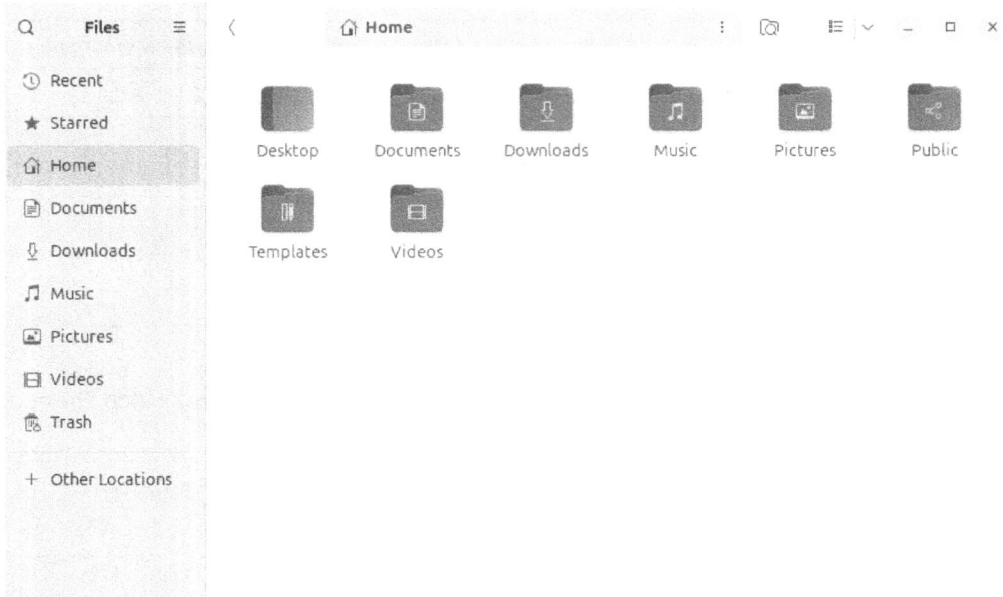

Figure 5.15 – Files app

Your **Home** directory is your local space to store your files. Ubuntu provides a basic skeleton of directories to organize your files based on content. However, you are free to organize files as you wish.

You start with the following skeleton:

- Desktop: Any files stored will be displayed on the desktop
- Documents: Used to store documents, PDFs, text files, and so on
- Downloads: Default location web browsers save content downloaded from the internet
- Music: Local music files
- Pictures: Photos and screenshots
- Public: For sharing files with other users on the same computer
- Templates: For storing templates used by applications such as LibreOffice and the Text Editor
- Videos: Videos and screen recordings

Figure 5.15 shows the contents of your **Home** directory displayed with the GNOME **Files** app. In the **Files** app, you can navigate through your files and folders and open files with a double-click. You can also right-click on any file or folder to get additional actions. For example, double-clicking on a .txt file will open the application configured to open text files by default. A right-click on that file will give you an **Open With** option to choose another application to open it with. The same right-click menu will provide you with a variety of actions available, depending on the file or folder you selected. For example, you can copy, move, and rename files and folders and view additional file properties, as seen in *Figure 5.16*.

File properties

Figure 5.16 shows the file properties displayed for an image file:

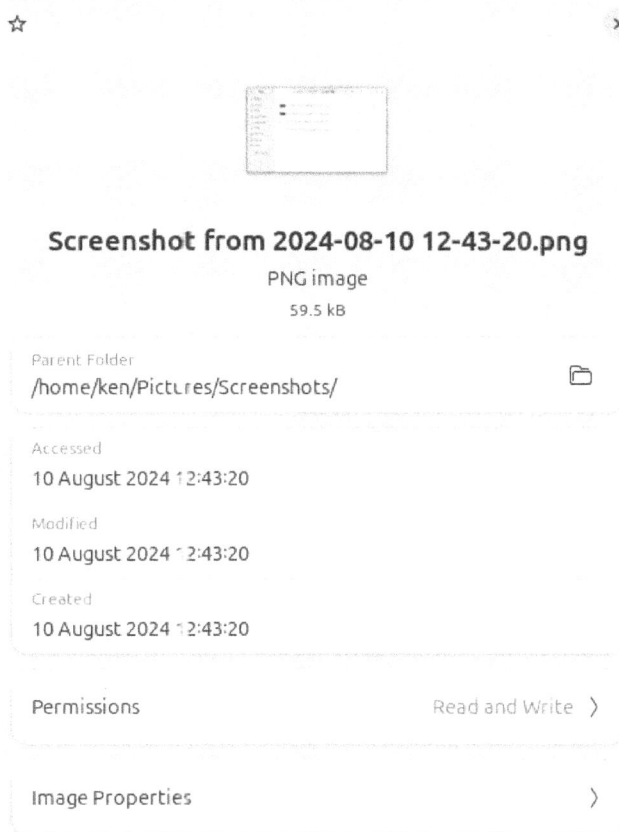

Screenshot from 2024-08-10 12-43-20.png

PNG image

59.5 kB

Parent Folder
/home/ken/Pictures/Screenshots/

Accessed
10 August 2024 12:43:20

Modified
10 August 2024 12:43:20

Created
10 August 2024 12:43:20

Permissions   Read and Write 〉

Image Properties   〉

Figure 5.16 – File properties

All files and folders display some basic information, such as the date and time when they were created, last modified, and accessed. You can also view and change the permissions on a file, limiting access to editing the file or even allowing it to be executed as if it were a program itself. Be careful when changing permissions; we'll learn more about file permissions in *Chapter 10*.

The details displayed vary depending on the type of file; for example, since this is an image, you can check **Image Properties**. If this file was a photo taken with a camera or phone, it could include very rich metadata such as information on the camera used and even the precise location the photo was taken if available.

Bookmarks

In *Figure 5.15*, you can see on the left-hand side that there is easy access to the content with bookmarks. These bookmarks will quickly open the directory the bookmark specifies. The default set of bookmarks roughly matches the skeleton directory structure listed previously. Creating custom bookmarks is easy by dragging and dropping any folder you like. Navigate to the folder you want to make a bookmark from and drag that folder to the bookmark bar on the left, and you'll see a hint created that says **New bookmark**. When you see that hint, you can drop it, and the bookmark will be created.

Figure 5.15 also shows some special bookmarks for **Recent**, **Starred**, and **Trash**:

- **Recent**: Files that have been recently accessed.
- **Starred**: Starring files and folders in the **Files** app is a handy way to mark them for quick access later.
- **Trash**: Deleted files and folders go to the trash. You can browse your trash and restore those files or empty the trash to delete the contents permanently.
- **Removable Media**: Dynamic bookmarks will be shown when available, such as when you plug in a USB stick or an external drive. These can be navigated like any other directory but include an eject action to safely remove the device without losing unsaved changes.

Views

The **Files** app allows you to navigate your files and folders using a grid or list view. You can change between grid and list views by toggling the emblem just to the right of the search, which looks like a grid or a list.

Grid view

The grid view is very simple and allows for easy drag-and-drop operations. It displays thumbnails for each file that are a bit larger, making it easier to use the thumbnail to preview what might be in the file, as seen in *Figure 5.17*:

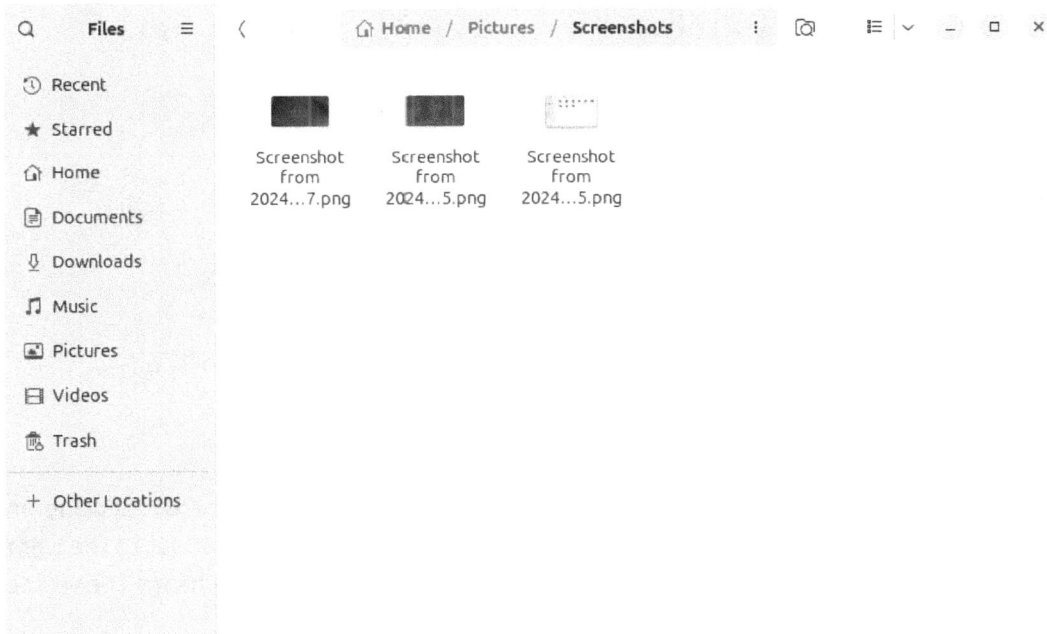

Figure 5.17 – Files grid view

List view

The list view is more compact, showing the files and folders in a list format, as seen in *Figure 5.18*:

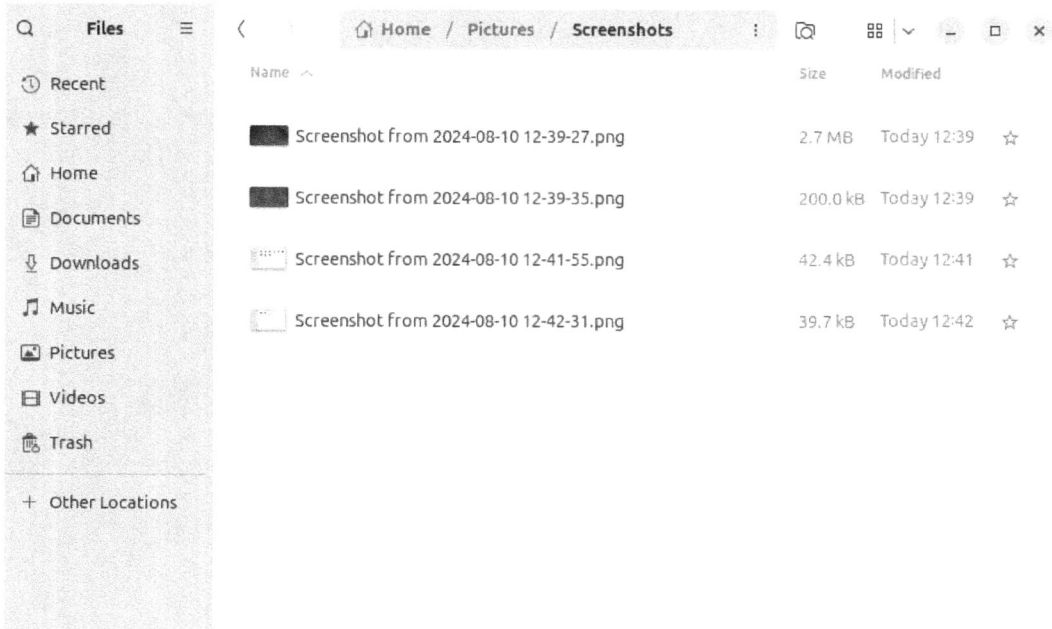

Figure 5.18 – Files list view

By default, there are columns for size, modified time and date, and starred. Clicking on the column heading will sort based on that column. Clicking on the expander to the right of the grid/list toggle shows additional sort options and an interface to change the visible columns in the list.

Search

The **Files** app has a powerful built-in search that can be used to search by file or folder name and contents. *Figure 5.19* shows a search for the word test, which displays results including a file named test.png, a text file that contains the word test, and a LibreOffice document with the word test:

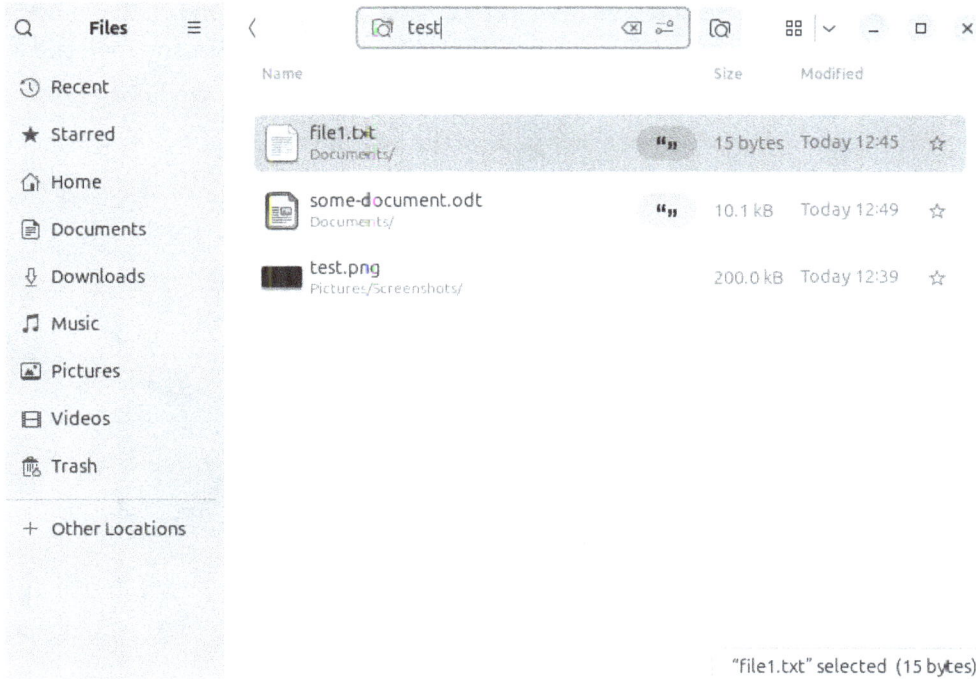

Figure 5.19 – Files search view

The **Files** app is a rich, powerful, yet easy-to-use file manager. We've discussed the most commonly used features necessary to be productive daily. There are other features that are intuitive enough to learn as you go, becoming a real power user.

So far in this chapter, we've discussed how to use and navigate your desktop. Now that we can be productive using Ubuntu, let's explore how we can have a bit of fun customizing our own user experience.

The power of customization – tailoring your Ubuntu experience

We've discussed the many ways you can interact with your Ubuntu Desktop. Let's explore more ways to make it your own! Customization is one of the things that attracts users to Linux, and some think Ubuntu isn't as customizable as some other distributions. This is not true! Ubuntu focuses on providing opinionated defaults that are intuitive and easy to use without overwhelming users. However, this doesn't mean you are limited in how you can customize your experience.

The **Settings** app provides some easy ways to customize the look and feel. Beyond the **Settings** app, you can install additional tools to further tweak the look and feel, and even some command-line tools allow access to thousands of settings!

As shown in *Figure 5.20*, the **Appearance** page in the **Settings** app makes it easy to change the wallpapers, choose light or dark modes, and set accent colors:

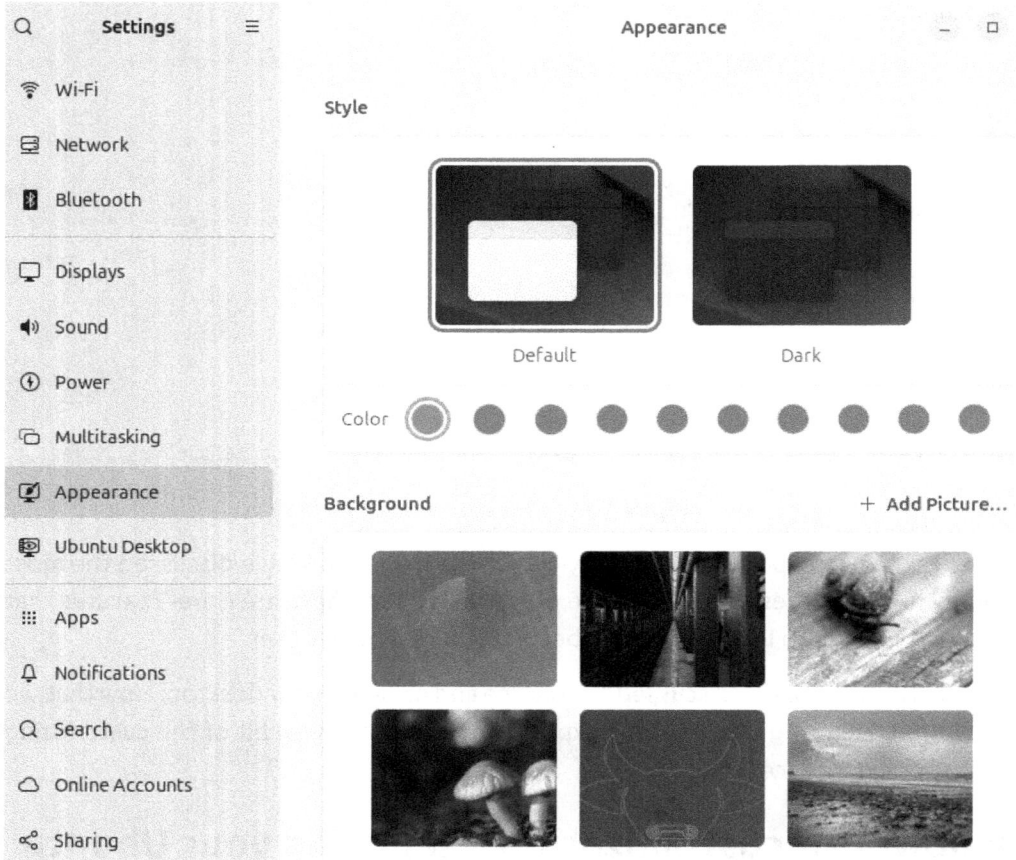

Figure 5.20 – Appearance Settings

Style

The **Style** section includes two settings: light/dark mode and accent color. What does this mean? The default (light) mode will display **user interface** (**UI**) elements with a very light color, making your screen bright and vibrant. All desktop operating systems have generally used this for many years, which is what we are accustomed to. Dark mode displays UI elements in a dark color, generally black. Dark mode has become popular in recent years and is even used by many websites to change the background color of sites you are browsing to match. Dark mode is often desirable when working in a dark space, such as an unlit room.

An accent color is a great way to add a personal touch to the desktop environment. With 10 colors to choose from, you are sure to find one you love. The accent color is visible in many places, such as the indicators in the top panel, the dock on the left, and UI elements in most applications.

Background

Often known as wallpapers, changing the background of your desktop has always been a stable feature in all operating systems. Ubuntu includes a great collection of official and incredible user-submitted wallpapers.

For every Ubuntu release, there is a wallpaper contest. Users can submit photos and other digital artwork to be considered for inclusion in the release. At the end of the submission period, the community votes, and the *eight* winning wallpapers are selected and included in the official Ubuntu release! So, not only are the wallpapers submitted by the community but the community decides which wallpapers are included. This is yet another example of how users can be part of shaping the amazing Ubuntu experience.

The wallpaper contest is run through the Ubuntu discourse, which can be found at https://discourse.ubuntu.com/tag/wallpapers.

GNOME Tweaks

Beyond what we covered in the **Settings** app, there are many other ways to customize the look and feel of your desktop. The **GNOME Tweaks** app provides a UI that allows even more settings to be changed:

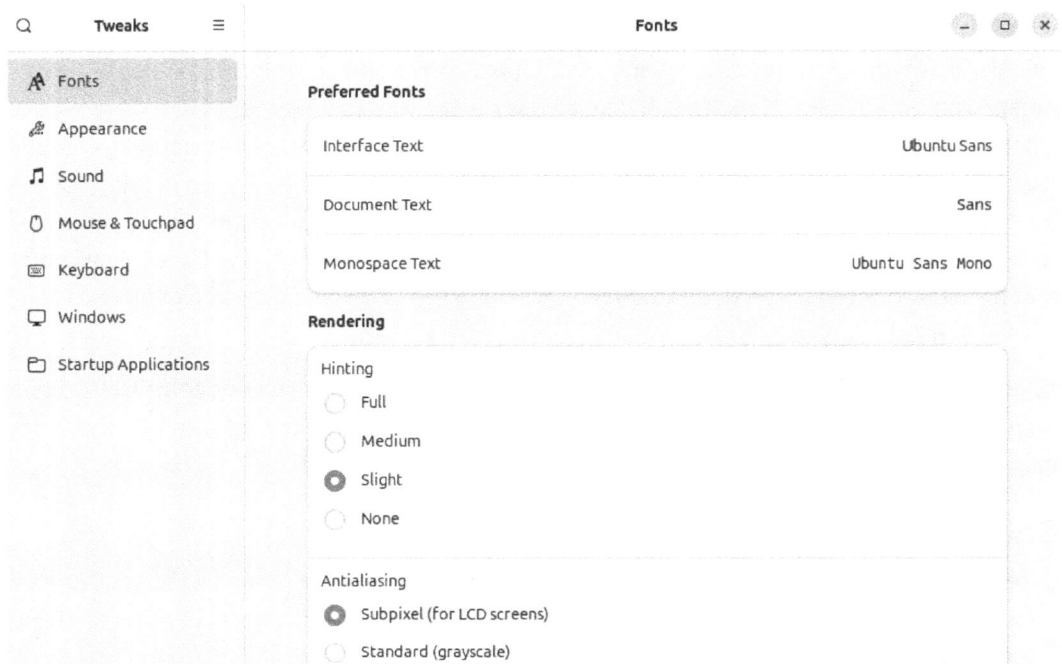

Figure 5.21 – GNOME Tweaks

The GNOME **Tweaks** app isn't included in the default installation, but it is easily installed from the App Center or Terminal. In the App Center, simply search for GNOME Tweaks and click **Install**, or in a Terminal, run this command:

```
sudo apt install gnome-tweaks
```

The GNOME **Tweaks** app provides an interface to change additional settings such as default fonts, themes, sounds, and more. You can navigate through the **Tweaks** app and experiment with making changes. If you end up in a situation where you changed something and you don't know how to get back to the default, there is a **Reset to Defaults** option in the menu near the top left.

GSettings

We all want to become power users, right? Well, **GSettings** exposes everything that can be configured. By using GSettings directly, we can tweak many things, some of which the original developers may not have meant to be tweaked, so use them with caution.

With that disclaimer out of the way, let me reassure you it's not really dangerous; just try not to make too many changes at a time so you can remember what might have caused things to go sideways. There is a built-in mechanism to reset any configuration settings you change back to the defaults.

GSettings is an **application programming interface (API)** that developers use to store configuration settings. It's designed for apps and other parts of the platform to use programmatically, but there is a handy command-line utility that allows you to view and change any setting you like.

On a fresh installation of Ubuntu 24.04, 1,470 settings are available to view and change. These settings include those exposed in the **System Settings** interface, the behavior of the GNOME Desktop shell, and even application settings. For example, the accent color setting we discussed earlier in this chapter is actually a setting in GSettings. The same goes for the wallpaper, the number of workspaces, and so on. Beyond that, many applications, such as the **Files** app, store settings in GSettings as well.

To see the value of any settings, use the `gsettings` command:

```
ken@monster:~$ gsettings get org.gnome.nautilus.preferences show-hidden-
files false
```

The preceding `gsettings get` command shows us that the `show-hidden-files` option is disabled.

If we enable that setting in the **Files** app and run the command again, you'll see it returns `true`.

You can also run a very similar `gsettings` command to set the value:

```
ken@monster:~$ gsettings set org.gnome.nautilus.preferences show-hidden-
files true
```

If you forget what the original setting was, you can easily reset it with the following:

```
ken@monster:~$ gsettings reset org.gnome.nautilus.preferences show-hidden-
files
```

Or, if you make a number of changes for the same app and want to reset them all to the defaults, use the following:

```
ken@monster:~$ gsettings reset-recursively org.gnome.nautilus.preferences
```

This will reset every setting in `org.gnome.nautilus.preferences` to their default values.

As a very wise fictional character once said, *With great power comes great responsibility*. Being able to leverage utilities such as GSettings to change anything exposes you to un-expected behavior, so use them with caution.

We just touched on using a command-line utility for the first time here, and we will cover command-line usage as well as much more advanced use of GSettings in *Chapter 10*.

It's been fun customizing the look and feel of our desktop experience, making it our own. Now, let's look at some of the applications in Ubuntu.

A tour of essential applications

Our computer wouldn't be of much use without applications, so take a tour of the open source software included in Ubuntu. When we think of essential applications in today's connected world, a web browser is at the top of the list.

Firefox browser

When considering Ubuntu's ethos, **Firefox** ticks all the boxes. It's open source, privacy-fo-cused, and has a thriving community of passionate users and developers. In *Chapter 3*, we discussed the many benefits of open source software and its role in Ubuntu. The openness of Firefox gives us a great deal of confidence and trust in Firefox. However, **Mozilla**, the organization behind Firefox, is about more than just openness. Mozilla invests in keeping our data safe with an ever-growing list of privacy features.

Learn more at https://www.mozilla.org/firefox.

Thunderbird email

Email is necessary. Sure, there are many web-based email options. However, many people prefer the feel of a native application for handling their email needs. Born out of the same Mozilla project as Firefox, **Thunderbird** shares the dedication to openness and protecting users' personal data. Privacy is front and center while still providing an intuitive, easy-to-use email application.

Learn more at https://www.thunderbird.net.

LibreOffice

Whether you are using Ubuntu for work or pleasure, you'll surely need to be able to view, edit, and create documents, spreadsheets, and presentations. **LibreOffice**, from the **Document Foundation**, does that while maintaining compatibility with other popular office suites.

LibreOffice uses the **OpenDocument Format** (**ODF**), an open standard file format by default. ODF files can be identified with the following file extensions:

- `.odt`: Text document
- `.ods`: Spreadsheet
- `.odp`: Presentation
- `.odg`: Graphic

LibreOffice isn't just one application; it's a suite of applications that provide practical and powerful capabilities for various tasks:

- **LibreOffice Writer**: A full-featured word-processor
- **LibreOffice Calc**: A powerful spreadsheet tool
- **LibreOffice Impress**: A presentation tool
- **LibreOffice Draw**: A graphics tool for creating sketches and diagrams
- **LibreOffice Math**: A formula editor often invoked within your documents

Learn more at `https://www.libreoffice.org`.

Text Editor

Sometimes, you need to take simple notes, edit configuration files, or quickly edit source code. **GNOME Text Editor** is perfect for these!

Clocks

GNOME Clocks provides all the features you would expect in a clock app: alarms, stopwatches, timers, and my favorite feature, world clocks. As we become increasingly connected, the world gets smaller and smaller, making the world clock feature in GNOME Clocks incredibly useful.

Adding clocks from different cities worldwide makes it easy to quickly figure out what time it is for your friends and colleagues. The world clock feature in GNOME Clocks also integrates into the desktop calendar, providing quick access by clicking on the date and time in the top panel of your desktop.

App Center

This is the app store for Ubuntu! Ubuntu includes a nicely curated collection of practical applications to get you started on your journey. However, many additional apps are available to meet your needs, and **App Center** is there to help you discover them.

App Center makes it easy to explore available software, starting with a view that includes popular applications recommended by the Ubuntu Desktop team. Built-in views range from featured applications to views focused on productivity, development, and games. All are dedicated to helping you discover great applications and games, clearly showing user ratings, descriptions, and screenshots. As you would expect, App Center allows installation and the ability to rate applications you have installed with a quick thumbs up or thumbs down.

GIMP – GNU Image Manipulation Program

GIMP is an image editor ideally suited for graphic designers and photographers, providing very powerful editing capabilities.

Learn more at `https://gimp.org`.

Inkscape

Inkscape is a powerful design tool ideally suited for illustrators and web designers.

Learn more at `https://inkscape.org`.

Visual Studio Code

Microsoft's **Visual Studio Code** has become a wildly popular developer tool, even among avid Linux enthusiasts. The Visual Studio Code experience on Ubuntu provides a familiar developer experience to many, supporting development in your language of choice.

Learn more at `https://code.visualstudio.com`.

Android Studio

Android Studio is an **Integrated Developer Environment (IDE)** for mobile development targeting mobile devices. It makes it easy to set up a development environment for Android apps, and a built-in Android emulator allows you to test and view your application as if it were running on a mobile phone.

Learn more at `https://developer.android.com/studio`.

Summary

In this chapter, we've covered a great deal! We dove into desktop concepts, such as navigating, launching apps, and effectively using our computer. We explored how to customize many aspects of the UI, given our style, and even dipped our toe into more advanced customizations requiring the command line.

Many users enjoy the ability to tweak and customize the user experience, and I hope you enjoy it too.

In the next chapter, we'll discuss the importance of software updates and how they are critical to the security and stability of our computers.

Further reading

*   Ubuntu Desktop guide: `https://help.ubuntu.com/stable/ubuntu-help/shell-overview.html.en`

*   Helpful keyboard shortcuts: `https://help.ubuntu.com/stable/ubuntu-help/shell-keyboard-shortcuts.html.en`

*   GSettings manual page: `https://manpages.ubuntu.com/manpages/man1/gsettings.1.html`

6

Software Discovery: Finding and Installing Applications

Over the last few chapters, we've learned more about **Ubuntu Desktop, installing the operating system (OS)**, and using the desktop like a pro. These are all essential topics, but all of this is meant to give you the tools necessary to use the applications you need for work or play. Ubuntu starts you off with a nicely curated selection of world-class open source software pre-installed, but it's just the tip of the iceberg. There's an ever-growing ecosystem of Linux applications to choose from.

Now that we know how to use our Ubuntu Desktop like a pro, we'll learn how to find and install the applications we need.

If you are coming from another OS, it's essential to understand that software installation on Ubuntu is a bit different. You may be used to downloading software from a website and installing it manually. There may be times on Ubuntu when you can do that, but it's often not the best, most robust, or most secure method.

Software installation usually requires **root** access, which means administrative access over the entire system. Any software you download from the internet and install as root could replace unrelated files or install unwanted files on your system. This could result in stability issues or even malware running on your computer.

The desired method for software installation is with either the apt or snap tool. apt installs Debian packages from trusted Ubuntu software repositories that Ubuntu developers have vetted. snap packages provide a means to get the software directly from the application publisher but run it in a confined sandbox, protecting the rest of your system.

We've tossed around the term *packages* here. Let's quickly touch on what software packages are. A package is a generic term for how software is bundled to be installed on a computer reliably. There are numerous software packaging technologies out there. For Ubuntu, we'll focus on Debian and Snap packages.

In this chapter, we will cover the following topics:

- Understanding software packages
- Debian packages
- Snap packages
- Finding and choosing software
- Installing packages

Introducing Debian packages

You may have heard of Debian, a well-known Linux distribution that was first released in 1993. Ubuntu is based on Debian, and many Ubuntu developers are also Debian developers. Debian contains tens of thousands of well-maintained software packages.

Debian packages were designed for use by dpkg, a command-line tool for working with Debian packages. These packages contain a bundle of files that are part of the application or sometimes a bundle of files necessary for other applications to run. Each package declares other packages it depends on, which are required to function as expected. Due to the nature of these dependencies, apt was invented as a tool to resolve dependencies based on an online repository of Debian packages. It also handles downloading these packages from the online repositories.

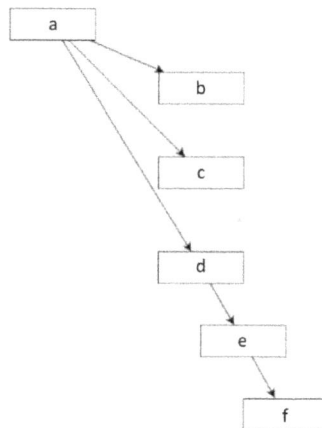

Figure 6.1 – Package dependency graph

The package dependency graph in *Figure 6.1* shows that package *a* depends on packages *b*, *c*, and *d*. Package *d* depends on package *e*, and package *e* depends on package *f*. This means if we install package *a* with apt, five additional packages will be installed, for a total of six packages.

apt has handled dependency management very well for many years. The technology is mature and well understood by packagers.

Your Ubuntu system comprises a collection of these Debian packages, all meticulously maintained by Ubuntu and Debian developers. Ubuntu cryptographically signs these packages, which have undergone extensive automated testing before being published to the official apt repository.

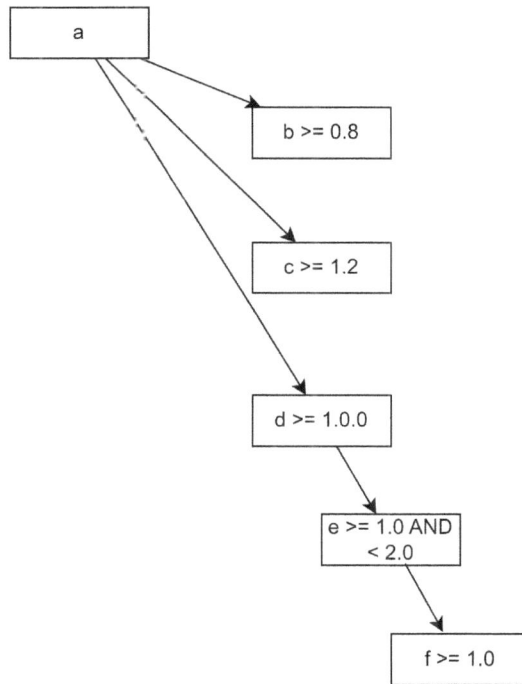

Figure 6.2 – Versioned package dependency graph

Let's consider a scenario where packages depend on specific versions of other packages. In *Figure 6.2*, each package dependency is articulated with a comparison method and a version to compare.

For example, *d >= 1.0.0* means the version of package *a* that you are installing requires version 1.0.0 or greater of package *d* to function correctly. In a more complex example, in

Figure 6.2, we see that package *d* depends on package *e* 1.0 or greater but less than 2.0. This means package *e* 2.0 introduced a change that breaks this particular version of package *d*.

These dependency graphs can get complicated, but you don't need to handle them yourself. apt handles them very well and does a good job of keeping your system usable.

So, if that's the case, why did we just go into such detail on how these dependencies work? It is important to understand the complexity of package dependencies and how you could break your system by utilizing other package repositories or installing software you might download from a website.

We'll start by learning about the available types of apt repositories.

Ubuntu repositories

The official Ubuntu apt repositories comprise four components: main, restricted, universe, and multiverse.

main

The main repository is for software officially supported by Canonical for the life of the release. Software in this repository will get bug fixes and security updates until it is **end-of-life (EOL)**. Everything in the main repository has to be free and open source software.

restricted

The restricted repository is for proprietary drivers necessary for some devices.

universe

The Ubuntu community maintains the universe repository, which is by far the most extensive collection of packages available. All software in the universe repository must be free and open source.

multiverse

The multiverse repository is for software that might be restricted by copyright, patent, or other potential legal issues.

Personal Package Archive

Launchpad is a software collaboration platform that provides the functionality necessary to build and distribute Linux software. It is essential for producing Ubuntu. Launchpad offers a **Personal Package Archive (PPA)** feature that allows anyone to create an apt repository and distribute software for Ubuntu or other Debian-based Linux distributions.

Anyone can create a PPA, which means packages installed from the PPA haven't been officially packaged, reviewed, or tested. Many resources on the internet reference these PPAs as solutions for solving specific problems or even getting a newer version of an application you really want.

It's important to understand that adding a PPA introduces risk. Some packages added to the PPA could be unrelated to the specific software you were looking for and end up on your system without you realizing it, replacing the trusted Ubuntu version.

Third-party package repositories

Other third-party package repositories exist, often from software vendors to distribute their software. These vendors usually try to ensure compatibility with LTS versions of Ubuntu and not introduce packages that cause stability problems. Just be aware that adding the repositories does introduce some risk, depending on your level of trust in the software vendor.

Back to the dependency graph in *Figure 6.2*. If a PPA you have enabled on your system adds version 2.0 of package *e*, there will be an unsatisfied dependency for package *d*. If you are installing package *a* for the first time and the PPA with version 2.0 of package *e* is already enabled on your system, apt will refuse to install.

You should prefer the packages in official Ubuntu repositories over downloading software on the internet, from PPAs, or other third-party repositories.

Introducing Snap packages

While the Debian package ecosystem has served Ubuntu well for the past 20 years, it does introduce complexity to software vendors who want to publish their applications for Linux. The Snap technology was created to solve the problems we discussed earlier while also providing means to control your level of trust in the applications you use.

At the simplest level, an application's Snap package bundles all the other dependent software, providing a complete runtime for the application. This ensures that the software functions as the vendor or developer intended, regardless of what version of Ubuntu or other Linux distribution you are using. This is incredibly important to the viability of Linux as a target for software developers. The Linux ecosystem is fragmented, and a software vendor such as Spotify doesn't want to build its software differently for the thousands of possible Linux distributions and versions. Historically, this has been the biggest hurdle in convincing these software vendors to publish software releases for Linux.

By being able to publish their application as a Snap, the vendor only has to build and test their application with the runtime defined by the Snap they control. In the Ubuntu case, this ensures the application functions the same on Ubuntu 18.04 as on Ubuntu 24.04, but also Fedora or other distributions. Since the Snap includes all the dependencies, installation can't cause stability problems with any other part of the OS or other applications.

Another critical piece of this story is the Snap Store, which provides a trusted source for users to install software published as a Snap. The Snap Store allows any software developer or vendor to publish their software in a way that's easy for users to install and use while providing the appropriate level of trust. This means Spotify is a verified publisher in the Snap Store, and you can trust that the version of Spotify you install from the Snap Store hasn't been tainted by anyone else.

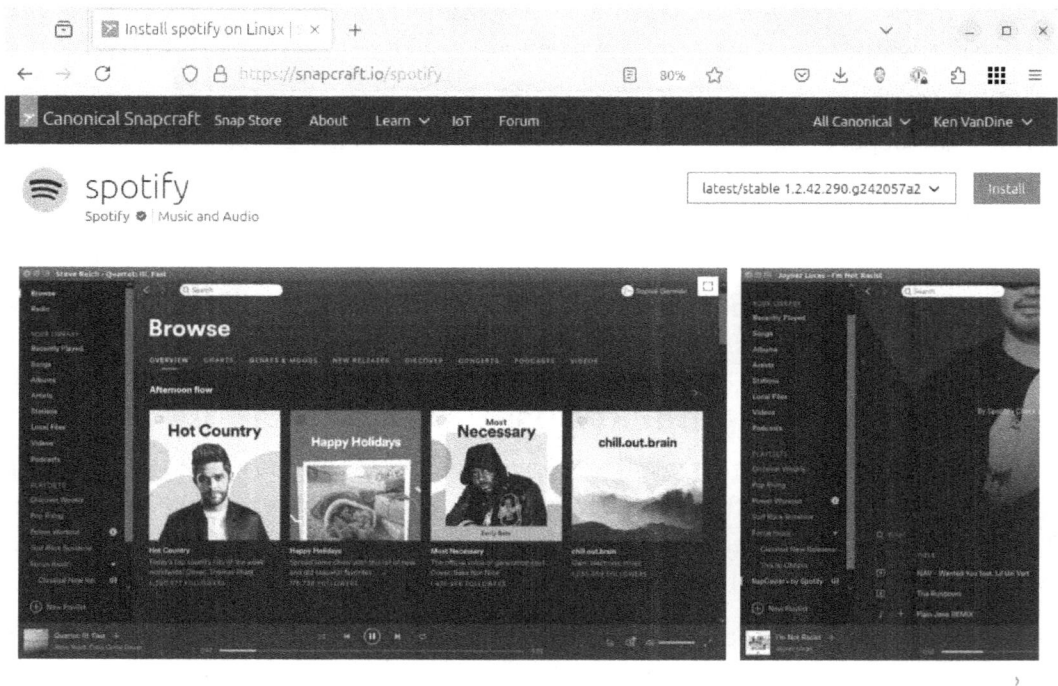

Figure 6.3 – Snap Store

Figure 6.3 shows the Snap Store page for the Spotify application. Notice that below the Snap name, the publisher is named with a small green check emblem. This shows that Canonical has verified that Spotify is the entity that published this Snap. This gives you peace of mind and lets you trust that the Snap is authentic.

While on the topic of trust, let's talk about the anatomy of a Snap. When you install a Snap from the Snap Store, SnapD fetches the Snap from the Snap Store behind the scenes. These are signed and verified to be indeed from the expected publisher and haven't been tainted on the way to your computer. When installed, SnapD configures permissions on the Snap based on the assertions from the Snap Store. We'll talk more about permissions later in this chapter when we discuss how the SnapD sandbox works.

The installed Snap is stored on your system as a single read-only file representing the filesystem of the runtime needed for the application. When you launch the application, installed as a Snap, the system verifies the integrity of the single read-only file and the cryptographic signature to match the expected publisher. After being verified, that file is mounted as a filesystem and runs the application inside a confined sandbox.

We'll discuss Snap technology more thoroughly later in this chapter. For now, just know that Snap is the ideal way to install any application you need, ensuring trust and stability.

Unveiling the Ubuntu App Center: your one-stop shop for applications

The Ubuntu App Center is a beautiful and intuitive application store for Linux, which should be familiar for anyone who has installed applications on a modern mobile phone or tablet.

Important note

The appearance and functionality of the Ubuntu App Center will change over the life of Ubuntu 24.04, with user interface changes occurring outside of the normal Ubuntu release cycle. The App Center must be capable of enabling users to discover and install software while maintaining compatibility with the Snap Store and other online services so it can see significant updates during the life of the Ubuntu LTS release.

Let's take a tour of the Ubuntu App Center, and learn more about finding useful software and key criteria to look at to determine quality.

Explore/Discover

As you would expect, App Center provides an intuitive way to discover and learn about applications you may need and install them if you wish. When launched, you'll likely notice a banner guiding you to learn more about applications recommended by the team that produces Ubuntu Desktop as a great way to jump-start your experience.

You can also browse for software by category, such as **Productivity**, **Development**, **Games**, and so on. Along with categories, you can also browse by a special **Featured** category, which provides a short list of applications that have been chosen to feature. This featured set of applications changes regularly.

Search

Of course, search is built right into the heart of the Ubuntu App Center experience, allowing you to search for anything. The **Search** field automatically searches for the text you entered in the application name, publisher name, category name, and so on. You can search for anything, and the results will match in various ways.

The obvious example is to enter a partial name of the application you are looking for. Still, you can also search for games, which will return everything in the **Games** category and any applications with games in the name or description. A search for VanDine will return all applications that I have published.

The app view

Regardless of how you find an application you are interested in, search for, or browse for it, the app view will be shown once selected. In the app view, you'll see the name of the application, who published it, the category, ratings, a helpful description, a series of screenshots, and other useful information.

Ratings

When choosing which applications to install, it's very helpful to see what other users think of the app. The App Center displays ratings from other users and allows you to give apps you have installed a thumbs up or thumbs down.

The ratings included in the App Center are calculated using a simple thumbs-up or thumbs-down from each user to display a favorable or unfavorable result.

Installation

Of course, the App Center allows you to install, uninstall, and launch applications. There are some more advanced options for managing already installed applications, which we'll discuss a bit later.

Exploring the power of Snap

As discussed earlier, Snap is the universal app package format for Linux. A Snap bundles the runtime necessary to run the app, making it portable to any Linux distribution with Snap support enabled. The portability aspect does solve the Linux fragmentation concerns that deterred application developers from publishing their software for Linux, but there's much more to the Snap technology.

Before discussing the benefits of the Snap technology, let's examine the various components that make it work.

Snap

A Snap is a bundle of an app and its dependencies that work without modification across Linux distributions.

SnapD

SnapD is the background service that automatically manages and maintains your Snaps.

Snap Store

The Snap Store is the universal app store for Linux. It allows application developers to upload Snaps and users to browse and install software.

Snapcraft

Snapcraft is the developer tool used to build and publish snaps.

Benefits of Snap

We've discussed portability, ensuring the application behaves the same on any Linux distribution with SnapD installed. Beyond that, Snap technology brings a level of trust to software that has never been seen before. Not only can you trust that the software is published by the developer listed as the publisher in the store but Snap also protects your system.

Every snap is run in its own sandbox, with limited access to system resources. By default, the application doesn't have access to anything outside of the software included in the snap, not even files on your system or network access. We call this **confinement**, and SnapD provides a mechanism to allow access to required resources while allowing the user to control that access.

SnapD automatically keeps your software up to date, ensuring that important security or bug fixes are applied promptly. If an application is running when SnapD determines there's an update, you'll see a notification that an update is available. When you quit the application, the update is applied immediately to ensure that when you launch it again, you have the latest version.

Updates are atomic, meaning the entire update has to be successful. Atomic updates ensure any failed update doesn't break your system or application experience. The Snap can provide a health check that runs on installation or update. If, for any reason, the health check fails, Snap will revert to the previous known good version. When the rollback happens, the application data also reverts to the data from the known good version.

Even if the automatic health check didn't fail, if you determine that the new version of the application doesn't work as expected, you can quickly revert the update. This also restores the snapshot of the data to ensure a consistent user experience. Speaking of snapshots, Snap also keeps a snapshot of application data for the latest two revisions of the Snap. The automatic snapshot is primarily used for revert or rollback operations. However, you can choose to restore from a snapshot at any time. Snap also allows you to take additional snapshots at any point, enabling you to take a backup of application data any time you like and restore from those snapshots at will.

What is confinement?

Imagine a hypothetical scenario of being able to install each application you need on a computer all by itself, and you only use that computer for that one piece of software. So, installing a video game can't go behind your back, find your contacts, and send all the contact information back to a remote server because your contacts are stored in another application on a completely different computer. Snap confinement looks like this, with the convenience of running each application on the same computer, completely isolated.

There are times when it is desirable for applications to share data or even access other resources on your computer. SnapD confinement allows for this by providing interfaces that can be connected to allow such access. The application developer that publishes the Snap needs to define which interfaces are needed and justify to the Snap Store security team why they should be allowed. Some of these are automatic, such as network access.

A great example is camera access. Suppose an application needs access to the camera. In that case, the developer must declare that Snap needs access to the camera interface and request that the interface be autoconnected at installation time. Suppose the Snap Store security team determines that the application can be trusted and that it is indeed an application that the user would expect to access the camera. In that case, the store can allow that interface to be autoconnected at installation time. While this allows that application to access the camera at runtime, the user can disconnect the camera interface at any time, denying access to the camera at runtime.

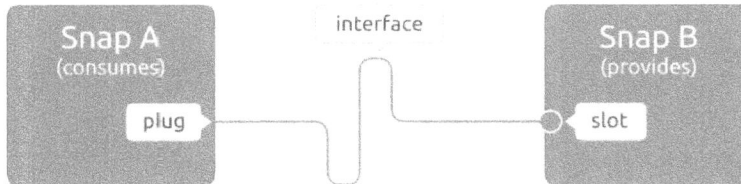

Figure 6.4 – Interface slot and plug

Figure 6.4 illustrates the plug-and-slot relationship of an interface. The slot side provides a resource, and the plug connects to the slot, allowing access to the resource. Some snaps provide a slot, as shown in *Figure 6.4*, but some slots are provided by SnapD, specifically for access to host resources such as camera, microphone, network, and so on.

Snapcraft

Snapcraft is a developer tool used to package software as a Snap. A simple YAML file declares the information necessary to compile the software, dependencies, and plugs. YAML is a declarative formatting language that Snapcraft can read. Snapcraft will use the declarative YAML file to compile and create the Snap, which can be installed locally or published to the Snap Store. Snapcraft also includes all the tools necessary to manage the Snap life cycle, including release management.

The power of the command line: installing software with APT and Snap

The App Center provides a great, intuitive interface for finding and installing applications. Let's explore how we can do that with our trusty command line.

For Debian packages, APT is the tool for finding and installing software from the Ubuntu software repositories. It's important to understand that APT relies on a local package cache for searches and dependency resolution. What does that mean? Well, APT downloads data from all configured software repositories to use later when searching, installing, or upgrading packages. This package cache includes a list of all software available in the repositories, including information such as version, description, dependencies, and much more.

Let's take a look at some common ways you may use APT with the command line.

apt show

The apt show command displays information in the package cache. The following example shows the information included in the APT package cache, which can be seen using the apt show gnome-calculator command, where gnome-calculator is the package for which we want information:

```
ken@monster:~$ apt show gnome-calculator


Package: gnome-calculator
Version: 1:46.1-1ubuntu1~24.04.1
Priority: optional
Section: math
Origin: Ubuntu
Maintainer: Ubuntu Developers <ubuntu-devel-discuss@lists.ubuntu.com>
Original-Maintainer: Debian GNOME Maintainers <pkg-gnome-maintainers@
lists.alioth.debian.org>
Bugs: https://bugs.launchpad.net/ubuntu/+filebug
Installed-Size: 3,383 kB
Depends: libadwaita-1-0 (>= 1.4~beta), libc6 (>= 2.34), libglib2.0-0t64
(>= 2.64.0), libgtk-4-1 (>= 4.11.4), libgtksourceview-5-0 (>= 5.3.0),
libmpc3 (>= 1.1.0), libmpfr6 (>= 3.1.3), libsoup-3.0-0 (>= 3.4.0), libxml2
(>= 2.7.4), dconf-gsettings-backend | gsettings-backend
Recommends: yelp, gvfs
Breaks: gcalctool (<< 6.7)
Replaces: gcalctool (<< 6.7)
Homepage: https://apps.gnome.org/Calculator/
Task: ubuntu-desktop-minimal, ubuntu-desktop, edubuntu-desktop-
gnome-minimal, edubuntu-desktop-gnome, edubuntu-desktop-gnome-raspi,
ubuntucinnamon-desktop-minimal, ubuntucinnamon-desktop, ubuntucinnamon-
desktop, ubuntucinnamon-desktop-raspi
Download-Size: 440 kB
APT-Sources: http://archive.ubuntu.com/ubuntu noble-updates/main amd64
Packages
```

```
Description: GNOME desktop calculator
The GNOME calculator is a powerful graphical calculator with financial,
logical and scientific modes. It uses a multiple precision package to do
its arithmetic to give a high degree of accuracy.
```

Most information displayed is intuitive, such as the package name, version, description, and home page. Other information that could be useful for users, such as the link to where to file bugs for the package, is usually linked to the package on Launchpad, which is the tool Ubuntu developers use to build and maintain the Ubuntu Linux distribution.

APT uses other information internally to ensure all dependencies are met when the application is installed. In the previous example, we can see that gnome-calculator requires libgtk-4-1 greater than or equal to version 4.11.4. APT will ensure that the requirement is met when installing gnome-software, and if it can't meet the requirement, the installation will fail with an error message.

apt update

As discussed earlier, APT downloads package information from software repositories and stores it locally on the computer. We call this the **local package cache**. This package cache needs to be periodically refreshed with the latest information in the software repositories, such as new versions. We can update that cache anytime with the sudo apt update command.

Important note

Some apt commands alter your system, requiring administrative privileges to run. You can run any program with administrative privileges by preceding it with sudo. The sudo command tells the system to run the following command as a super user. I strongly advise only using sudo when necessary. In this book, when there is an example of a command that requires sudo, it will be included in the reference.

apt search

The apt search command searches the descriptions of all packages in the package cache. This is the best way to find the software you are looking for.

Sticking with the calculator example in the *apt show* section earlier, if we search for the term calculator, we get 135 results. It's important to note that not all 135 results are calculator applications that can be used for math homework. Since the search looks for the search term in the descriptions, any package that uses that term will be shown. For example, one of the packages in the result is used to connect a Texas Instruments hand-held calculator to your computer, which might not be what you are looking for.

Continuing with this example, assuming you are looking for an application to use as a calculator, it's probably safe to assume a package name that contains the term calculator is more likely to meet our needs. We can instruct APT to search only package names, not package descriptions, by adding the `--names-only` argument, or `-n` for short:

```
ken@monster:~$ apt search calculator --names-only
Sorting... Done
Full Text Search... Done
deepin-calculator/noble 5.7.21-2build2 amd64
  Calculator for DDE (Deepin Desktop Environment)

gnome-calculator/noble-updates 1:46.1-1ubuntu1~24.04.1 amd64
  GNOME desktop calculator

libwww-google-calculator-perl/noble,noble 0.07-2.1 all
  Perl interface for Google calculator

lomiri-calculator-app/noble,noble 4.0.1-1 all
  Calculator App for Lomiri Operating Environment

unity-scope-calculator/noble,noble 0.1+14.04.20140328-0ubuntu5 all
  Calculator scope for Unity
```

The previous example shows that by adding `--names-only` to the `apt search` command, we get only five results, which are more likely to provide the application we are looking for.

Also, the results show the package name, version, and just the first line of the description, which may not be enough information. We can add the `--full` argument, or `-f` for short, to display the full description in the results.

apt install

Now that we understand how to find the software we need with APT, it's time for installation. APT is intuitive, and I'm sure you've already guessed that the `apt install` command is the best way to achieve this. There are some useful tricks, though, so let's dig in!

Most likely, all you need to do is run apt install gnome-calculator, and you're done. APT will install the latest version of the package and all its dependencies. However, there are cases where you might want to specify the exact version to install or perhaps the version from a different pocket.

That's a concept we haven't covered yet, pockets. The Ubuntu APT repositories are organized by release and pocket. The release is self-explanatory: the code name for the Ubuntu releases the package is compatible with. The repository is further organized into different pockets:

- **Release**: Packages included in the release version.
- **Updates**: Updates that have been thoroughly tested.
- **Security**: Security fixes.
- **Proposed**: Proposed fixes that haven't been verified yet. This pocket isn't enabled by default.
- **Backports**: Major version updates from future versions of Ubuntu that have been backported to this release. This pocket isn't enabled by default.

We can use the apt policy command to determine which versions are available for a package:

```
ken@monster:~$ apt policy gnome-calculator
gnome-calculator:
  Installed: (none)
  Candidate: 1:46.1-1ubuntu1~24.04.1
  Version table:
   1:46.1-1ubuntu1~24.04.1 500
      500 http://archive.ubuntu.com/ubuntu noble-updates/main amd64
Packages
   1:46.0-1ubuntu1 500
      500 http://archive.ubuntu.com/ubuntu noble/main amd64 Packages
```

Back to the preceding gnome-calculator example, we can see that version 46.1 is available in noble-updates (the updates pocket of 24.04), and version 46.0 is in noble (the release pocket of 24.04). Simply install it with sudo apt install gnome-calculator, which will install 46.1 as it's the latest version.

Since Ubuntu 24.04 was released, an update to 46.1 has been published. This is the best version to install, likely fixing bugs found in 46.0. But let's say you want to install 46.0 from the release pocket. You can do this with sudo apt install gnome-calculator=1:46.0-1ubuntu1.

apt reinstall

Reinstall is exactly what it sounds like. Once you've installed a package, using the same install command will just tell you the package is already installed.

apt reinstall is used the same as an APT install, but it downloads the package again and installs it over the existing installed package, overwriting files as necessary.

apt remove

To uninstall a package that has been installed with APT, simply use the sudo apt remove command. For example, use sudo apt remove gnome-calculator to uninstall the gnome-calculator package.

apt purge

Some packages include configuration files that can be modified over time. When the package is uninstalled, the changes to those files are kept around in case you install it again. apt purge is like remove but also purges any configuration files associated with the package.

apt autoremove

When a package is installed, APT installs any other packages necessary as declared by the package dependencies. This is great; you don't need to know what packages are necessary for gnome-calculator to work, just install gnome-calculator and APT does the hard work. Well, when you remove a package, those dependencies aren't automatically removed. Over time, the number of packages you have installed on your system that aren't actually needed will grow.

APT makes it easy to automatically remove those packages with the autoremove command. The autoremove command is more of a housekeeping thing, not requiring a particular package name to be declared. Simply run sudo apt autoremove any time and you'll be presented with all packages currently installed on your system that were installed just to satisfy a dependency for packages no longer installed.

autoremove isn't necessary, but it can be a good idea from time to time.

apt autopurge

Similar to autoremove, the sudo apt autopurge command removes those unneeded packages along with any modified configuration files, just like the purge command does.

apt autoclean

APT downloads files as part of keeping the package cache updated as well as Debian packages files needed to install packages. These downloaded files are just there to speed up any APT operation that might utilize them without the need to download them again. You can use `sudo apt autoclean` to automatically clean up these temporary files at any time.

apt-file find

Sometimes you'll run into an error where you'll see a file not found error message. It's not always obvious how to find the package you need to install to solve the issue. The `apt-file` command is incredibly useful but sadly is not included in the default Ubuntu installation. I always strongly recommend everyone install `apt-file`. The `apt-file` command is included in the `apt-file` package – run `sudo apt install apt-file` to install it:

```
ken@monster:~$ apt-file find /usr/bin/gnome-calculator
gnome-calculator: /usr/bin/gnome-calculator
```

The previous example demonstrates how to use `apt-file` to find which package provides `/usr/bin/gnome-calculator`.

command-not-found

This is a little-known piece of magic that really makes your life easier. You might have seen it but probably didn't know what provides it. The `command-not-found` utility keeps a mapping of many possible commands, and which packages provide them to display a useful message when you attempt to run the command and it's not installed:

```
ken@monster:~$ gnome-calculator
Command 'gnome-calculator' not found, but can be installed with:
sudo snap install gnome-calculator  # version 46.1, or
sudo apt  install gnome-calculator  # version 1:46.1-1ubuntu1~24.04.1
See 'snap info gnome-calculator' for additional versions.
```

In the previous example, you can see that when I tried to run the `gnome-calculator` command, it wasn't installed, but `command-not-found` showed me that it was available to install with `snap` or `apt`, including the exact command necessary to install it.

snap find

When searching for software in the Snap Store, the `snap find` command is your friend. Searches match the package name and other data relevant to the Snap. You can even search by publisher, so searching for `vandine` will show all the snaps I've published.

snap info

The snap info command will show you more details on the Snap, including publisher, description, store link, and version availability:

```
ken@monster:~$ snap info neofetch-desktop
name:      neofetch-desktop
summary: Neofetch Desktop
publisher: Ken VanDine◯
store-url: https://snapcraft.io/neofetch-desktop
contact: https://github.com/kenvandine/neofetch-desktop
license: GPL-3.0+
description: |
  Shows Linux System Information with Distribution Logo
commands:
  - neofetch-desktop
snap-id:    ELDfufW5r9Zdi8oii92DDsgAqcSro9Ga
tracking:   latest/stable
refresh-date: 40 days ago, at 14:37 EDT
channels:
  latest/stable:  0.3 2024-07-25 (65) 1MB -
  latest/candidate: ↑
  latest/beta:    ↑
  latest/edge:    0.3 2024-07-24 (65) 1MB -
installed:        0.3        (65) 1MB -
```

The previous example shows the output of snap info neofetch-desktop as an example. In addition to the obvious summary, description, and publisher information, notice the channels and tracking information. You can see in this example that I installed version 0.3 from the stable channel, which was last updated 40 days ago. We'll discuss this in more detail later in this chapter when we cover advanced Snap concepts.

snap list

It's useful to quickly see what snaps are installed on your system with a simple snap list command.

snap install

As expected, the `snap install` command will install a snap from the Snap Store. The syntax is simple: `sudo snap install neofetch-desktop` will install the latest stable version of `neofetch-desktop`.

snap remove

The `snap remove` command will remove the snap from your system. Most commonly, you would use `sudo snap remove neofetch-desktop` to uninstall the `neofetch-desktop` snap. When removing the snap, SnapD will keep snapshot data on your system to handle revert operations. This is usually desirable, and we'll go into more detail about why later when discussing reverting. But there are cases where a snap might store large amounts of data, using disk space you might be looking to free up. In this case, you can instruct SnapD to purge that data during removal. You just add the `--purge` argument to the command to purge on removal – for example, `sudo snap remove --purge neofetch-desktop`. Just note this will uninstall the Snap *and* remove any data that would have been stored, making it impossible to revert the removal.

snap refresh

SnapD automatically updates all snaps on your system, ensuring you always have the latest published version. This happens a few times per day, but there might be cases when you know there's a newer version available and you would rather not wait for the auto-refresh. To trigger a forced refresh of all snaps on your system, run `sudo snap refresh`. Or if you want to refresh just a single snap, run `sudo snap refresh neofetch-desktop`.

snap revert

Any Snap operation can be reverted if the outcome isn't what you expected. SnapD stores all the necessary data to switch you back to the previous version of the snap and revert the data to match the data associated with the snap to the last revision. This is particularly useful after an update when the application no longer functions as expected. You can use `sudo snap revert neofetch-desktop` to revert to the previous version of `neofetch-desktop`.

snap connections

Snap permissions are managed as plugs connected to slots for defined interfaces, as shown in *Figure 6.4*. Interfaces are defined in SnapD as a set of rules for allowing access to system resources. The rules for each interface vary depending on the access required. For example, the camera interface defines the rules for accessing your webcam.

The Snap publisher declares which interfaces are necessary to use the software, but you, as the user, can control which interfaces are allowed for each Snap installed on your system. Use the `snap connections` command to see which interfaces are connected or available to be connected. This command will output every interface for every snap installed on your system, which is probably not what you typically need. To reduce that to what's relevant, you can specify the snap to view its connections. The `snap connections firefox` command will display all interfaces for the Firefox Snap:

```
ken@monster:~$ snap connections firefox
Interface        Plug                    Slot
audio-playback   firefox:audio-playback  :audio-playback
audio-record     firefox:audio-record    :audio-record
camera           firefox:camera          :camera
network          firefox:network         :network
```

In the previous example, we can see a list of connections made for the Firefox Snap. This is only an excerpt; quite a few more interfaces are necessary for a full-featured web browser such as Firefox. In this example, we can see that Firefox has access to the audio-record interface, which allows access to your microphone, and the camera interface, which allows access to your camera.

snap interface

To get more details on an interface, we can use the `snap interface` command, for example, `snap interface camera`:

```
ken@monster:~$ snap interface camera
name:          camera
summary:       allows access to all cameras
documentation: https://snapcraft.io/docs/camera-interface
plugs:
  - 1password
  - cheese
  - chromium
  - discord
  - element-desktop
  - firefox
  - gnome-boxes
  - telegram-desktop
  - whatsie
```

```
slots:
  - snapd
```

In the previous example, we can see that the camera interface allows access to all cameras and a link to the online documentation. The `snap interface` command also displays a list of snaps that *plug* the camera interface and what provides the *slot* to the camera interface. The diagram in *Figure 6.4* should help visualize the relationship.

In the case of the camera interface, the slot is provided by SnapD, which is generally the case for any hardware resources on the system. It's also possible for other snaps to provide a slot for an interface, allowing access to resources controlled by that snap.

snap connect and disconnect

Snap provides `connect` and `disconnect` commands to manage interface connections. To prevent Firefox from accessing our microphone, `sudo snap disconnect firefox:audio-record` will disconnect the plug. You could do the same for any of the interfaces, such as the camera plug, to prevent access to your camera. Conversely, you can allow access with `suco snap connect firefox:audio-record`.

snap help

As you can see, Snap is a very powerful tool with many commands. The `snap help` command provides a full list of available commands:

```
ken@monster:~$ snap help
The snap command lets you install, configure, refresh anc remove snaps.
Snaps are packages that work across many different Linux distributions,
enabling secure delivery and operation of the latest apps and utilities.

Usage: snap <command> [<optiors>...]

Commonly used commands can be classified as follows:

        Basics: find, info, install, remove, list
       ...more: refresh, revert, switch, disable, enable, create-cohort
       History: changes, tasks, abort, watch
       Daemons: services, start, stop, restart, logs
   Permissions: connections, interface, connect, disconnect
 Configuration: get, set, unset, wait
    App Aliases: alias, aliases, unalias, prefer
```

```
        Account: login, logout, whoami
      Snapshots: saved, save, check-snapshot, restore, forget
         Device: model, remodel, reboot, recovery
   Quota Groups: set-quota, remove-quota, quotas, quota
Validation Sets: validate
    ... Other: warnings, okay, known, ack, version
    Development: validate


For more information about a command, run 'snap help <command>'.
For a short summary of all commands, run 'snap help --all'.
```

The previous example shows all the available Snap commands. To get more information on any one of those commands, you can specify the command name, such as snap help install, for more detailed help on the install command.

That's a lot of information on the basics of using APT and Snap commands to manage software on your system. This will most likely cover anything you need regularly.

Advanced Snap concepts

Now that we understand how Snaps work and how to install and manage them on our Ubuntu system, let's learn about some of the more advanced Snap concepts on our journey to mastering Ubuntu.

Snap channels

Snap technology has a well-defined, sophisticated software lifecycle built in. What does this mean? It sounds very complicated. Perhaps it's a bit complicated but incredibly robust and powerful.

Overall, we refer to this as **snap channels**. A channel comprises a track, risk level, and branch.

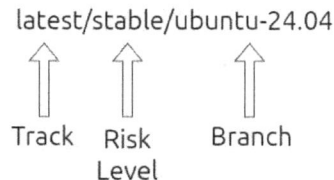

Figure 6.5 – Snap channels

Tracks

Tracks allow software publishers to distinguish between major versions or feature releases of the software. All Snaps have the *latest* track defined, and typically, that's all that's used. However, some publishers will utilize tracks to give early access to new features or even provide important bug and security fixes for software on an extended support version.

For example, Microsoft often publishes the latest stable releases of VS Code on the default latest track and provides an insider track for new features that have yet to be released in the latest stable release. Mozilla utilizes tracks as well for Firefox:

```
channels:
  latest/stable:    129.0.2-1       2024-08-20 (4793) 282MB
  latest/candidate: 130.0-2         2024-08-29 (4848) 284MB
  latest/beta:      130.0b9-1       2024-08-23 (4813) 283MB
  latest/edge:      131.0a1         2024-09-02 (4869) 303MB
  esr/stable:       115.14.0esr-2   2024-08-06 (4707) 257MB
  esr/candidate:    115.15.0esr-1   2024-08-27 (4834) 257MB
  esr/beta:         ↑
  esr/edge:         ↑
```

Using Mozilla's Firefox snap in the previous example, we can see versions released on the *latest* track as well as the *ESR* track. Mozilla publishes new **Extended Support Releases (ESR)** once per year while still regularly publishing crash and security fixes to that series. Some users or organizations may prefer the slower release cadence and follow the ESR track while not compromising security.

Risk levels

Snap defines four risk levels:

- **Stable**: Stable release
- **Candidate**: Potentially the next stable release, usually pending testing
- **Beta**: Experimental release
- **Edge**: Latest development snapshot

You should generally stick to the stable releases, which provide a more reliable experience. However, there may be times when you want to try out new features or perhaps participate in testing what's coming next.

Each track automatically has all four risk levels available, but there might not be versions of the Snap published for each risk level.

Branches

Not all channels include a branch, but these can be useful in further defining the software we use. The most common case of branch use is for any software included in the default Ubuntu installation, as a snap will have a branch that specifies the Ubuntu release. For example, Firefox is included in Ubuntu and tracks `latest/stable/ubuntu-24.04`. Note, in that example, the branch name matches a specific Ubuntu release.

The Ubuntu Release Team can use this as a mechanism to provide critical bug fixes that apply to Ubuntu 24.04 users without affecting other users of the Firefox Snap.

The branch can also be used by software publishers to provide bug fixes that users can easily test and validate.

In the *snap info* section covered earlier, the output of `snap info` shows the tracking channel is `latest/stable`. We can also see any revisions released on other channels. If there is a new version on the `latest/candidate` channel that we want to try, we can refresh from that channel with `sudo snap refresh --channel=latest/candidate neofetch-desktop`. This command will refresh the snap to the version published on the `latest/candidate` channel and change the tracking information we saw in `snap info`. Future refreshes will automatically use the `latest/candidate` channel until we change the tracking channel again.

We can also use the `snap switch` command to just switch the tracking channel without actually performing the `refresh` operation immediately, but will automatically refresh eventually. The command to switch is `sudo snap switch --channel=latest/candidate neofetch-desktop`.

As mentioned earlier, all snaps have a `latest` track and all snaps have those four risk levels. Snap understands the shorthand for switching just the risk level on the same track. So, the preceding example can also be performed with `sudo snap refresh --candidate neofetch-desktop` with the same result.

The same shorthand for specifying the risk level as well as the `--channel` argument works on the `snap install` command as well. So, if you don't already have `neofetch-desktop` installed, you can use `sudo snap install --candidate neofetch-desktop` to install directly from the `candidate` channel.

Snap tasks

As mentioned earlier, Snap operations are all atomic, meaning each operation must be completed successfully, or the entire operation will be reverted to ensure your system is still usable. These operations are known as **changes**, and they are made up of a group of tasks.

For example, a `snap install` operation consists of a change to the installation, which includes many tasks necessary for the installation to be complete. These tasks involve downloading the snap, checking the snap authenticity, running the health checks, connecting all the required interfaces, and more. If any of these tasks fail, the entire installation fails.

You can see changes with the `snap changes` command. This will output a table that includes ID, Status, Spawn, Ready, and Summary columns:

- **ID**: A number that can be used to get further information on the change
- **Status**: Abort, Do, Doing, Done, Error, Hold, Undo, Undoing, and Wait
- **Spawn**: The timestamp for when the task started
- **Ready**: The timestamp for when the task was complete
- **Summary**: Description of the task

For each ID found in the output of the `snap changes` command, you can get more detail with `snap task ID`, replacing ID with the appropriate ID:

```
ken@monster:~$ snap changes
ID Status Spawn                  Ready               Summary
2833 Done  today at 12:34 EDT today at 12:35 EDT Install "yaru-widgets-
example" snap from "edge" channel
```

The previous example shows the change with task ID 2833 for installing the yaru-widgets-example snap from the edge channel.

```
ken@monster:~$ snap tasks 2833
Status   Spawn            Ready              Summary
Done   today at 12:34 EDT  today at 12:34 EDT  Ensure prerequisites for
"yaru-widgets-example" are available
Done   today at 12:34 EDT  today at 12:34 EDT  Download snap "yaru-widgets-
example" (494) from channel "edge"
Done   today at 12:34 EDT  today at 12:34 EDT  Fetch and check assertions
for snap "yaru-widgets-example" (494)
Done   today at 12:34 EDT  today at 12:34 EDT  Mount snap "yaru-widgets-
example" (494)
Done   today at 12:34 EDT  today at 12:34 EDT  Copy snap "yaru-widgets-
example" data
Done   today at 12:34 EDT  today at 12:34 EDT  Setup snap "yaru-widgets-
example" (494) security profiles
Done   today at 12:34 EDT  today at 12:34 EDT  Make snap "yaru-widgets-
example" (494) available to the system
```

```
Done  today at 12:34 EDT  today at 12:34 EDT  Automatically connect
eligible plugs and slots of snap "yaru-widgets-example"
Done  today at 12:34 EDT  today at 12:35 EDT  Set automatic aliases for
snap "yaru-widgets-example"
Done  today at 12:34 EDT  today at 12:35 EDT  Setup snap "yaru-widgets-
example" aliases
Done  today at 12:34 EDT  today at 12:35 EDT  Run install hook of "yaru-
widgets-example" snap if present
Done  today at 12:34 EDT  today at 12:35 EDT  Run default-configure hook
of "yaru-widgets-example" snap if present
Done  today at 12:34 EDT  today at 12:35 EDT  Start snap "yaru-widgets-
example" (494) services
Done  today at 12:34 EDT  today at 12:35 EDT  Run configure hook of "yaru-
widgets-example" snap if present
Done  today at 12:34 EDT  today at 12:35 EDT  Run health check of "yaru-
widgets-example" snap
Done  today at 12:34 EDT  today at 12:34 EDT  Connect yaru-widgets-
example:desktop to snapd:desktop
Done  today at 12:34 EDT  today at 12:34 EDT  Connect yaru-widgets-
example:desktop-legacy to snapd:desktop-legacy
Done  today at 12:34 EDT  today at 12:34 EDT  Connect yaru-widgets-
example:network to snapd:network
Done  today at 12:34 EDT  today at 12:34 EDT  Connect yaru-widgets-
example:opengl to snapd:opengl
Done  today at 12:34 EDT  today at 12:34 EDT  Connect yaru-widgets-
example:wayland to snapd:wayland
Done  today at 12:34 EDT  today at 12:34 EDT  Connect yaru-widgets-
example:x11 to snapd:x11
Done  today at 12:34 EDT  today at 12:34 EDT  Connect yaru-widgets-
example:gnome-42-2204 to gnome-42-2204:gnome-42-2204
Done  today at 12:34 EDT  today at 12:34 EDT  Connect yaru-widgets-
example:gsettings to snapd:gsettings
Done  today at 12:34 EDT  today at 12:34 EDT  Connect yaru-widgets-
example:gtk-3-themes to gtk-common-themes:gtk-3-themes
Done  today at 12:34 EDT  today at 12:34 EDT  Connect yaru-widgets-
example:icon-themes to gtk-common-themes:icon-themes
Done  today at 12:34 EDT  today at 12:34 EDT  Connect yaru-widgets-
example:sound-themes to gtk-common-themes:sound-themes
Done  today at 12:34 EDT  today at 12:35 EDT  Setup snap "yaru-widgets-
example" (494) security profiles for auto-connections
```

The previous example shows all the tasks associated with task ID 2833. If any of these tasks fail, task 2833, which was installing yaru-widgets-example, will fail.

Changes in progress can be aborted with snap abort ID, replacing ID with the task ID to abort.

Managing updates

SnapD ensures all snaps are automatically refreshed every four hours if a new version is available. However, there are two scenarios in which SnapD won't automatically refresh.

Running

If a new version is available but the software provided in the Snap is currently in use, SnapD will download the update but only apply it once you exit the application. This is desirable for long-running applications as they might behave differently when the version changes without restarting the application. For example, most users leave their web browser, such as Firefox, open all day. If Firefox is open when an update is available, SnapD will download the new version but not update it until it exits. As a user, you will get a notification explaining a new version.

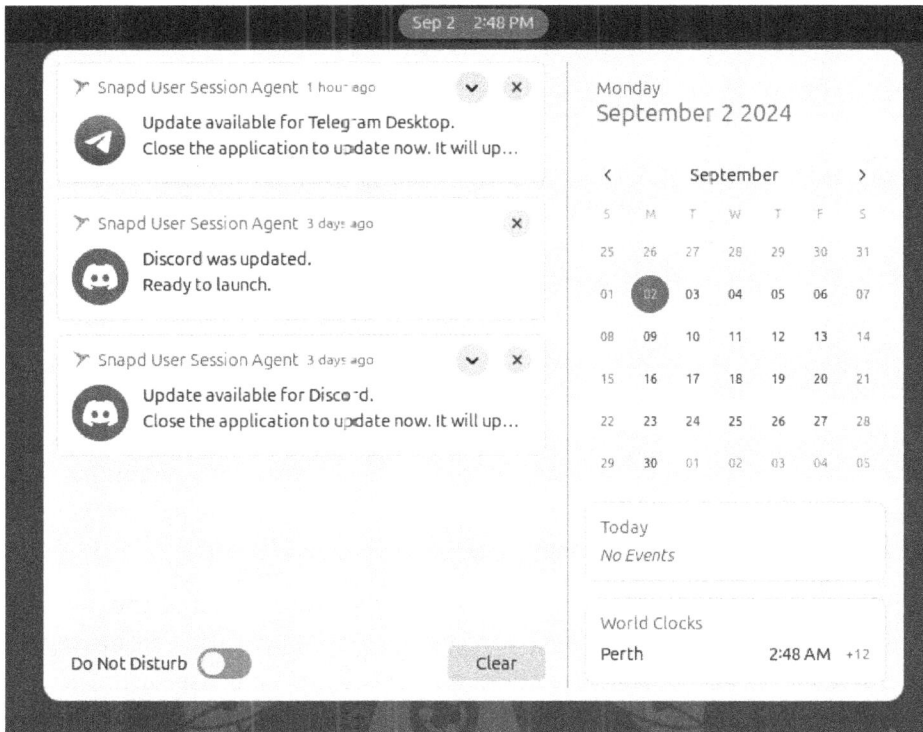

Figure 5.6 – Snap refresh awareness

Figure 6.6 shows that I was notified of an update available for Discord three days ago. I exited Discord, and SnapD completed the refresh. Then, SnapD notified me again that the new version of Discord was now ready to launch.

Held

SnapD allows you to pause or stop automatic updates for individual snaps or your entire system. You can add a hold for an individual snap by specifying a duration with the `hold` argument to the `snap refresh` command. For example, `sudo snap refresh --hold=24h firefox` will hold Firefox refreshes for 24 hours. You can replace 24 hours with any desired duration; if you omit the duration, refreshes will be held indefinitely.

You can also hold automatic refreshes of all snaps by omitting the Snap name. So, `sudo snap refresh --hold` will stop automatic refreshes of all snaps indefinitely.

> **Important note**
>
> Pausing automatic refreshes is precisely that, and it only applies to automatic refreshes. If you hold refreshes of all snaps indefinitely and run the `sudo snap refresh` command, it will refresh all snaps.

To cancel a hold, simply use the `--unhold` argument to the `snap refresh` command, just as we did when we created the hold. So, `sudo snap refresh --unhold firefox` will remove the hold for Firefox.

You can see the `held` status with the `snap info` and `snap list` commands. The `snap list` command, of course, lists all installed snaps. You'll see `held` in the `Notes` column to the right. Using `snap info firefox`, you will see `held` shown to the right of the installed version if it's held.

snap enable/disable

A unique feature of Snap technology is the ability to change the state of an installed snap without removing it. When installing a snap, SnapD automatically enables it, allowing you to run the application. At any time, you can disable the snap, which prevents it from running. Later, you can enable the snap again.

When disabled, you can't run the snap from the command line, and the launcher will not be available on your desktop, as if you removed the application from your system. However, all the data and the app are still there. Usage is simple: use `sudo snap disable gnome-calculator` or `sudo snap enable gnome-calculator` to disable or enable the gnome-calculator snap, respectively.

Snap services

Snaps support much more than just desktop applications. There are snaps for services that run in the background as well. For example, the **Common UNIX Printing System (CUPS)** provides a service that runs in the background to allow other applications to print. The cupsd service is provided by the cups snap.

The snap services command lists all services provided by snaps on your system. The same command shows you the current status of the service:

```
ken@monster:~$ snap services cups.cupsd
Service     Startup  Current  Notes
cups.cupsd  enabled  active -
```

The previous example shows the cupsd service provided by the cups snap. This service is necessary for any application on your system to print.

Snap provides several ways to manage these services. As shown in the following example, you can see the current status of the service with the snap services command:

```
ken@monster:~$ sudo snap restart cups.cupsd
2024-09-02T15:32:41-04:00 INFO Waiting for "snap.cups.cupsd.service" to
stop.
Restarted.
ken@monster:~$ sudo snap stop cups.cupsd
2024-09-02T15:33:19-04:00 INFO Waiting for "snap.cups.cupsd.service" to
stop.
Stopped.
ken@monster:~$ sudo snap start cups.cupsd
Started.
```

Snap also provides restart, stop, and start commands, as demonstrated in the previous example.

To get log output from a running service, Snap provides a logs command such as snap logs cups.cupsd to see the runtime log output from the service, which is helpful for debugging issues.

Snapshots

A snapshot is a copy of the user, system, and configuration data stored by SnapD for one or more snaps. Snapshots are generated manually with the `snap save` command and automatically when a snap is removed. To prevent this snapshot from being saved on removal, use `sudo snap remove --purge SNAPNAME`.

Snapshots created automatically during removal are retained for 31 days before being deleted automatically.

These snapshots are commonly used to restore data for a specific Snap version, such as when reverting a `snap remove` operation. However, this snapshot feature is useful far beyond that case. Any snapshot can be exported and later imported, which is great when integrated with your data backup strategy or even when moving application data to a new computer.

The `snap save` command creates new snapshots. Using `sudo snap save SNAPNAME` will generate a snapshot for the specific snap while omitting `SNAPNAME`, creating snapshots of all installed snaps:

```
ken@monster:~$ sudo snap save neofetch-desktop
Set  Snap             Age     Version  Rev  Size    Notes
10 neofetch-desktop   523ms   0.3      65   1.51MB  -
ken@monster:~$ snap saved
Set  Snap             Age     Version  Rev  Size    Notes
8   hollywood         13.0d   1.21     3      248B  auto
10 neofetch-desktop   4m37s   0.3      65   1.51MB  -
```

Saved snapshots can be listed with the `snap saved` command, as shown in the previous example. They can also be exported as ZIP archives for backup and restore purposes.

```
ken@monster:~$ snap export-snapshot 10 neofetch-desktop-10.zip
Exported snapshot #10 into "neofetch-desktop-10.zip"
ken@monster:~$ sudo snap import-snapshot neofetch-desktop-10.zip
Imported snapshot as #10
Set  Snap             Age     Version  Rev  Size    Notes
10 neofetch-desktop   11.5m   0.3      65   1.51MB  -
```

The previous example demonstrates exporting a snapshot to a file named `neofetch-desktop-10.zip`, which is suitable for backing up and importing the snapshot later.

These are some of the most useful Snap concepts. To learn more, I'd encourage you to review the built-in documentation with the `snap help` command and the online reference material available at `https://snapcraft.io/docs`.

The Ubuntu APT repositories and the Snap Store include a nearly endless array of open source software to meet your needs for both work and play. I'd encourage everyone to explore, discover what's available, and engage with the developer communities.

Summary

In this chapter, we've learned how software, such as Debian or Snap packages, is made available to you and gained an understanding of how they differ. We should be able to find the software we need or want, install it, and use it effectively.

As we've learned in this chapter, Debian packages are an important part of the Ubuntu ecosystem. However, Snaps are much more advanced and offer many benefits. I strongly encourage you to choose the Snap option whenever it is available.

Further reading

- Ubuntu APT repositories: `https://help.ubuntu.com/community/Repositories/Ubuntu`

- Snap documentation: `https://snapcraft.io/docs`

7

Software Updates: Enhancing Security and Stability

We've learned that Ubuntu is a distribution comprised of software from many open source projects and software vendors. We've discussed finding new software and the necessary considerations when installing such software. Most significantly, we must consider the ongoing need to update that software. We don't always need the latest and greatest version upgrades, but installing security and critical bug fixes in a timely manner is essential.

This chapter covers the following topics:

- The importance of updates: constantly vigilant
- Keeping your system updated: exploring update methods
- Best practices for smooth updates: a proactive approach
- Ubuntu Pro
- Troubleshooting update issues: when things don't go as planned

The importance of updates: constantly vigilant

The transparent nature of open source software gives us a significant advantage regarding system security. However, it's important to understand that all software has bugs and the potential to exploit our systems. Security vulnerabilities usually surface because the code evolves and changes over time.

It is possible that a malicious developer intentionally introduces exploitable code, such as the *XZ* example from *Chapter 3*. Thankfully, those types of attacks are incredibly rare.

Due to how usage evolves, code that was safe when it was developed initially could become exploitable later. The important thing to understand is while software isn't perfect, it's essential to ensure you apply, at a minimum, all critical security updates.

But how do we know what a critical security update is?

Thankfully, we have well-established mechanisms for reporting such vulnerabilities and tracking their status. Let's start with **Ubuntu Security Notices**, a service the Ubuntu Security Team provides to issue notices for known security vulnerabilities in Ubuntu packages: `https://ubuntu.com/security/notices`.

For each known vulnerability, a unique **Ubuntu Security Notice** (**USN**) is posted. The service provides a few methods to subscribe to these notices, if needed. Usually, we don't need to subscribe, just trust you get the necessary security updates in a timely fashion. But knowing how the USN service works means you can quickly look up more information as needed.

A USN will list a unique USN number as a reference, a brief title, the date of the notice, the name of the package, which Ubuntu releases are affected, and a description of the vulnerability. The notice also lists which package versions include the fix:

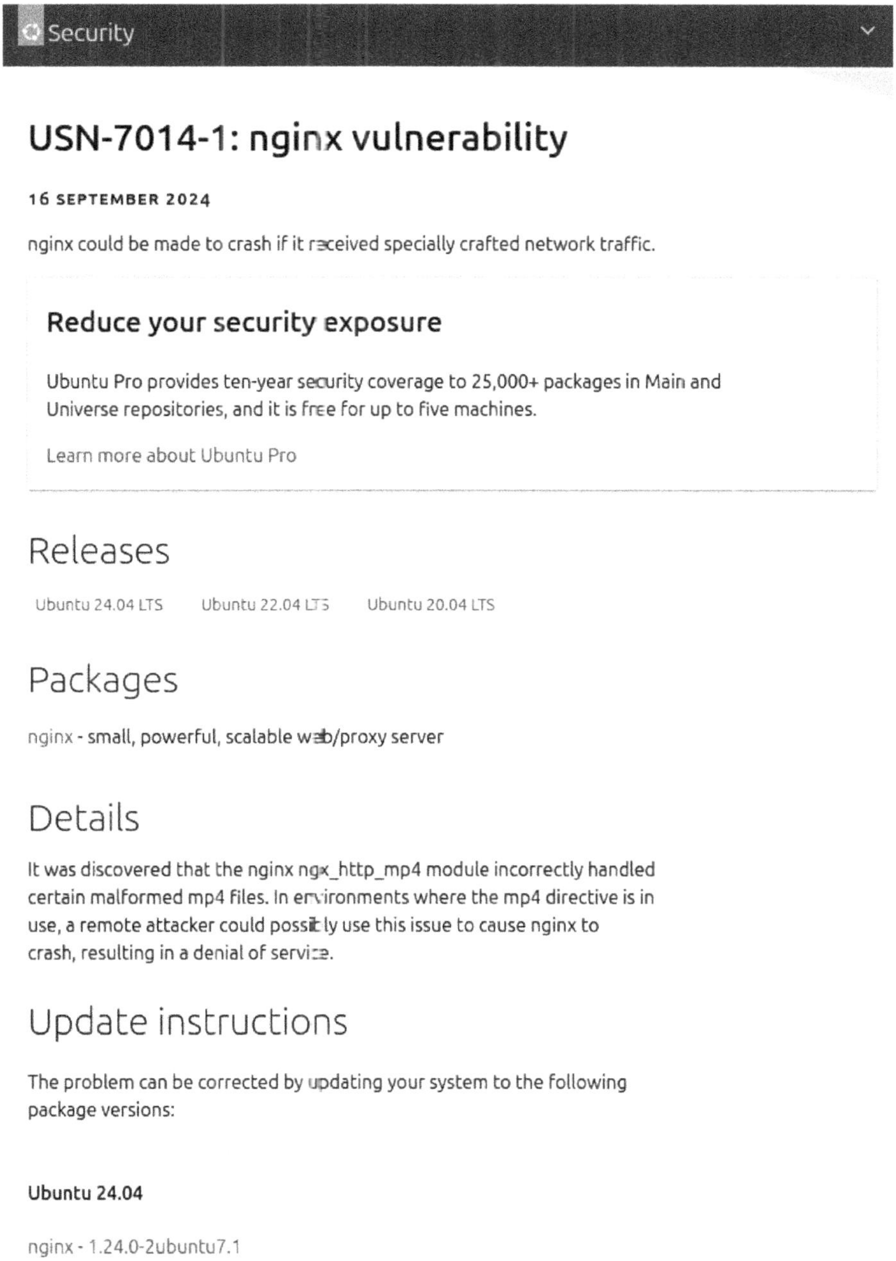

Security

USN-7014-1: nginx vulnerability

16 SEPTEMBER 2024

nginx could be made to crash if it received specially crafted network traffic.

Reduce your security exposure

Ubuntu Pro provides ten-year security coverage to 25,000+ packages in Main and Universe repositories, and it is free for up to five machines.

Learn more about Ubuntu Pro

Releases

Ubuntu 24.04 LTS   Ubuntu 22.04 LTS   Ubuntu 20.04 LTS

Packages

nginx - small, powerful, scalable web/proxy server

Details

It was discovered that the nginx ngx_http_mp4 module incorrectly handled certain malformed mp4 files. In environments where the mp4 directive is in use, a remote attacker could possibly use this issue to cause nginx to crash, resulting in a denial of service.

Update instructions

The problem can be corrected by updating your system to the following package versions:

Ubuntu 24.04

nginx - 1.24.0-2ubuntu7.1

Figure 7.1 – Ubuntu Security Notice

Another critical part of the information provided in the USN is the reference **Common Vulnerabilities and Exposures (CVE)** number.

As an Ubuntu user, following the updates made available on Ubuntu and the USNs published for your Ubuntu version is enough information. However, it is also good to understand how vulnerabilities are reported and when the USN is issued. A catalog of all known CVEs is maintained as part of the **CVE Program**, an international, community-driven effort to identify and catalog publicly disclosed vulnerabilities.

Notice I said publicly disclosed vulnerabilities. Often, it's best not to disclose a vulnerability publicly until there is a known fix. To handle this, part of the CVE submission process includes an embargo period, which allows developers time to provide a fix for the vulnerability before it's publicly known. Why is this important? Without a fix, the public disclosure could just be a place for malicious hackers to look for ways to exploit the vulnerabilities.

Part of the CVE process includes having a CVE severity assigned to articulate risk:

- No Risk
- Low Risk
- Medium Risk
- High Risk
- Critical Risk

CVE-2024-7347

Publication date	14 August 2024
Last updated	14 October 2024

UBUNTU PRIORITY	CVSS 3 SEVERITY SCORE
📶 **Medium**	📶 **4.7 · Medium**
Why this priority?	Score breakdown

NGINX Open Source and NGINX Plus have a vulnerability in the ngx_http_mp4_module, which might allow an attacker to over-read NGINX worker memory resulting in its termination, using a specially crafted mp4 file. The issue only affects NGINX if it is built with the ngx_http_mp4_module and the mp4 directive is used in the configuration file. Additionally, the attack is possible only if an attacker can trigger the processing of a specially crafted mp4 file with the ngx_http_mp4_module. Note: Software versions which have reached End of Technical Support (EoTS) are not evaluated.

Read the notes from the security team

Status

PACKAGE	UBUNTU RELEASE	STATUS
nginx	24.10 oracular	✅ Not affected
	24.04 LTS noble	✅ Fixed 1.24.0-2ubuntu7.1
	22.04 LTS jammy	✅ Fixed 1.18.0-6ubuntu14.5
	20.04 LTS focal	✅ Fixed 1.18.0-0ubuntu1.6
	18.04 LTS bionic	✅ Fixed 1.14.0-0ubuntu1.11+esm1 (Ubuntu Pro)
	16.04 LTS xenial	✅ Fixed 1.10.3-0ubuntu0.16.04.5+esm6 (Ubuntu Pro)
	14.04 LTS trusty	✅ Fixed 1.4.6-1ubuntu3.9+esm5 (Ubuntu Pro)

Figure 7.2 – CVE

Using the example from *Figure 7.1*, following the link to the CVE record as seen in *Figure 7.2*, we can see the severity was medium, which will help us understand how likely it is that this vulnerability will be exploited. We can also see Ubuntu's priority to fix it was also medium. These priorities consider the severity and how broad the exposure might be so the Ubuntu Security Team can prioritize fixing vulnerabilities appropriately.

Keeping your system updated: exploring update methods

We've talked about how critical it is to ensure the software installed on our system is kept up to date with the latest security fixes; now, let's learn how we can most effectively do that in practice.

Snaps

Let's start by covering **snap** updates, which are pretty simple. Snaps are automatically updated regularly. More specifically, your system will check for updates to installed snaps approximately every four hours and automatically apply any available updates for applications that aren't currently in use. Why not apply updates for running applications? That could cause instability, so we hold updates for running applications for up to 14 days. If an update is available for an application that's in use, you'll get a notification letting you know to restart the application at your convenience to install the update. In the background, **SnapD** downloads the update and waits for the process to end before finishing the update. If the update isn't available immediately, you will see a dialog showing you the progress:

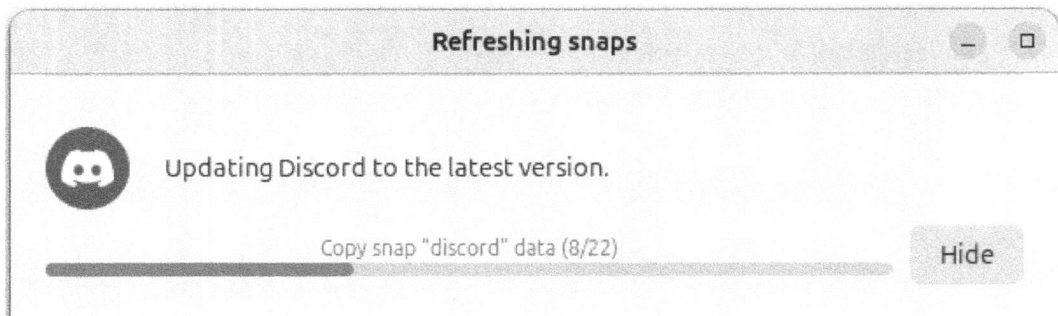

Figure 7.3 – Snap refresh progress

This could happen if an application needs data migrated to a new version. In *Figure 7.3*, Discord is handling data migration from one version to the next. When the update is complete, you will be notified, and the application will be available.

Unattended upgrades

Important security-related updates will be installed automatically, quietly behind the scenes, to help ensure your system's security. You can configure this behavior in **Software & Updates**:

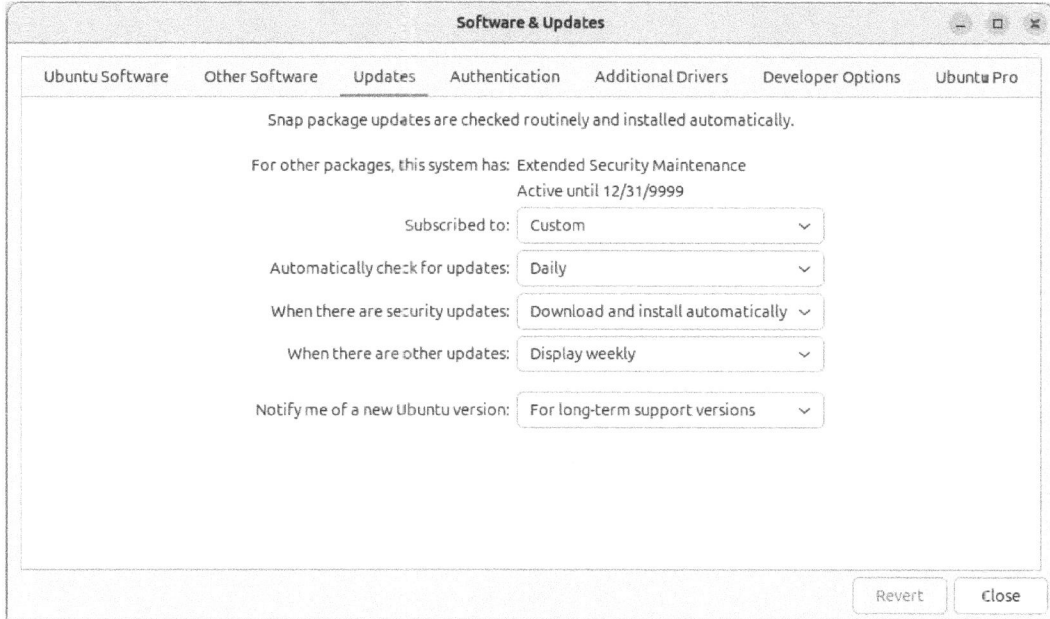

Figure 7.4 – Software & Updates

In *Figure 7.4*, under the **Updates** tab in **Software & Updates**, we can see settings for how often to check for updates and what to do when security updates are found. The default settings are to check daily and automatically download and install security updates.

If an unattended update is being installed when you power off or restart your computer, you will see a message saying that an unattended upgrade is being installed and to please wait. It is important to wait for this to finish; do not force power off your computer, as this will likely leave things in a corrupt state.

Update Manager

For updates other than security updates, you will get prompted by **Update Manager**, showing you what updates are available as well as other relevant information about each update:

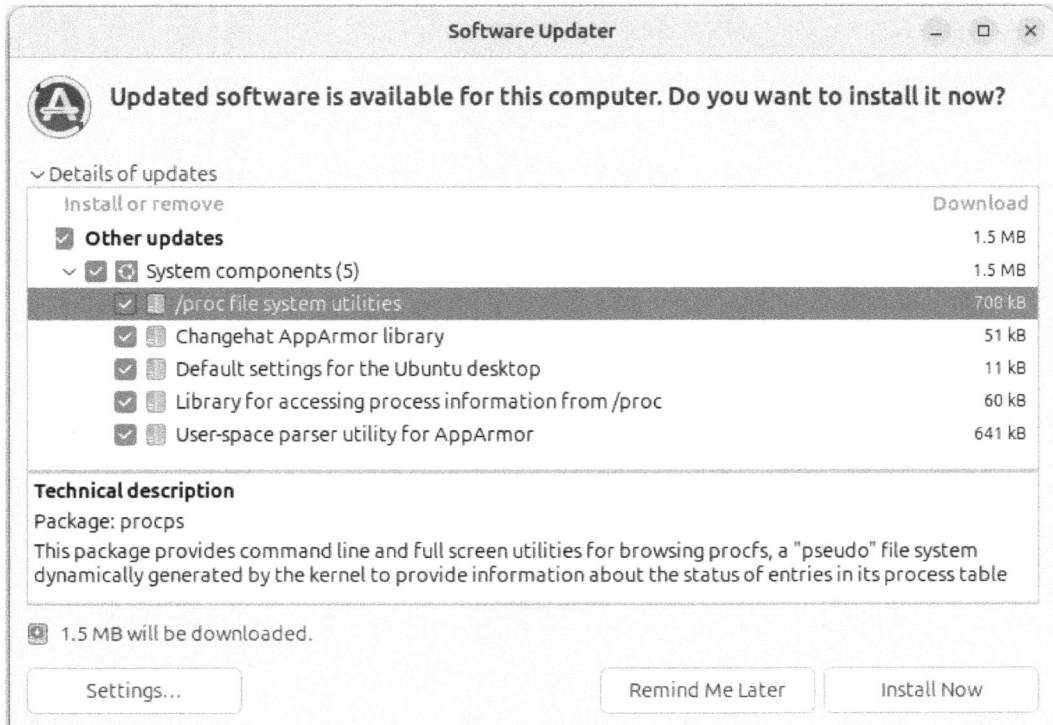

Figure 7.5 – Software Updater

Update Manager will notify you regularly for available updates based on the schedule, which can be seen in *Figure 7.5*. If you want to look at Update Manager to see what updates are available and install them, you can launch the Update Manager application.

apt updates

Package updates can be done anytime using the command-line **apt** utility. To check for updates for all installed packages and install them, run the sudo apt upgrade command. However, this command has a limitation: if a package update requires installing a new package as a dependency or perhaps even removing a package that now conflicts, it will ignore that package. This won't cause a problem, and it will just upgrade the packages it can and show you a message in the terminal listing the packages it couldn't update.

You can use the `sudo apt dist-upgrade` command to handle these cases with dependency changes. This will attempt to resolve those dependency changes, such as installing new packages or removing conflicting packages as necessary.

Both `apt upgrade` and `apt dist-upgrade` are interactive, meaning they show you what they're going to do and allow you to confirm before installing the update.

An important thing to know about `dist-upgrade` is that since it handles dependency changes, you should be really careful before confirming the operations. The update could uninstall necessary packages, so you should look for things that might make your system not function as expected.

Release upgrades

Release upgrades refer to upgrades to a new Ubuntu release. For example, if you are a user of Ubuntu 22.04, you would have gotten a notification that a release upgrade was available to Ubuntu 24.04.

Release upgrades are from LTS version to LTS version incrementally. This means you can't skip an LTS version. For example, as an Ubuntu 20.04 user, you would have to do a release upgrade to 22.04 before you could do a release upgrade to 24.04. The same applies to interim releases, such as Ubuntu 23.04, which would need to upgrade to 23.10 before upgrading to 24.04.

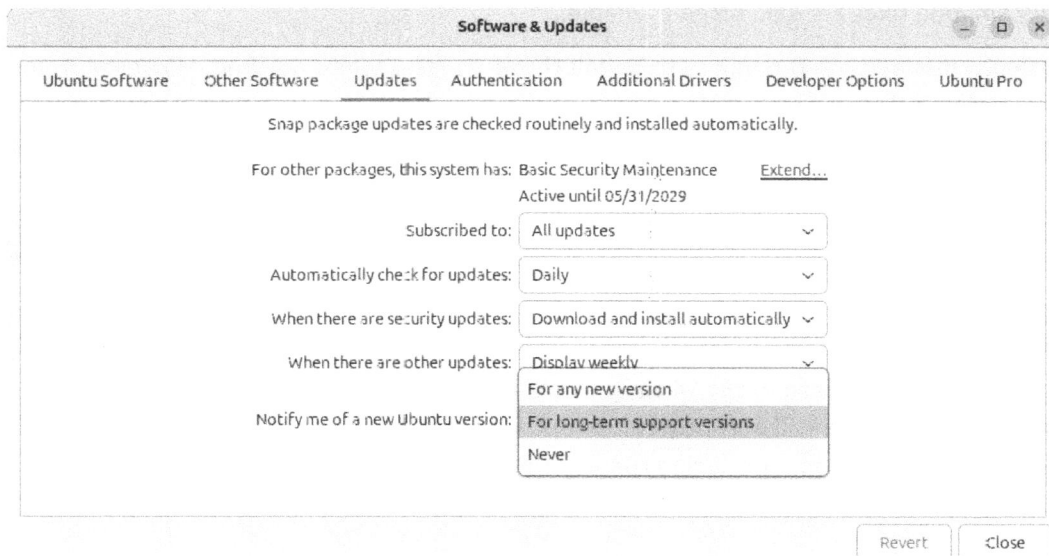

Figure 7.6 – Software & Updates

In *Figure 7.6*, you can see a setting for which versions of Ubuntu to look for in release upgrades. If you are an LTS user, such as Ubuntu 24.04, that setting will be set to **For long-term support versions**. You can change that to **For any new version** or **Never**. Any new version would mean you'll be notified when the next release is available, regardless of LTS or interim.

As mentioned, release upgrades are primarily driven by notifications. You'll get a notification when a new release upgrade is available, but the term *available* is tricky here. As a user of Ubuntu 22.04, you wouldn't see a notification that a release upgrade is available until Ubuntu 24.04.1 is released. The first *point release* after an LTS release gives Ubuntu developers time to gather bug reports from users of the new LTS version to fix critical issues and release the first point release a few months later, before existing Ubuntu LTS users are prompted to update. You can, of course, update to 24.04.0 from 22.04 at any time.

To do a release upgrade without the notification, you will need to run the release upgrade tool from a terminal. The command is simply `sudo do-release-upgrade`.

Best practices for smooth updates: a proactive approach

Keeping your software updated is important, but the road might get bumpy if you make updates an afterthought. Besides the more obvious security aspect of updating your system, bug fixes are also often available.

Usually, it is quick and painless to install these updates when notified. However, if you neglect to install updates when available, they will accumulate over time. The longer you wait to install the update, the more additional updates accumulate, which could lead to unexpected behavior as the Ubuntu development teams providing these updates test the update on a fully updated system. I always recommend installing the updates soon after being notified to ensure your system is as close to what has been tested as possible.

It's great that your snaps will automatically update, ensuring the best possible scenario. But as mentioned earlier, if the application is running, SnapD will notify you and defer installing the update for up to 14 days. This is a long time, and you could easily forget that, in 14 days, your app will abruptly exit to update. I'd recommend saving anything you are working on in the app and closing the app to allow it to update.

Ubuntu Pro

Ubuntu Pro is all you need to ensure you have access to all the best security updates. Ubuntu Pro is a subscription service provided by Canonical, providing extended security updates for over 25,000 packages not covered by the Ubuntu LTS commitment.

Don't fret about the service being a subscription. Ubuntu Pro is free for personal use and reasonably priced for enterprise use.

Ubuntu Pro encompasses some valuable services, but we'll focus on just a few for this chapter. For more information, see https://ubuntu.com/pro.

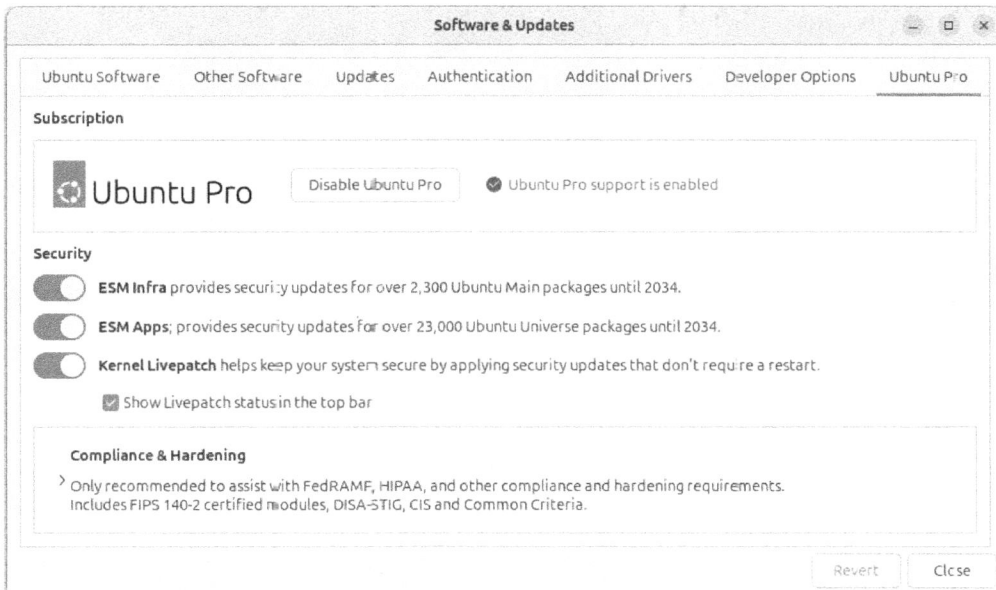

Figure 7.7 – Ubuntu Pro

Expanded Security Maintenance

As you probably recall from earlier in the book, we talked about main and universe repositories for software. Canonical provides free security and bug-fix updates for all packages in the main Ubuntu repository for the life of the LTS release (five years from release). However, there are over 25,000 packages in the universe repository, which are maintained by the broader Ubuntu community. Many of these packages in the universe repository are used heavily in many production and development environments. Ubuntu Pro provides access to security updates for all packages in the main and universe repositories for 10 years from the LTS release date.

To see the **Extended Security Maintenance** status of the software on your computer, use the pro command:

```
ken@monster:~$ sudo pro security-status
3630 packages installed:
     2488 packages from Ubuntu Main/Restricted repository
     1089 packages from Ubuntu Universe/Multiverse repository
     53 packages no longer available for download

To get more information about the packages, run
     pro security-status --help
for a list of available options.

This machine is attached to an Ubuntu Pro subscription.

Main/Restricted packages are receiving security updates from
Ubuntu Pro with 'esm-infra' enabled until 2034.

Universe/Multiverse packages are receiving security updates from
Ubuntu Pro with 'esm-apps' enabled until 2034. You have received 10
security
updates.
```

In the preceding command block, we can see how many packages are installed on the system from the main and universe repositories and what's covered under Ubuntu Pro. We can also see 53 additional packages installed that are no longer available.

Livepatch

The **Canonical Livepatch** service provides security fixes for your kernel without rebooting, allowing you to keep your systems secure without jeopardizing uptime for essential infrastructure. This doesn't mean you don't need to reboot, but the kernel livepatch service will apply security fixes to the kernel without rebooting. You should schedule a time to reboot when it's convenient.

Landscape

Landscape is a management and administration tool for Ubuntu, making it trivial to manage large-scale deployments of Ubuntu systems. You can install, update, and remove packages from a single web UI, reboot, and perform most systems administration tasks. With Landscape, you can also view reports showing essential compliance information:

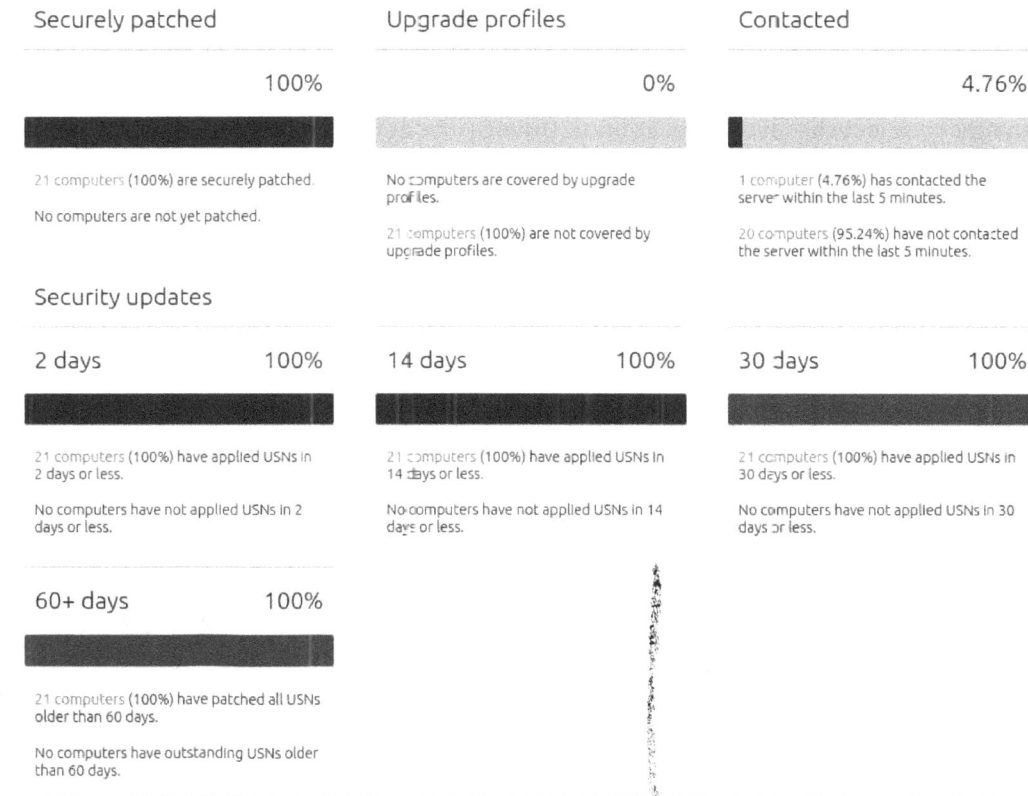

Securely patched

100%

21 computers (100%) are securely patched.

No computers are not yet patched.

Upgrade profiles

0%

No computers are covered by upgrade profiles.

21 computers (100%) are not covered by upgrade profiles.

Contacted

4.76%

1 computer (4.76%) has contacted the server within the last 5 minutes.

20 computers (95.24%) have not contacted the server within the last 5 minutes.

Security updates

2 days   100%

21 computers (100%) have applied USNs in 2 days or less.

No computers have not applied USNs in 2 days or less.

14 days   100%

21 computers (100%) have applied USNs in 14 days or less.

No computers have not applied USNs in 14 days or less.

30 days   100%

21 computers (100%) have applied USNs in 30 days or less.

No computers have not applied USNs in 30 days or less.

60+ days   100%

21 computers (100%) have patched all USNs older than 60 days.

No computers have outstanding USNs older than 60 days.

Figure 7.8 – Landscape reports

As you can imagine, Ubuntu Pro is essential if you work in an environment that values security and compliance.

Troubleshooting update issues: when things don't go as planned

Of course, nothing is perfect, and sometimes an update will fail or your computer will not work as expected after the update.

Recovery mode

If the hardware doesn't work as expected after a software update, for example, WiFi doesn't function, you can reboot into the previous kernel. To do this, you must use the boot manager to select the last kernel at boot. Ubuntu's boot manager is **GRUB**, which can be accessed during boot by pressing the *Esc* or *Shift* key while the BIOS screen is shown. For example, this might be the screen that shows your manufacturer's logo early in the boot process. You can tap and hold the appropriate key during that screen. If your system uses UEFI boot, it will be the *Esc* key; if it's using legacy boot, it will be the *Shift* key.

The GRUB boot manager screen provides a menu of kernels or boot modes, which could also include other operating systems. The top entry should be the latest kernel, and the second menu entry should be recovery mode. Recovery mode will disable networking, extra drivers, and so on to give you a minimal boot configuration and create an environment where you can make necessary repairs:

Figure 7.9 – GRUB (boot manager)

The following menu entry is for advanced options, which include the option to select a previous kernel. Ubuntu, by default, keeps the latest two kernels installed on the system. The updated kernel you installed may have a bug in your device's WiFi driver. Selecting the previous kernel should boot and get you working network access:

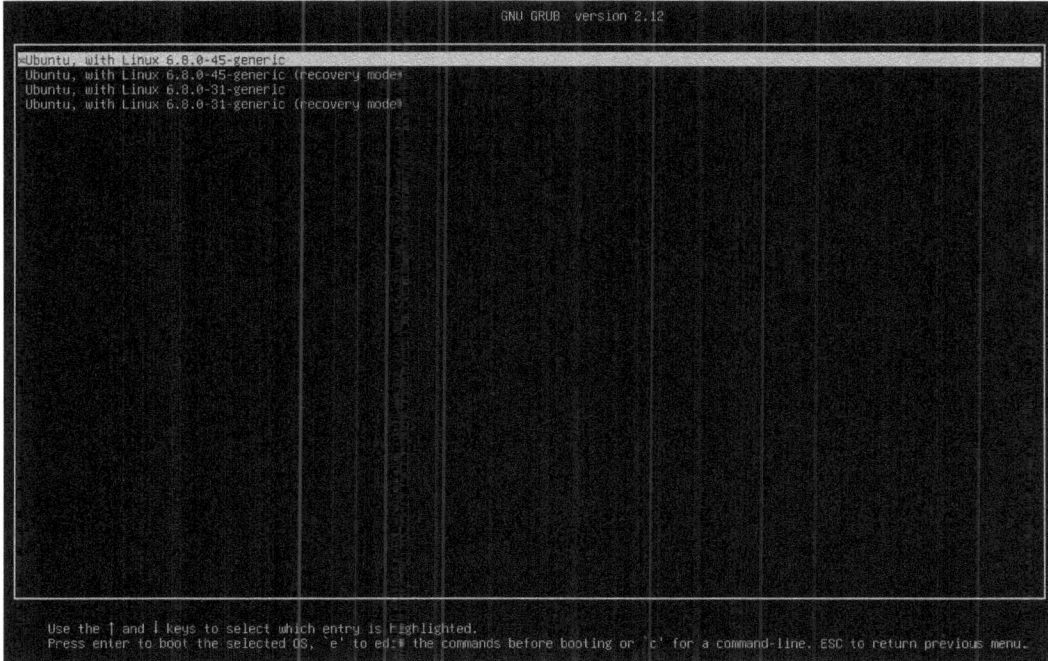

GNU GRUB version 2.12

```
*Ubuntu, with Linux 6.8.0-45-generic
 Ubuntu, with Linux 6.8.0-45-generic (recovery mode)
 Ubuntu, with Linux 6.8.0-31-generic
 Ubuntu, with Linux 6.8.0-31-generic (recovery mode)
```

```
Use the ↑ and ↓ keys to select which entry is highlighted.
Press enter to boot the selected OS, 'e' to edit the commands before booting or 'c' for a command-line. ESC to return previous menu.
```

Figure 7.10 – GRUB advanced options

If you select the recovery option in GRUB, as seen in *Figure 7.10*, your system will boot into a very minimal environment. This environment doesn't provide a graphical user interface or networking, and your hard drive is read-only. To make changes to your system in recovery mode, you must *remount the root partition in read-write mode*.

```
Recovery Menu (filesystem state: read-only)

        resume            Resume normal boot
        clean             Try to make free space
        dpkg              Repair broken packages
        fsck              Check all file systems
        grub              Update grub bootloader
        network           Enable networking
        root              Drop to root shell prompt
        system-summary    System summary




                        <Ok>
```

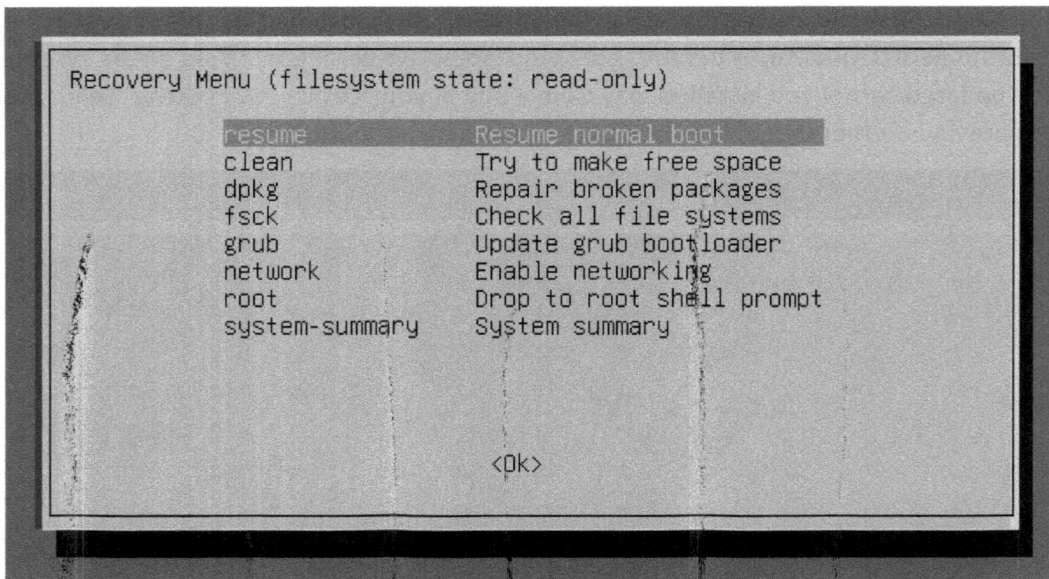

Figure 7.11 – Recovery mode

Choosing the root option in the recovery menu shown in *Figure 7.11* will get you a command-line shell with root (administrative) privileges. As mentioned before, your hard drive is in a read-only state in recovery mode; to make changes, you will need to remount your hard drive as writable:

```
root@monster:~# mount -o remount,rw /
```

Summary

In this chapter, we've learned about the importance of software updates. These updates are essential for maintaining system security, stability, and functionality. By regularly applying updates, users can protect themselves from vulnerabilities, enhance system performance, and enjoy the latest features and bug fixes.

Ubuntu makes it easy to stay on top of essential updates with unattended upgrades, automated snap updates, and notifications for routine updates.

In the next chapter, we'll learn how to get help using the extraordinary Ubuntu community. We'll learn where to find documentation, where to ask for help, and how to engage with Ubuntu developers and the broader Ubuntu community to help improve Ubuntu.

Further reading

- **Example CVE:** https://ubuntu.com/security/CVE-2024-3094
- **Ubuntu Pro:** https://ubuntu.com/pro
- **Ubuntu Security Notices:** https://ubuntu.com/security/notices

Join the CloudPro Newsletter with 44000+ Subscribers

Want to know what's happening in cloud computing, DevOps, IT administration, networking, and more? Scan the QR code to subscribe to **CloudPro**, our weekly newsletter for 44,000+ tech professionals who want to stay informed and ahead of the curve.

https://packt.link/cloudpro

8

Getting Help: The Ubuntu Community and Beyond

In the ever-evolving world of Ubuntu, whether you are new to Ubuntu or a seasoned veteran, having access to reliable and up-to-date documentation is crucial. This chapter will discuss Ubuntu documentation resources and explore the vast Ubuntu community and all it offers.

In this chapter, we will cover the following topics:

- Documentation
- Ubuntu community
- Beyond Ubuntu
- Bug reporting

Official Ubuntu documentation: a reliable reference

Sources for the official Ubuntu documentation can vary, including a user guide that is built right into your Ubuntu installation and online documentation.

The Ubuntu Desktop Guide

Ubuntu includes thorough documentation resources bundled together as the Ubuntu Desktop Guide. Look for the icon on the Ubuntu Dock with the question mark. Search for help in the application spread if you've unpinned it from your dock.

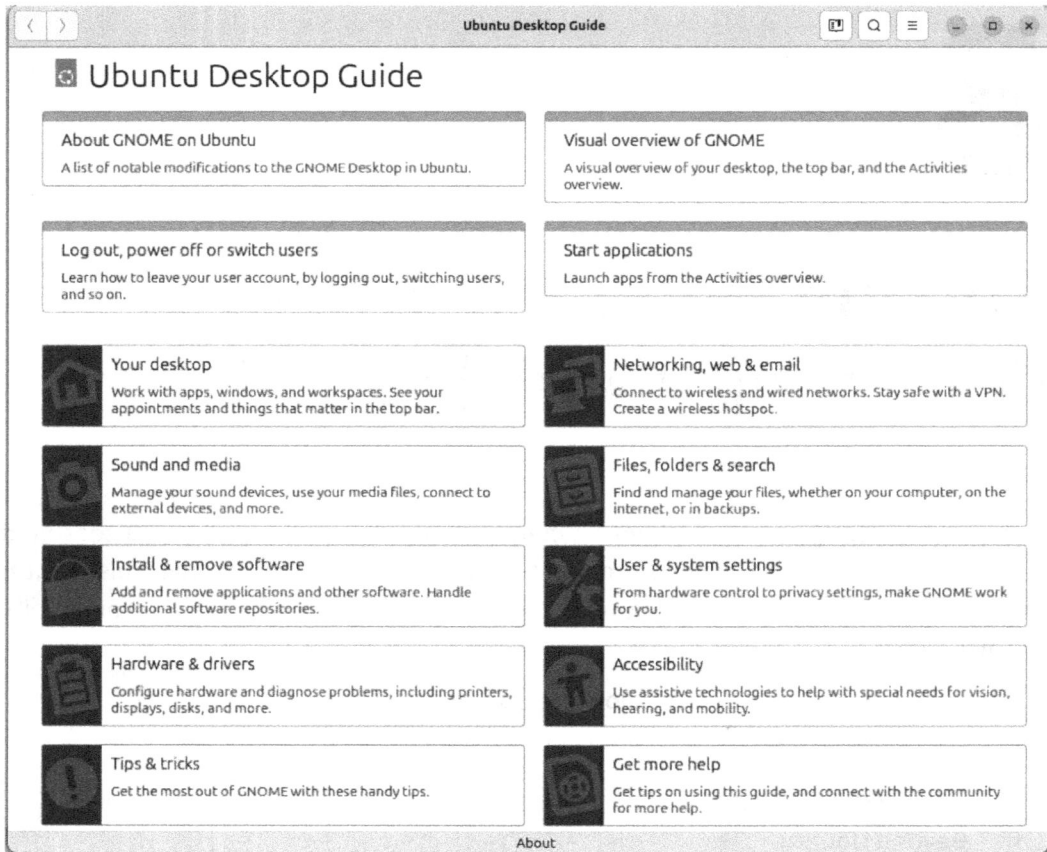

Figure 8.1 – The Ubuntu Desktop Guide

The Ubuntu Desktop Guide is a well-organized collection of documentation you can navigate from the front page by section and drill down into the topic you are looking for using the tiles on the main page.

As shown in *Figure 8.1*, the window has back and forward controls at the top left for basic navigation, as well as a search button near the top right for searching the integrated documentation.

The guide also supports bookmarks, which are just to the left of the search button. You can easily bookmark any resource in the guide that you might need to return to.

Online documentation

The official online documentation is divided into the Ubuntu Desktop Guide and the Ubuntu Server Guide, allowing users to find the appropriate information more easily. These guides can be found at `https://help.ubuntu.com` and are organized by Ubuntu release versions. The Ubuntu Desktop Guide is available in many languages and will automatically be displayed in your browser's suggested language.

Use the search bar on the website to find relevant documentation based on keywords or topics quickly.

When selecting the Desktop Guide for Ubuntu 24.04 on the main page, you will notice something closely resembling the integrated Ubuntu Desktop Guide app, as seen in *Figure 8.1*.

Contributing

Of course, all the official documentation is also open source, allowing you to contribute fixes and improvements or even expand to cover more topics. Information on contributing is at the bottom of the guide.

The Ubuntu community: a wealth of knowledge and support

Throughout this book, we've talked about community and the importance of community to Ubuntu. This really can't be emphasized enough, and when it comes to getting help, the Ubuntu community is a powerful resource.

Let's break down the Ubuntu community into four distinct resources you should consider when looking for help or finding ways to contribute:

- **Ubuntu Discourse**: The ultimate hub to discuss anything Ubuntu
- **Ask Ubuntu**: The place to go to ask questions and find answers
- **Ubuntu Matrix**: Messaging platform to talk about anything
- **Launchpad**: The place to go to report bugs and much more

It's important to remember that you are expected to follow the Ubuntu Code of Conduct when participating in the Ubuntu community: `https://ubuntu.com/community/ethos/code-of-conduct`.

Before covering the various Ubuntu community resources, let's discuss some simple concepts to help you get the most out of your experience:

- **Asking effective questions**:
    - Clear and concise problem statements:
        - Providing essential details and context
        - Avoiding ambiguity and vagueness
    - Relevant information:
        - Sharing system information such as Ubuntu version, error messages, and recent changes
    - Showing effort:
        - Demonstrating that you've already tried to solve the problem
    - Respectful and polite communication:
        - Adhering to community guidelines and etiquette (Ubuntu Code of Conduct)
- **Receiving and providing help**:
    - Understanding different help styles:
        - Recognizing various approaches to assistance
    - Offering help to others:
        - Contributing to the community by answering questions and providing support
    - Building relationships:
        - Fostering connections with other community members

Regardless of where you engage with the Ubuntu community, if you keep those things in mind and ensure you follow the Code of Conduct, I'm sure you'll be pleasantly surprised.

Ubuntu Discourse

The Ubuntu Discourse is the ultimate hub for Ubuntu discussions. You can find release notes, announcements, meeting minutes from various teams, and much more here. The Ubuntu Discourse is a resource for finding information; you can also actively engage in any topic, asking questions, expressing your thoughts, or simply adding your reactions.

More information can be found at https://discourse.ubuntu.com.

Ask Ubuntu

Ask Ubuntu is a question-and-answer community for Ubuntu. You may be familiar with Stack Exchange, where you can ask questions, answer questions, or simply find information and vote on the best answers. Well, Ask Ubuntu is a Stack Exchange dedicated to the Ubuntu community! Join Ask Ubuntu. Chances are, if you have a question, it's likely been asked before, and Ask Ubuntu will help you determine which answer is best. If you don't find what you're looking for, simply ask your question, and someone who follows Ask Ubuntu will answer. I would also encourage you to engage with the Ask Ubuntu community by answering questions you are confident about and earning some flair, which is great for building credibility in the community.

More information can be found at https://askubuntu.com.

Ubuntu Matrix

Matrix is an open source instant messaging platform for real-time chat used across the Ubuntu community. Ubuntu chose Matrix because it is both open source and an open standard, encouraging a rich ecosystem of software that can interact with it.

Using the Ubuntu Matrix server, you can easily interact with other users and developers in topic-specific rooms. You are welcome to join, whether you just want to lurk and see what others are discussing or want to join the vibrant, open, diverse, and transparent community for discussions.

More information can be found at https://ubuntu.com/community/communications/matrix.

Ubuntu Hideout on Discord

Discord is a wildly popular online chat medium that is hard to ignore, so it should be no surprise to see a Discord server dedicated to the Ubuntu community. It's an *unofficial* server, meaning Ubuntu or Canonical doesn't officially sanction it, but that shouldn't discourage you from using it. If you are a Discord user, I'd encourage you to join the Ubuntu Hideout community!

More information can be found at https://ubuntuhideout.com.

Launchpad

Launchpad is a software collaboration platform used to build Ubuntu. It provides the package build infrastructure to build all the packages in Ubuntu. Launchpad also provides code hosting, translation tooling, and mailing lists. However, the primary reason you will likely want to visit Launchpad is to search for or file bugs for Ubuntu software. Launchpad is the de facto place for filing Ubuntu bugs!

More information can be found at `https://launchpad.net`.

Beyond Ubuntu: exploring online resources

Ubuntu, the most popular Linux distribution used worldwide, is pretty easy to find information about using your favorite internet search provider. You can often just search for any question you have, preceded with `Ubuntu`, and you will likely find plenty of results. If you don't find what you're looking for, you can search for `Linux` results, and what you find will likely be relevant.

Be careful when following advice on the internet. It can be easy to copy and paste malicious commands found online without understanding the implications. My recommendation is to do additional research on any solution you find to better understand it.

Reporting bugs

Earlier, we discussed Launchpad as the de facto place to track bugs in Ubuntu. It's great to be able to find existing bugs that have been reported as a reference; however, it depends on Ubuntu users reporting those bugs to be effective. Without bug reports, Ubuntu developers will be less likely to be able to fix them.

Ubuntu includes a handy tool to make filing effective bug reports on Launchpad easier. The tool is called `ubuntu-bug`, and it automatically attaches information about your system, the version of the package with the bug, and useful logs.

If you know the Ubuntu package name, simply run the tool in a terminal with the package name specified:

```
ken@monster$ ubuntu-bug <package-name>
```

You will see a window open with information collected from your system that will be sent to Launchpad. The window will give you the **Send** or **Don't Send** options. If you send it to Launchpad, you will see a web browser window opened to guide you through the rest of the process.

If you do not know the package name, don't fret! Simply running the `ubuntu-bug` command without any package name will give you a window to guide you through the process.

Regardless of what resource you are using to ask for help, be sure to include the information necessary to help you. A bug report or a Discourse post that simply states something doesn't work on Ubuntu isn't useful and will likely be ignored as it's too much effort to go back and forth getting the information needed.

Always provide the following information:

- Ubuntu version, available in `/etc/os-release`
- Specific software you are having issues with, including version
- Detailed steps to reproduce the issue
- Any recent updates or changes you've made to your system
- A courteous closing, ensuring readers understand that you will be thankful for any help

I can't stress enough the importance of being part of the Ubuntu community while you are on this journey. Even asking questions is essential to engaging in the community, but don't be shy when you can help others!

Summary

In this chapter, we've discussed the many ways to find help when help is needed. Getting help is much more than knowing which online resources are available. Understanding how to ask your question, which resource is most appropriate for the issue, and how to best act on the answers you find is essential.

In the next chapter, we'll learn how Ubuntu can integrate with enterprise login services, provisioning, and management in larger enterprise environments.

Further reading

- The Ubuntu Code of Conduct: `https://ubuntu.com/community/ethos/code-of-conduct`
- Official online documentation: `https://help.ubuntu.com`
- Ubuntu Discourse: `https://discourse.ubuntu.com`
- Ask Ubuntu: `https://askubuntu.com`
- Ubuntu Matrix: `https://ubuntu.com/community/communications/matrix`
- Ubuntu Hideout on Discord: `https://ubuntuhideout.com`
- Launchpad: `https://launchpad.net`

9

Ubuntu in the Enterprise and at Scale

Ubuntu has become a popular choice for enterprise environments due to its stability, security, and scalability. This chapter will explore leveraging Ubuntu for enterprise-level deployments and management. Most enterprises that incorporate Ubuntu are heterogeneous, often catering to Microsoft Windows. There are several key requirements when adding another operating system to your environment: identity management, provisioning, and security. Ubuntu is a viable option offering authd for identify management integration with Microsoft Entra ID and Google IAM, and Landscape for systems management at scale. By the end of this chapter, you will understand how to set up secure authentication, manage large-scale deployments and maintain your Ubuntu infrastructure efficiently.

In this chapter, we will cover the following topics:

- Landscape for management at scale
- authd for identity management
- Practical examples of Landscape to deploy authd configuration

What is Landscape?

Managing a fleet of Ubuntu systems in an enterprise setting can quickly become complex. Landscape is a powerful systems management tool designed specifically for Ubuntu. Developed by Canonical, Landscape allows you to monitor, manage, and maintain multiple Ubuntu systems (desktop, server, and WSL) from a single web-based interface. Whether you're managing a small network or thousands of machines, Landscape provides the tools and features needed to streamline administrative tasks and ensure your systems run smoothly.

Why use Landscape?

Managing large-scale Ubuntu deployments manually can be tedious, inefficient, and error-prone. Using Landscape offers numerous advantages:

- **Centralized management**: You can manage all your Ubuntu machines from one interface, simplifying administrative tasks and reducing the time required for routine maintenance
- **Scalability**: Whether you have a handful of servers or thousands, Landscape scales with your needs, making it ideal for enterprises of any size
- **Automation**: Automate repetitive tasks such as updates, upgrades, and package installations, freeing time for more strategic work
- **Compliance and auditing**: Ensure compliance with corporate policies and industry regulations by tracking changes and generating detailed reports

Landscape provides an overview of your entire Ubuntu estate at a glance, as shown in *Figure 9.1*.

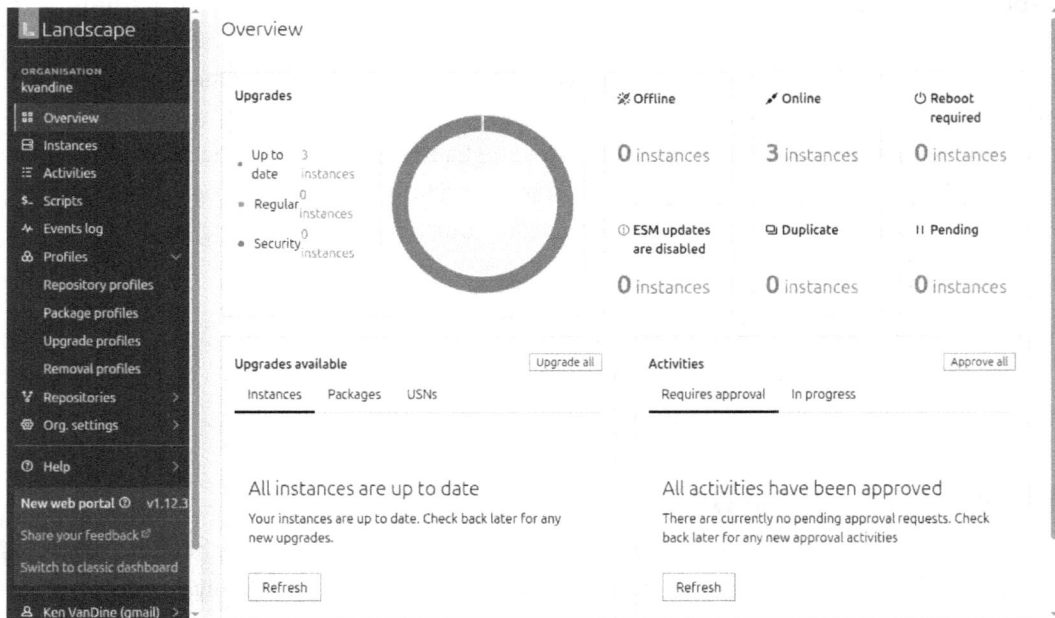

Figure 9.1 – Landscape overview

Key features of Landscape

Let's take a tour of the key features of Landscape, providing all the essentials to effectively manage your enterprise.

System monitoring

Effective system monitoring is crucial for ensuring the stability, security, and overall performance of your Ubuntu systems.

- **Real-time monitoring**: Keep track of system health, resource usage, and performance metrics in real time
- **Alerts and notifications**: Receive alerts for potential issues, enabling proactive management and reducing downtime

Package management

Managing software across your enterprise is a critical task that includes installing, updating, and removing software packages installed on your Ubuntu systems.

- **Centralized updates**: Manage software updates and security patches across all your systems from a single interface
- **Repository profiles**: Create and manage custom package repositories tailored to your organization's needs.
- **Package profiles**: Ensure and enforce the installation of specific packages on systems

Configuration management

Properly configuring and managing your Ubuntu systems is a vital task that requires attention to detail and repeatability.

- **Automated configuration**: Define and apply configurations consistently across multiple machines
- **Templates and scripts**: Use predefined templates and custom scripts to automate configuration tasks

Compliance reporting

Auditing your Ubuntu systems and generating reports is essential for maintaining organizational security, integrity, and transparency requirements.

- **Audit trails**: Maintain a detailed audit trail of all changes and actions performed on your systems
- **Compliance reporting**: Generate compliance reports to meet regulatory requirements and internal policies

User management

As a systems management platform, it's necessary to be able to manage who has access to the powerful capabilities within Landscape.

- **Role-Based Access Control (RBAC)**: Assign roles and permissions to users to ensure appropriate access to management functions within Landscape

Any changes made to systems managed by Landscape are reflected as activities. The **Activities** view in *Figure 9.2* shows activities that have been completed as well as ones that are in progress. This is useful as a means to audit changes that have been made via Landscape in the past, as well as tracking the status of management tasks as a whole.

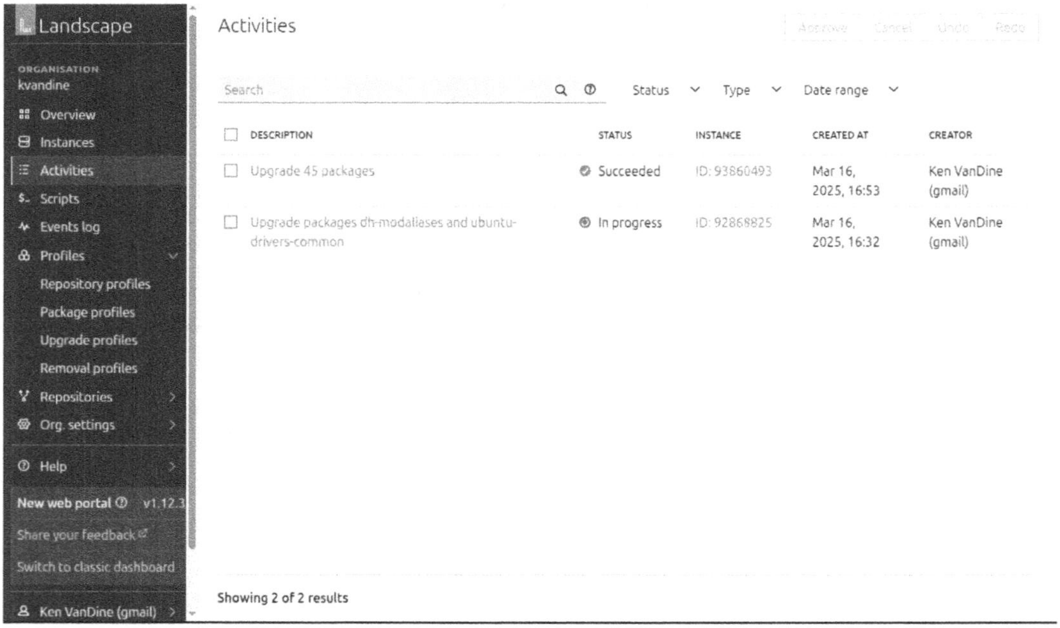

Figure 9.2 – Landscape activities

Identity management

Integration with corporate identity management services is a key requirement for any enterprise, particularly in a mixed environment with Windows systems. Common services in these environments include Microsoft Active Directory, Microsoft Entra ID (formerly Azure Active Directory), and Google IAM.

Fortunately, Ubuntu 24.04 supports these services, and more identity brokers are in development.

This chapter will explain how to utilize the Microsoft Entra ID and Google IAM identity services and how to use Landscape to onboard your fleet of Ubuntu systems.

Configuring Microsoft Entra ID

To enable Ubuntu authentication with Microsoft Entra ID, follow these steps to register an application, set permissions, and generate credentials.

Step 1: Registering the application

1. Sign in to the Microsoft Entra ID portal at https://entra.microsoft.com.
2. Navigate to **Identity** | **Applications** | **App registrations** | **New registration**, as shown in *Figure 9.3*.
3. Provide a name for your application and select the appropriate supported account types.
4. Click **Register**.

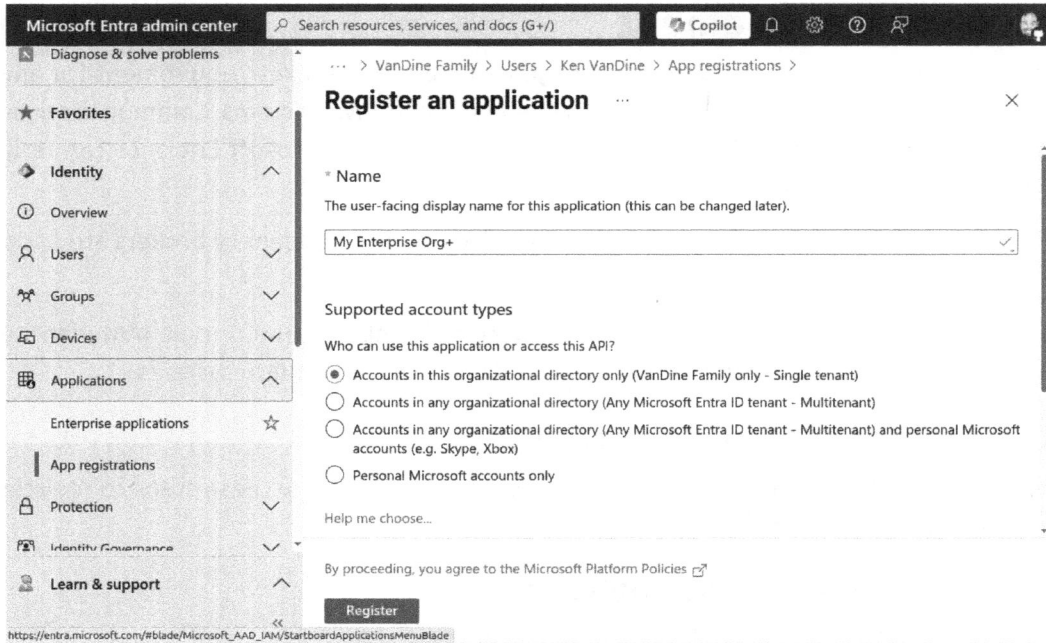

Figure 9.3 – Microsoft Entra ID – App registrations

Step 2: Configuring API permissions

1. As shown in *Figure 9.4*, in the registered application, navigate to **API permissions**.

2. Click **Add a permission**, select **Microsoft Graph**, and add the necessary permissions.

3. Ensure you grant admin consent for the required permissions.

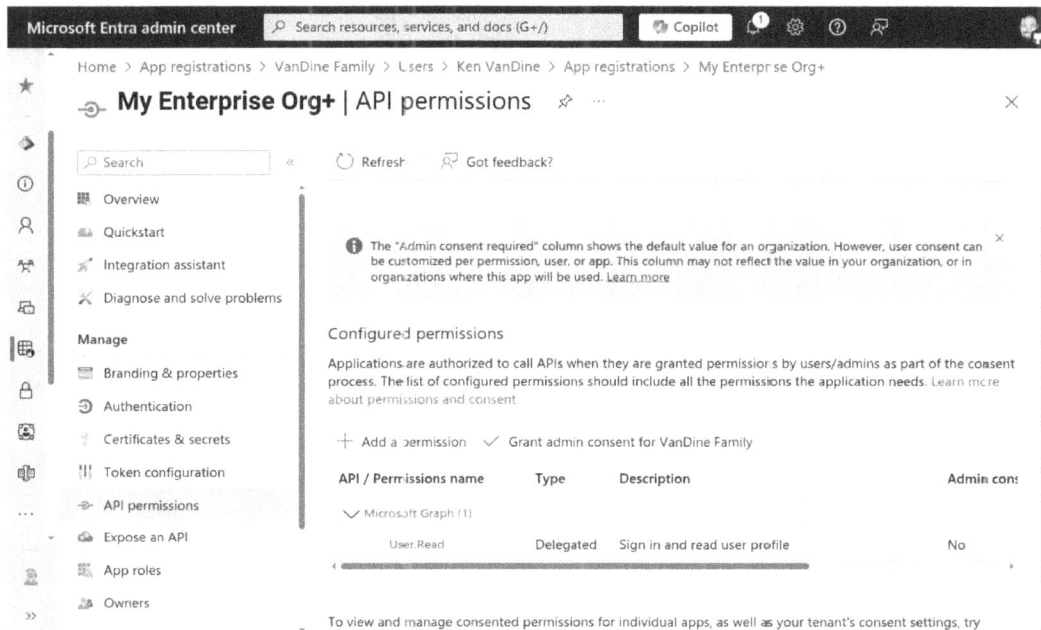

Figure 9.4 – Microsoft Entra ID – API permissions

Step 3: Generating a client secret

1. Navigate to **Certificates & secrets,** as shown in *Figure 9.5*.
2. Click **New client secret**, provide a description, and set an expiry period.
3. Save the generated client secret value securely.

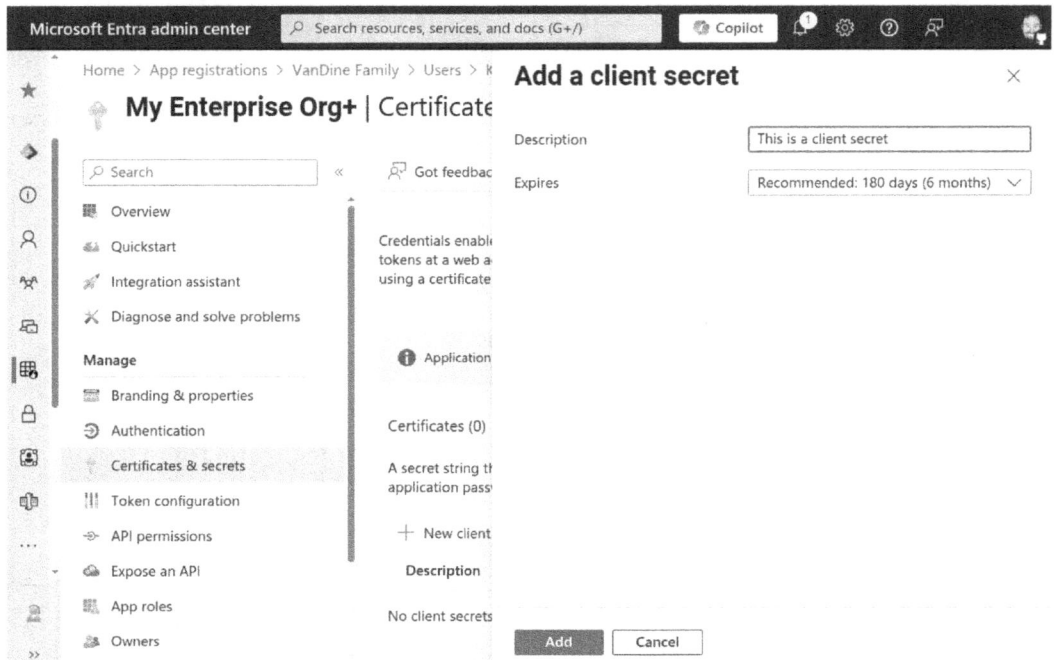

Figure 9.5 – Microsoft Entra ID – Client secret

Configuring Google IAM

To enable Ubuntu authentication with Google IAM, follow these steps to create a service account and generate credentials.

Step 1: Setting up Google IAM

1. Sign in to the Google Cloud console at `https://cloud.google.com`.

2. Navigate to **IAM & Admin** | **Service accounts** | **Create service account**, as shown in *Figure 9.6*.

3. Provide a name and description for the service account and click **Create and continue**.

4. Assign the necessary roles to the service account and click **Continue**.
5. Click **Done** to complete the creation of the service account.

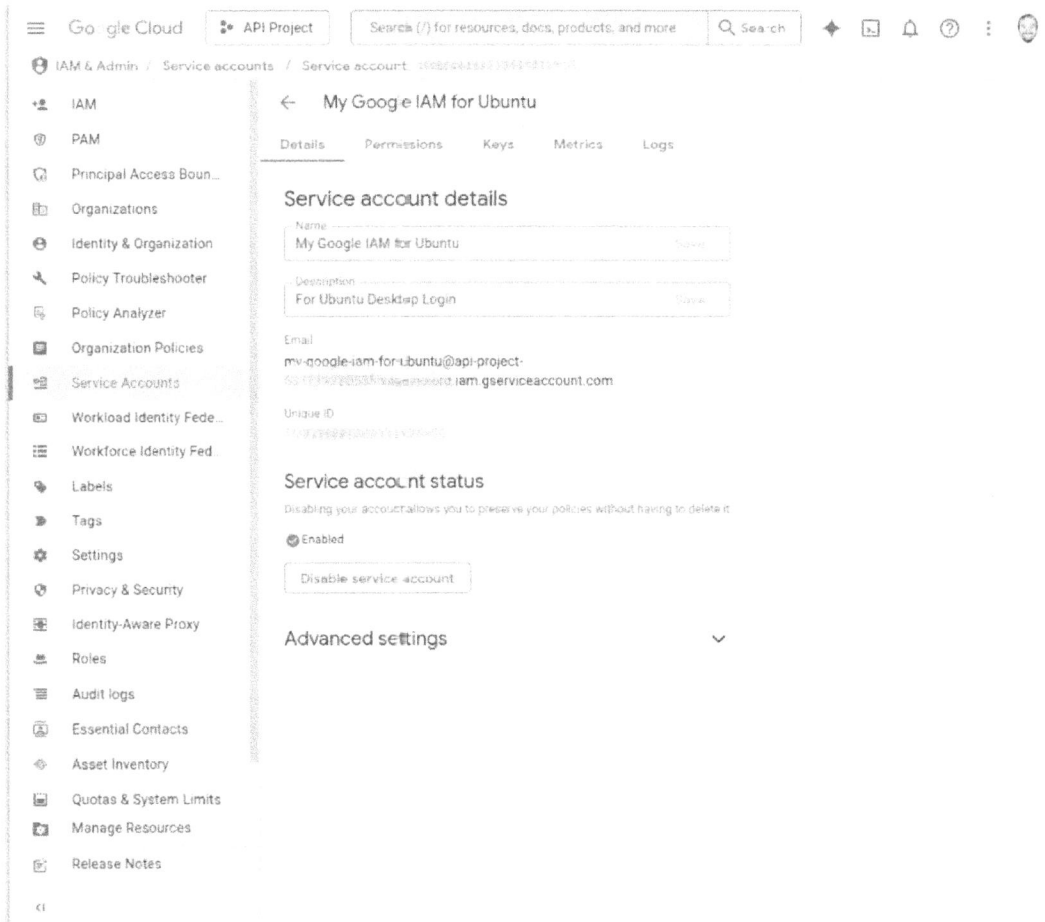

Figure 9.6 – Google IAM – Create service account

Step 2: Generating an OAuth 2.0 client ID

1. In the Google Cloud console, navigate to **APIs & Services** | **Credentials** | **Create credentials** | **OAuth client ID**, as shown in *Figure 9.7*.
2. Configure the OAuth consent screen by providing the required information.
3. Select **TVs and Limited Input devices** (which supports QR code login) as the application type, and provide a name.

4.   Click **Create** and save the generated client ID and client secret securely.

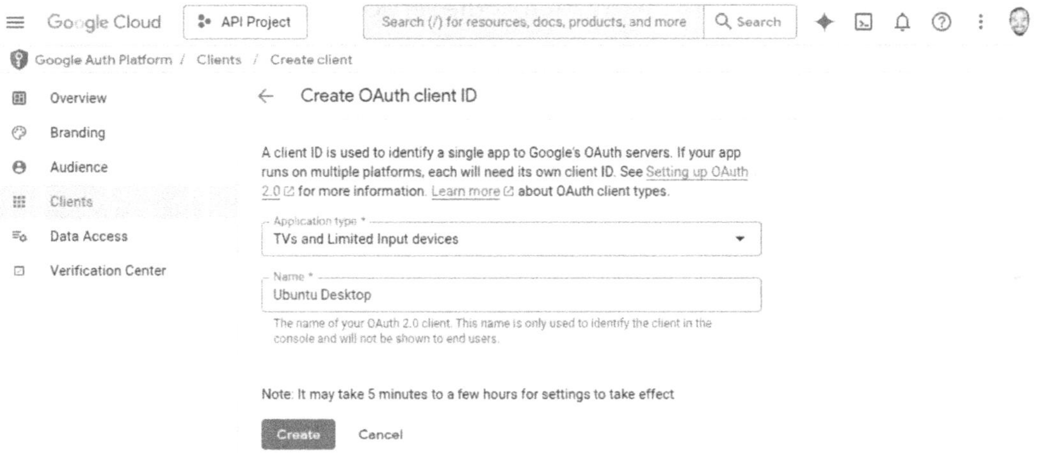

Figure 9.7 – Google IAM – Create OAuth credentials

Installing and configuring authd

The packages necessary for authd for Ubuntu 24.04 are in an additional repository that must be enabled. *Note that the additional* apt *repository will not be required for Ubuntu 26.04 and beyond*:

```
ken@monster:~$ sudo add-apt-repository ppa:ubuntu-enterprise-desktop/authd
ken@monster:~$ sudo apt update
ken@monster:~$ sudo apt install authd gnome-shell yaru-theme-gnome-shell
```

Installing and configuring the necessary identity broker

To enable authentication via Microsoft Entra ID or Google IAM, you need to install and configure the appropriate identity broker. The following steps outline the installation process and necessary configuration changes.

For Microsoft Entra ID, do the following:

```
ken@monster:~$ sudo snap install authd-msentraid
ken@monster:~$ sudo mkdir -p /etc/authd/brokers.d/
ken@monster:~$ sudo cp /snap/authd-msentraid/current/conf/authd/msentraid.
conf /etc/authd/brokers.d/
```

Set the issuer ID and client ID in the broker configuration file. Using your favorite editor, open /var/snap/authd-msentraid/current/broker.conf:

```
[oidc]
issuer = https://login.microsoftonline.com/<ISSUER_ID>/v2.0
client_id = <CLIENT_ID>
```

For Google IAM, do the following:

```
ken@monster:~$ sudo snap install authd-google
ken@monster:~$ sudo mkdir -p /etc/authd/brokers.d/
ken@monster:~$ sudo cp /snap/authd-google/current/conf/authd/google.conf /
etc/authd/brokers.d/
```

Set the client ID and client secret in the broker configuration file. Using your favorite editor, open /var/snap/authd-google/current/broker.conf:

```
[oidc]
issuer = https://accounts.google.com
client_id = <CLIENT_ID>
client_secret = <CLIENT_SECRET>
```

The broker.conf configuration files include extensive comments explaining other configuration settings you may want to set. At a minimum, you should set allowed_users and optionally set owner. If you do not explicitly set a value for owner, the first user who successfully logs in will become the owner.

After the configuration is complete, reboot. On the login screen, you will notice the option to log on with the configured identity broker.

Logging in with your identity broker

Now that our system is configured, we will see the option to log in with Microsoft Entra ID or Google IAM in the Ubuntu login manager, as shown in *Figure 9.8*.

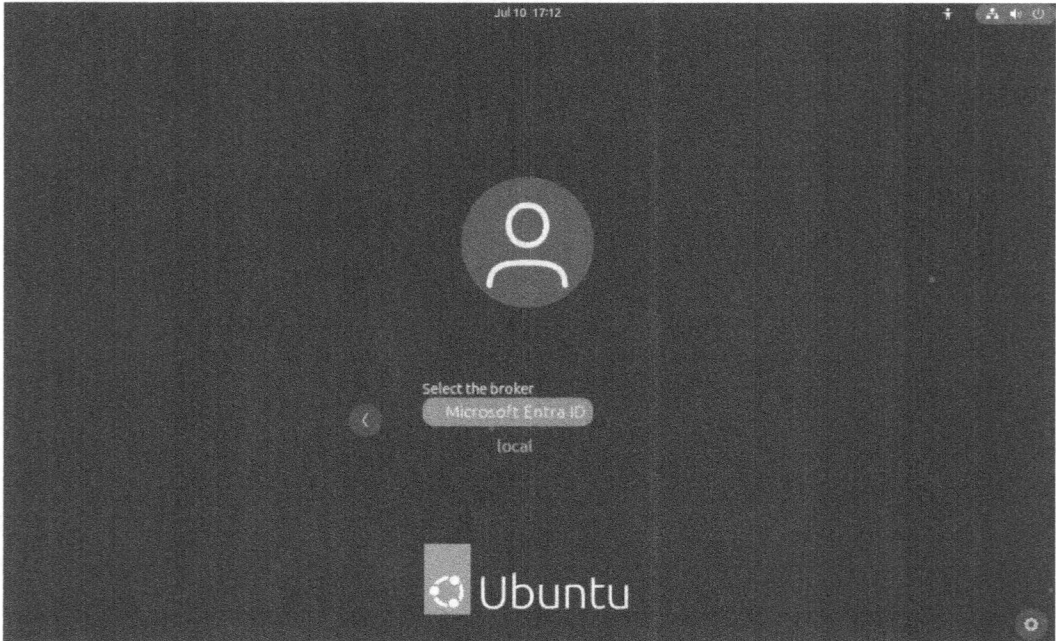

Figure 9.8 – Login manager with Microsoft Entra ID login

Selecting your configured identity broker will show a QR code, shown in *Figure 9.9*, that can be scanned with your login device, such as Microsoft Authenticator or Google Authenticator.

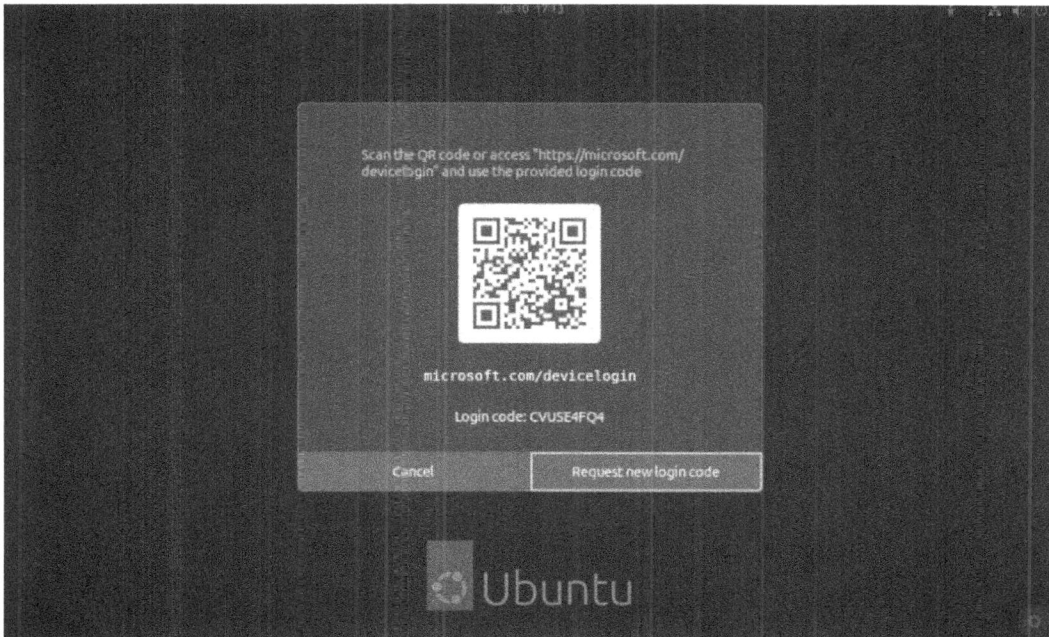

Figure 9.9 – Login manager displaying QR code for login using your authentication device

Integration with identity services such as these is essential for many enterprises, streamlining user authentication and management.

Configuring authd at scale with Landscape

Now that you understand how to enable authd with your enterprise's identity broker, let's learn how to configure your entire fleet of devices.

As described earlier in this chapter, Landscape is a powerful tool that allows total control over every Ubuntu device in your enterprise. This chapter will focus on configuring authd using Landscape, but Landscape isn't limited to just authd. You can configure any aspect of your Ubuntu systems using the concepts you'll learn here.

As we learned in *Chapter 7*, Landscape is available for all systems attached to an Ubuntu Pro subscription. Any device attached to an Ubuntu Pro subscription can enable Landscape support with a simple command:

```
ken@monster:~$ sudo pro enable landscape
```

When we enroll the system with our Landscape instance, we need to ensure a few optional features are enabled in the client.

First, install the `landscape-client` package:

```
ken@monster:~$ sudo apt install landscape-client
```

Edit `/etc/landscape/client.conf` with your favorite editor:

```
[client]
log_level = info
url = https://landscape.canonical.com/message-system
ping_url = http://landscape.canonical.com/ping
data_path = /var/lib/landscape/client
computer_title = monster
account_name = standalone
include_manager_plugins = ScriptExecution
script_users = root,landscape,nobody
```

Ensure the `url` and `ping_url` values are correct for your Landscape instance. These default values will work if you use Canonical's hosted landscape.

As shown, you must add `computer_title`, `account_name`, `include_manager_plugins`, and `script_users`. `computer_title` is a string used to identify the system when registered with Landscape, and `account_name` is the identifier for your tenant in Canonical's hosted Landscape, or `standalone` if you are using a self-hosting Landscape server. The last two configuration options allow Landscape to run scripts on the device.

Once configured as desired, restart the `landscape-client` service to enroll in Landscape with the desired settings.

If the system was already enrolled in Landscape, restart the service:

```
ken@monster:~$ sudo service landscape-client restart
```

If not previously registered with Landscape, register now by running the following command and accepting all the default values (already specified in the configuration file):

```
ken@monster:~$ sudo landscape-config
ken@monster:~$ sudo landscape-config --is-registered
```

The last command, with `--is-registered`, should include `Registered: True` in the output.

We have now ensured that our system is registered with Landscape. Log in to the Landscape server and navigate to **Scripts**:

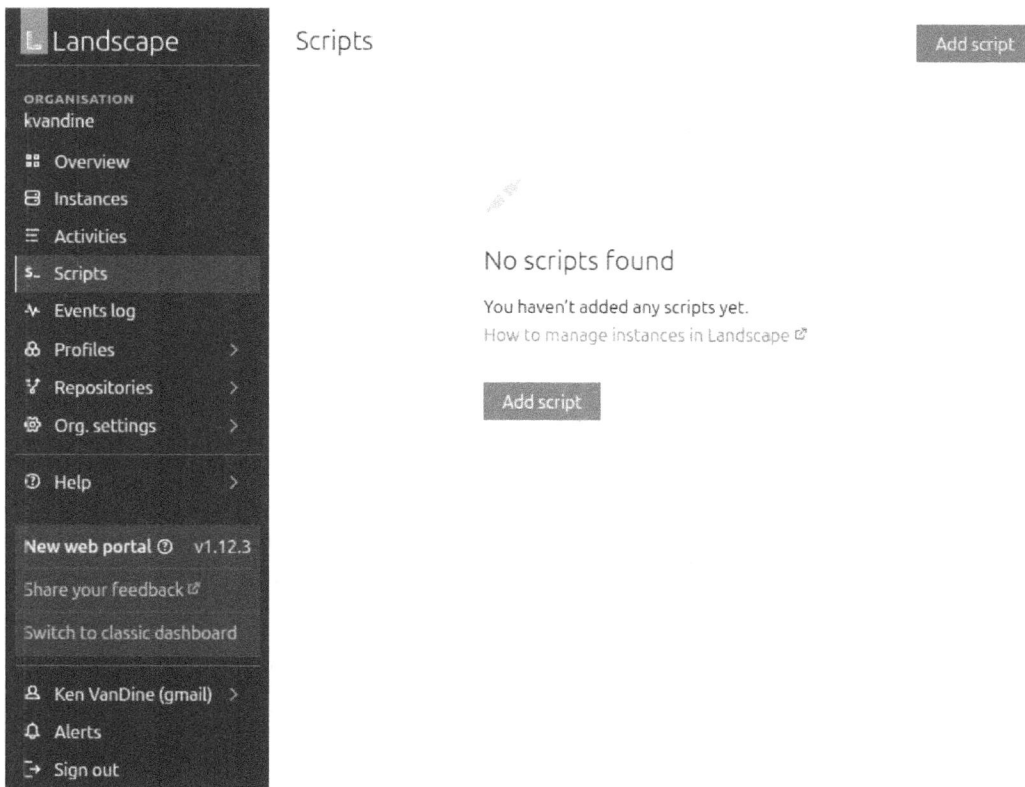

Figure 9.10 – Landscape – Add script

Click **Add script** to open the web UI to add a new script:

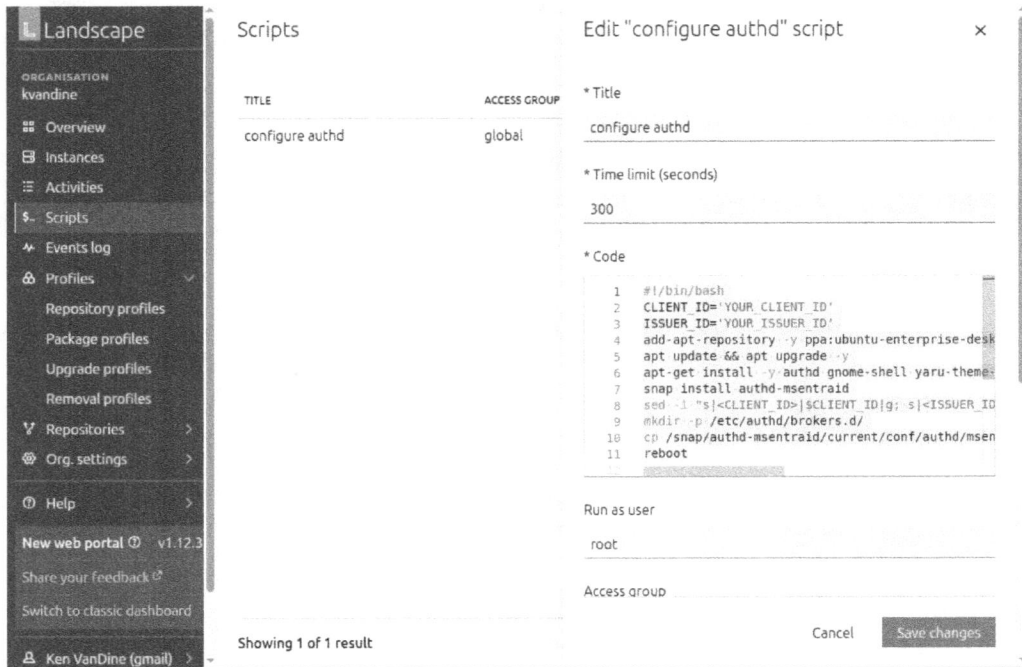

Figure 9.11 – Landscape – Adding a new script

Set the **Title** and **Run as user** values, as shown in *Figure 9.11*, and insert the script's content in the **Code** block.

For Microsoft Entra ID, your script should look something like this, replacing YOUR_CLIENT_ID and YOUR_ISSUER_ID with the respective values:

```bash
#!/bin/bash
CLIENT_ID='YOUR_CLIENT_ID'
ISSUER_ID='YOUR_ISSUER_ID'
add-apt-repository -y ppa:ubuntu-enterprise-desktop/authd
apt update && apt upgrade -y
apt-get install -y authd gnome-shell yaru-theme-gnome-shell
snap install authd-msentraid
sed -i "s|<CLIENT_ID>|$CLIENT_ID|g; s|<ISSUER_ID>|$ISSUER_ID|g" /var/snap/
authd-msentraid/current/broker.conf
mkdir -p /etc/authd/brokers.d/
cp /snap/authd-msentraid/current/conf/authd/msentraid.conf /etc/authd/
brokers.d/
reboot
```

For Google IAM, your script should look something like this, replacing YOUR_CLIENT_ID and YOUR_CLIENT_SECRET with the respective values:

```bash
#!/bin/bash
CLIENT_ID='YOUR_CLIENT_ID'
CLIENT_SECRET='YOUR_CLIENT_SECRET'
add-apt-repository -y ppa:ubuntu-enterprise-desktop/authd
apt update && apt upgrade -y
apt-get install -y authd gnome-shell yaru-theme-gnome-shell
snap install authd-google
sed -i "s|<CLIENT_ID>|$CLIENT_ID|g; s|<CLIENT_SECRET>|$CLIENT_SECRET|g" /
var/snap/authd-google/current/broker.conf
mkdir -p /etc/authd/brokers.d/
cp /snap/authd-google/current/conf/authd/google.conf /etc/authd/brokers.d/
reboot
```

Click **Add script** to save the script. Once your script is saved, you will see a list of available scripts, each with a small running icon, as shown in *Figure 9.12*:

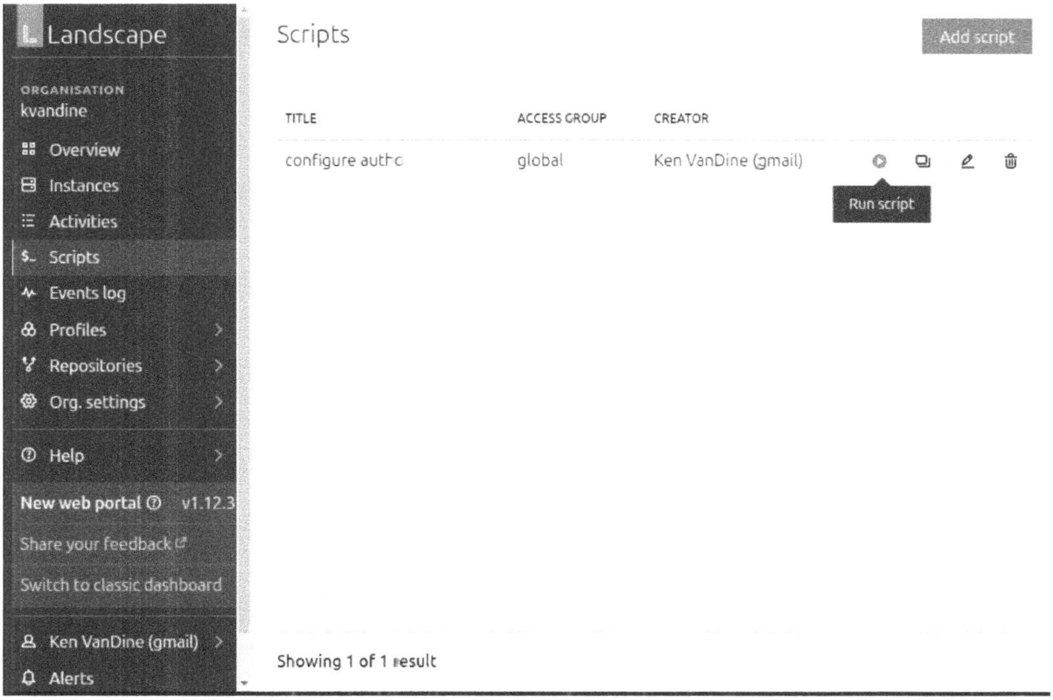

Figure 9.12 – Landscape scripts

Clicking the **Run script** icon will show you the **Run "configure authd" script** view, where you can select systems to run the script by name or tags, choose the user to run the script as, and choose when to run it.

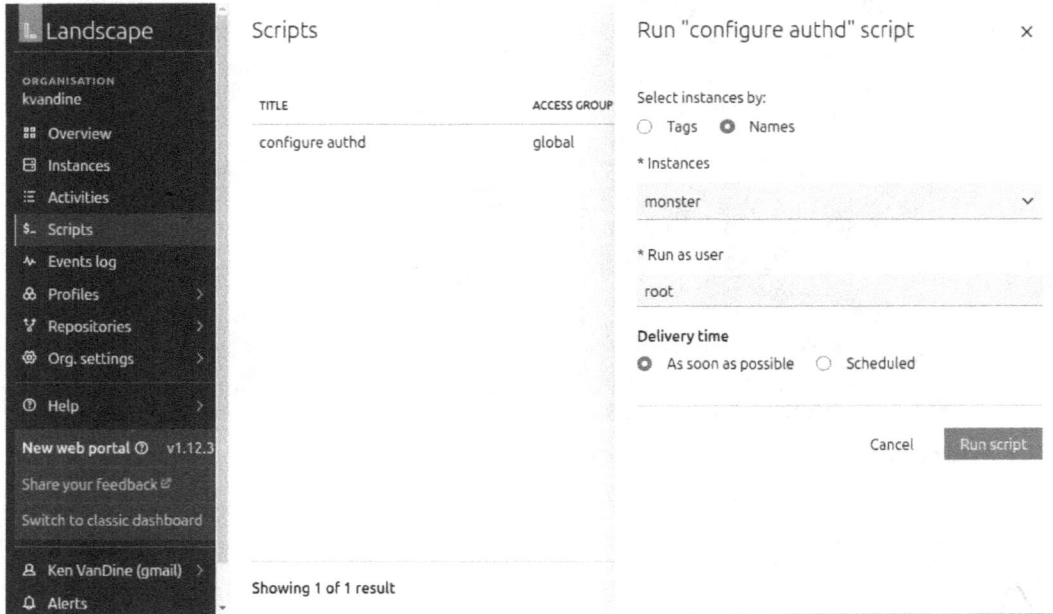

Figure 9.13 – Landscape – Run script

Within a few minutes, any systems selected will run this script if they're online; if not, they will run it when they come online.

As you can imagine, the ability to run scripts on any system managed by Landscape gives it the ultimate flexibility.

Summary

In this chapter, we've explored how to integrate enterprise login using authd with Microsoft Entra ID and Google IAM and how to manage large-scale Ubuntu deployments with Landscape. These tools enable you to enhance security, streamline management, and ensure the efficient operation of your Ubuntu infrastructure in an enterprise environment.

In the next chapter, we'll learn more about the benefits of using the command line to get things done, including plenty of tips and tricks to get comfortable.

Further reading

- Landscape: https://ubuntu.com/landscape
- authd: https://documentation.ubuntu.com/authd/en/latest/

10

Command-Line Tricks and Shortcuts: Boosting Your Efficiency

Welcome to *Chapter 10*, where we'll demystify the command line and unlock its potential to supercharge your Ubuntu workflow. The terminal initially intimidates many users, but it's a powerful tool that can save time, automate tasks, and give you fine-grained control over your system. This chapter aims to make you comfortable with the command line, showcasing its benefits and demonstrating that it's not something to fear. We'll start with the basics and gradually introduce more advanced concepts, giving you the confidence to navigate and manage your Ubuntu system like a pro.

In this chapter, we will cover the following topics:

- Navigating directories
- Working with files and directories
- Input, output, and pipes
- Process control
- Useful tools
- Scripting basics

Mastering navigation: moving around with ease

The command line, also known as the terminal or shell, is a text-based interface. Instead of clicking buttons and icons, you type commands to interact with your operating system. Mastering navigation is the first step to becoming comfortable with it.

> Important note
>
> Using the command line can be very powerful and is the ideal way to follow carefully outlined instructions.
>
> As you are learning your way around and using resources on the internet to help get the most out of your Ubuntu system, be cautious about copying and pasting commands found online. Read them carefully and ensure you understand what they are doing before you run them yourself. A malicious person on an online forum could hide a command in those instructions that could do anything, even delete everything on your computer.

Opening the terminal

You can open the terminal like any other graphical application by clicking the **Terminal** icon. You can also open the terminal with a handy keyboard shortcut by pressing *Ctrl + Alt + T*.

Once in the terminal, there are a couple of important things to note. You are familiar with *Ctrl + C* to copy selected text in other applications and *Ctrl + V* to paste. However, in a terminal, those shortcuts do different things. *Ctrl + C* kills the current running process. To copy in the terminal, select the text to copy and press *Ctrl + Shift + C*, and to paste, press *Ctrl + Shift + V*.

The current directory

When you open the terminal, you start in your home directory. Use the pwd (**print working directory**) command to see where you are.

Listing files

Use the ls (list) command to view the files and directories in your current location. Adding options such as ls -l (long listing) or ls -a (all files, including hidden ones) provides more detailed information. Hidden files and folders start with a leading period, such as .bashrc. This is useful to prevent accidentally moving or deleting something important in a graphical file manager.

Changing directories

Use the cd (**change directory**) command to move to a different directory. For example, cd Documents will take you to a folder named Documents located inside your current folder. Use cd .. to go back one directory, and cd ~ will take you back to your home directory. The ~ character is a shorthand for your home directory, so ~/Documents refers to the Documents folder in your home directory. This is true for any commands you may use that reference paths to directories and files. It's also handy to note that the cd command, with no arguments, also changes to your home directory.

Tab completion

This is a crucial time-saver! Start typing a command or filename and press the *Tab* key. If there are multiple possibilities, the shell will try to complete them for you. Press the *Tab* key twice to see a list of options.

Essential file and directory management: taking control

Now that you can navigate, let's learn how to manage files and directories.

Creating directories

Use mkdir directory_name to make a new directory.

Creating files

The touch file_name command creates an empty file.

Copying files

Use cp source destination to copy a file. cp -r source_directory destination_directory is used to copy an entire directory recursively.

Moving/renaming files

Use mv source destination to move or rename a file. For example, mv old_name new_name. mv source_directory destination_directory will move or rename directories.

Deleting files

Use rm file_name to remove a file. Be careful with this command! rm -r directory_name removes a directory and all its contents. Be *extra* cautious with rm -rf, which will force the recursive deletion of files and directories.

Viewing file content

Running `cat filename` displays the content of a file in the terminal. `less filename` is better for larger files, allowing you to scroll through the content. Running `head filename` displays the first 10 lines of a file, and `tail filename` shows the last 10. The `head` and `tail` commands have an optional `-n` argument for the number of lines to display. For example, `head -n 1 filename` will display just the first line.

Finding files and directories

We often have many files and directories stored on our computers that can be hard to find. The `find` command is here to help! If you have an idea of the name or part of the name of a file or directory you need to find, you can leverage the power of the `find` command to help.

To find a file or directory with the exact name `something` within your home directory, run `find ~ -name "something"`. If you don't know the exact name but know the name includes `omethin`, you can run `find ~ -name "*omethin*"`. Note that we are using the argument of `-name` in these examples, but there are many ways to search, including type, modification time, and so on.

To find all files in your home directory that have been modified in the past 24 hours, use `find ~ -type f -mtime -1`. In this example, we are limiting the types to files, but you could also use `-type d` for directories. And `-mtime -1` instructs `find` to look for modification time in the past one day.

Advanced techniques: working with permissions and ownership

Linux file permissions control who can read, write, and execute files.

Understanding permissions

Use `ls -l` to see file permissions. They look like `-rwxr-xr-x`. The first character indicates the file type (`-` for a regular file, and `d` for a directory), and the following nine characters represent the permissions: read (`r`), write (`w`), and execute (`x`) for the owner, group, and others.

Changing permissions

Use the `chmod` command to change permissions. For example, `chmod u=rwx,g=rx,o=rx filename` sets read, write, and execute permissions for the owner, and read and execute permissions for the group and others.

Ownership

Use `chown user:group filename` to change the owner and group of a file.

Elevated permissions

Sometimes, you will need to temporarily elevate your privileges to run specific commands as an administrator. Ubuntu assumes that tasks that require administrative permissions are run with the `sudo` command rather than using a dedicated administrator account such as root.

Using `sudo` is pretty simple. Prepend `sudo` to any command you run, and it will execute that command with administrative rights, assuming your user account is allowed to do so. Please use `sudo` with caution; elevated permissions can alter things on your system that may cause stability or security risks, and you may even lose essential data.

Mastering text manipulation with powerful tools

The command line has powerful tools for parsing and manipulating text.

> Important note
>
> **Regular expressions**, also known as **regexes**, are a sequence of characters that form a search pattern used to match, validate, and extract data from strings. It is a powerful tool used in programming, text processing, and data analysis to search, validate, and manipulate text. Regexes can be quite complex, but they are incredibly powerful. Many of the examples covered next can leverage regexes.

grep

`grep pattern filename` searches for a pattern within a file. `grep -r pattern directory` searches recursively within a directory. In this case, `pattern` can be a regex, as described in the preceding note.

sed

`sed 's/old/new/g' filename` replaces old with new in a file.

awk

`awk '{print $1}' filename` prints the first column of a file. `awk` splits the text in the file into columns based on white space. You can instruct `awk` to split on any character or series of characters with the `-F` option. For example, `awk -F : '{print $1}' filename` will split on the colon character and print just what's before the first colon. You can print additional columns; `awk -F : '{print $1 " " $3}' filename` will print the first and third columns split on the colon character with a space between the columns.

`awk` is actually a programming language and can be used for far more complex text processing. To learn more, see the manual page with `man awk`.

Input and output

Any command you run can produce output and usually does something meaningful with input. What does this mean? The text you see printed on the screen when you run `cat somefile.txt` is an example of output, specifically, `stdout` (**standard output**). This output can then be used as input, `stdin` (**standard input**), for another command. Commands can also produce `stderr` (**standard error**), which is used to display error messages and can be handled separately. You can manage `stdin`, `stdout`, and `stderr` using pipes or redirection.

Pipes connect the output of one command to the input of another. For example, `ls -l | grep .txt` lists files and then filters the list to show only those containing `.txt`. In this example, the output for the `ls -l` command is used as input to the `grep` command.

We can also redirect the output from any command to a file. For example, `ls -l > output.txt` will redirect output to a file (overwriting if it already exists) instead of printing to the screen. In this example, even though we redirected the output to a file, any errors will still be printed to the screen and will not be included in the `output.txt` file. You can also handle `stdout` and `stderr` separately by specifying different files for each. The number 1 represents `stdout`, and the number 2 represents `stderr`. For example, the `ls -l 1> output.txt 2> error.txt` command will create two files, `output.txt` will contain the standard output, and `error.txt` will contain any error messages. It can also be handy to ignore all errors by redirecting `stderr` to a special file, `/dev/null`. To ignore all errors and still print the output to the screen, you can run `ls -l 2> /dev/null`.

Process control

Every command on your computer, whether run from a terminal, a graphical app, or a running background service, is reflected as a process. Information about running processes, such as memory and CPU usage, is available.

The ps command outputs running processes and information related to the processes.

Just running ps with no arguments only prints processes running within the current shell, which is not very useful. There are many options available and an overwhelming number of combinations that change how the ps command works. For the sake of this chapter, I'll demonstrate what I feel is the most useful way to use the ps command.

To see all running processes on your system with all available information about each process, you can run ps auxww. As mentioned, this will print all running processes, likely much more than you need. You may want information about specific processes, which you can combine with the grep command. To find all Firefox processes, ps auxww | grep firefox will display all processes with the term firefox. This will include information such as the user account running the process, the **process ID (PID)**, CPU and memory usage, and much more. This output is nicely separated into columns of data, which can be easily parsed with the awk command. So, to see just the PID, you can pipe the output to awk and print the second column containing the PID, such as ps auxww | grep firefox | awk '{print $2}'.

So why is the PID interesting? One reason you might look for process information is that the program isn't behaving correctly. It could be using too many resources, such as memory or CPU, or it might be hung and not responding as expected. Getting the PID gives you the information necessary to kill that process and restore your system to a functional state.

Using the earlier example to find the PID (or multiple PIDs) for the Firefox process, you can then use the kill command to end it. For example, kill 11290 will kill the process with the PID 11290. Sometimes, a process won't die with a standard kill command; in such cases, you can use kill -9 11290 to forcefully stop it.

As you can see in this example, we needed to run several commands to find the PID of a process and kill it. There's also a handy `killall` command that will attempt to find and end any associated processes for an application. You can use `killall firefox` or `killall -9 firefox` as needed to accomplish the same task. This eliminates the need to run that `ps` command to find the PID and nicely handles the case of a single application with numerous associated processes. Using the Firefox example again, I actually have 13 Firefox processes currently running. Using `killall` will handle ending all of those processes.

top

You might wonder which processes are using excessive memory or CPU. Ubuntu also includes the `top` command, which displays a live view of system information, including running processes, which are sortable by memory, load (CPU), and other criteria.

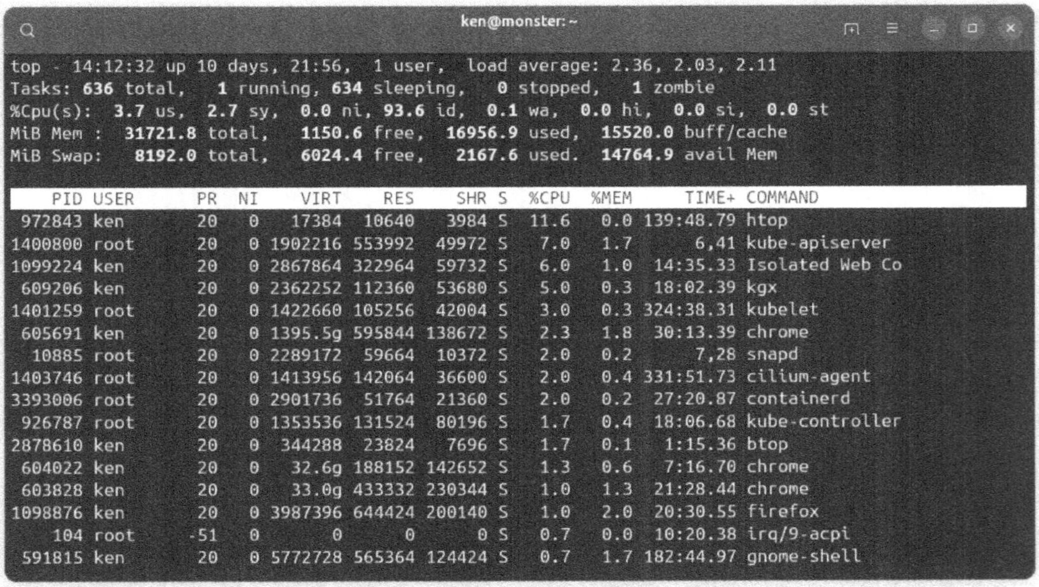

```
                                        ken@monster: ~                                  ⊡  ≡  _  ▭  ×

top - 14:12:32 up 10 days, 21:56,  1 user,  load average: 2.36, 2.03, 2.11
Tasks: 636 total,   1 running, 634 sleeping,   0 stopped,   1 zombie
%Cpu(s):  3.7 us,  2.7 sy,  0.0 ni, 93.6 id,  0.1 wa,  0.0 hi,  0.0 si,  0.0 st
MiB Mem :  31721.8 total,   1150.6 free,  16956.9 used,  15520.0 buff/cache
MiB Swap:   8192.0 total,   6024.4 free,   2167.6 used.  14764.9 avail Mem

    PID USER      PR  NI    VIRT    RES    SHR S  %CPU  %MEM     TIME+ COMMAND
 972843 ken       20   0   17384  10640   3984 S  11.6   0.0 139:48.79 htop
1400800 root      20   0 1902216 553992  49972 S   7.0   1.7      6,41 kube-apiserver
1099224 ken       20   0 2867864 322964  59732 S   6.0   1.0  14:35.33 Isolated Web Co
 609206 ken       20   0 2362252 112360  53680 S   5.0   0.3  18:02.39 kgx
1401259 root      20   0 1422660 105256  42004 S   3.0   0.3 324:38.31 kubelet
 605691 ken       20   0 1395.5g 595844 138672 S   2.3   1.8  30:13.39 chrome
  10885 root      20   0 2289172  59664  10372 S   2.0   0.2      7,28 snapd
1403746 root      20   0 1413956 142064  36600 S   2.0   0.4 331:51.73 cilium-agent
3393006 root      20   0 2901736  51764  21360 S   2.0   0.2  27:20.87 containerd
 926787 root      20   0 1353536 131524  80196 S   1.7   0.4  18:06.68 kube-controller
2878610 ken       20   0  344288  23824   7696 S   1.7   0.1   1:15.36 btop
 604022 ken       20   0   32.6g 188152 142652 S   1.3   0.6   7:16.70 chrome
 603828 ken       20   0   33.0g 433332 230344 S   1.0   1.3  21:28.44 chrome
1098876 ken       20   0 3987396 644424 200140 S   1.0   2.0  20:30.55 firefox
    104 root     -51   0       0      0      0 S   0.7   0.0  10:20.38 irq/9-acpi
 591815 ken       20   0 5772728 565364 124424 S   0.7   1.7 182:44.97 gnome-shell
```

Figure 10.1 – The top command displays process information

Using `top`, you can easily see real-time information about running processes, as shown in *Figure 10.1*.

However, there are even more powerful alternatives that aren't included in Ubuntu by default but can be easily installed. Both htop and btop have exciting features.

htop

htop provides all the same information as top, but with improved readability and more intuitive controls for sorting, searching, and killing processes. You may need to install it using sudo apt install htop. You can see htop in *Figure 10.2*.

Figure 10.2 – The htop command displays process information

btop

btop is even more powerful than htop, offering additional information such as current battery status, CPU temperature, network activity, and disk usage, all in a nice, easy-to-read interface. You may need to install it using sudo apt install btop. An example of btop is shown in *Figure 10.3*; it's my go-to application for system monitoring.

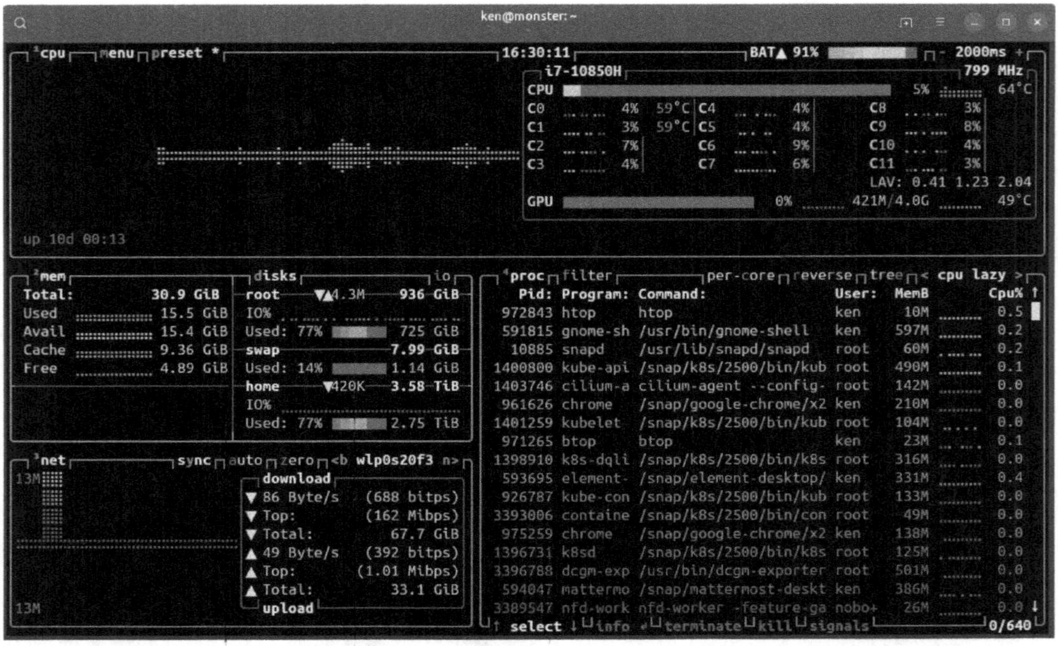

Figure 10.3 – The btop command displays process information

Foreground and background

We often run long-running processes from a terminal, such as graphical applications or text editors. We can easily *pause* an application and get our prompt back to run other commands. Pressing *Ctrl + Z* will pause the current process and give us a prompt to allow running further commands. Note that while the process is paused, you cannot interact with it. For example, if you pause Firefox, the browser window remains visible, but it won't respond to any input. To resume the process in the foreground, use the fg command. This brings the application back into focus and resumes interaction. Alternatively, you can run bg to resume the process in the background. This allows the application to continue running while keeping your prompt available for other commands.

History

All commands you run are added to your shell's history, which can be accessed in several ways. You can run the history command to display a list of recently executed commands. As with other commands, you can pipe its output to other utilities, such as grep, to narrow the output to something more useful. Let's say you are looking for some specific command you ran recently but can't remember all the command arguments you used. Something like `history | grep someterm` will find all occurrences of `someterm` and the output will be in the form of two columns; the first column is a number and the second column is the full command. You can use this output as a reference, or if you want to rerun the same command, you can use the number in the first column to execute it again. Simply run `!321` to run the command that has 321 in the first column.

You can also easily access your history by simply using the *Up* and *Down* arrow keys in the terminal. Pressing the *Up* key will show you the previous command, and each additional press steps further back through your history. Another handy shortcut to repeat the previous command is simply `!!` followed by *Enter*.

The shell also has a built-in reverse history search, which lets you quickly rerun a previous command by searching through your command history. To do this, press *Ctrl + R* and simply start typing the command. You'll see the command begin to complete as the search is refined. When you see the command you want to run, hit *Tab* to complete it and *Enter* to execute it:

```
(reverse-i-search)`git pul': git pull --rebase origin main
```

In this example, I had typed `git pul`, and the rest was completed from my history. I could press *Tab* to complete the command with that result.

Disk usage

Managing your computer's storage usage can be a tricky endeavor. Running out of disk space can cause stability issues and even data loss. This chapter isn't intended to teach you how to be a systems administrator, but it is essential to determine where these sorts of problems could be and how to take corrective action.

Your desktop system likely only has one disk, but you could have multiple. If you followed the guided installation as suggested, you would have a nice, simple storage layout, which is the scenario we will assume in this part of the chapter.

Report filesystem space usage: df

The `df` command shows information about the space used and available on your filesystem.

The `df` command is quite simple, and you can pass various arguments, but I always recommend just using `-h`, which tells `df` to print the output in human-readable values. Specifically, sizes will be formatted as easy-to-understand values such as megabytes, gigabytes, terabytes, and so on.

To see the current utilization of the disk/drive where your home directory is located, run df −h /home:

```
ken@monster:~$ df -h .
Filesystem      Size  Used Avail Use% Mounted on
/dev/nvme0n1    3.9T  2.9T  942G  76% /
```

In this example, you can see my storage drive is 3.9T (terabytes), with 2.9T currently used and 942G (gigabytes) of free space. This is more easily readable than without the -h argument; you will get sizes reported in 1K blocks, which isn't as meaningful.

Estimate file space usage: du

Now that you know how much space is being used, you might want to figure out where that space is being used. This is where the du command comes in handy. Like the df command, I always recommend printing the output as human-readable and summarizing that output. To do that, we can run du -hs ~, which will print the total space used by your home directory:

```
ken@monster:~$ du -hs ~ 2>/dev/null
2.2T    /home/ken
```

This example shows that my home directory uses 2.2T of my 2.9T total (as shown in the previous example of df). I also utilized the redirection of stderr to /dev/null to ignore errors output by the du command. For example, files and directories within my home directory that might be owned by root will generate errors.

Report memory usage: free

free is essential for understanding your system's memory usage. Running free -h (the -h option makes the output human-readable with units such as GB and MB) will show you the total amount of RAM, how much is currently used, how much is free, and how much is being used for buffers and cache (which can be reclaimed by applications if needed). It's your go-to command for checking whether your system is running low on memory.

Hardware information

Let's explore how to peek under the hood of your Ubuntu system right from the command line! These ls commands are your go-to tools for getting a quick and informative snapshot of your hardware.

Ubuntu manages your hardware well, but sometimes you need to know exactly what's what. These commands give you that insight without opening up your computer case:

- lshw (**list hardware**): This is the big one! lshw provides a comprehensive overview of your system's hardware components. Run it with sudo lshw (you'll likely need administrator privileges to see all the details) and prepare to see a detailed tree-like structure listing everything from your CPU and memory to your network interfaces and storage devices. You can even filter the output to focus on specific types of hardware using the -c option followed by a class. For example, to display only memory-related information, run sudo lshw -C memory.

- lsusb (**list USB devices**): As the name suggests, lsusb displays information about all the USB buses and the devices connected to them. This is super handy for identifying peripherals such as your mouse, keyboard, webcam, or external hard drives. You'll see details such as the vendor ID and product ID, which can be useful for troubleshooting or identifying specific devices.

- lspci (**list PCI devices**): **Peripheral Component Interconnect (PCI)** is a standard interface for connecting hardware components inside your computer. lspci lists all the PCI devices found on your system, such as your graphics card, network card, and sound card. Like lsusb, it provides vendor and device IDs, which can be invaluable for finding drivers or diagnosing hardware issues.

- lscpu (**list CPU information**): Want to know the specifics about your processor? lscpu gives you detailed information about your CPU architecture, including the number of cores, threads, model name, CPU family, cache sizes, and more. It's a quick way to get a clear picture of your system's processing power.

- lsblk (**list block devices**): Block devices are storage devices such as hard drives, SSDs, and partitions. lsblk provides a clear, tree-like view of these devices, their sizes, mount points (where they are accessible in the filesystem), and any associated logical volumes or RAID arrays. It's a great way to understand how your storage is organized.

These commands are your allies when you need to understand the hardware of your Ubuntu system. They provide a wealth of information at your fingertips, empowering you to diagnose issues, verify configurations, and get better acquainted with your machine.

Fun and useful utilities

We've learned the essentials of using the command line to work with files and directories, control processes, and gather information about your system. But the command line isn't all business. You can have some fun while streamlining the way you work.

asciinema and asciinema-agg

asciinema is a fun tool for creating animated recordings of your terminal session. It will record each keystroke and any output generated in the terminal until you press *Ctrl + D* to stop recording. The animated replay can be easily posted online, but I think it's even more useful to convert the animated results to an animated GIF with **asciinema-agg**. Both of these apps are available in the Snap Store and are easily installed, as demonstrated in the following code. You can see what the output looks like here:

```
ken@monster:~$ sudo snap install --classic asciinema
asciinema 2.2.0 from asciinema installed
ken@monster:~$ snap install asciinema-agg
asciinema-agg 1.3.0 from Guillaume Beuzeboc (gbeuzeboc) installed
ken@monster:~$ asciinema rec ubuntu.cast
asciinema: recording asciicast to ubuntu.cast
asciinema: press <ctrl-d> or type "exit" when you're done
ken@monster:~$ cowsay "Ubuntu is awesome"
 _____
< Ubuntu is awesome >
 -------------------
        \   ^__^
         \  (oo)_____
            (__)\       )\/\
                ||----w |
                ||     ||
ken@monster:~$ echo "that was fun"
that was fun
ken@monster:~$
exit
asciinema: recording finished
asciinema: asciicast saved to ubuntu.cast
ken@monster:~$ asciinema-agg ubuntu.cast ubuntu.gif
```

In this example, I used the (also fun) **cowsay** app to create ASCII art of a cow saying **Ubuntu is awesome** and I echoed **that was fun**. Then, I converted the resulting ubuntu.cast file into an animated GIF saved as ubuntu.gif. I encourage you to try these steps yourself and check out the result!

ImageMagick

ImageMagick is a collection of image-related utilities that are incredibly powerful. I'll highlight one of them right now and let you explore the rest if you are interested. The convert command, provided by the ImageMagick package (installable via sudo apt install imagemagick), can convert just about any image format into another.

Usage is simple; convert input_file output_file will detect the input file format and determine the format to convert to based on the file extension of output_file. For example, convert someimage.jpg someimage.png will convert a JPEG image named someimage.jpg to a PNG and save it as someimage.png.

You can even use it to convert an animated GIF, such as the one we created with asciinema, to a web-friendly video format such as WebM. To do this, we do need to specify a couple of arguments to handle the GIF, which is compressed, and to only loop once. For example, convert -layers coalesce -loop 9 ubuntu.gif ubuntu.webm will create a WebM video.

This is a tool I use regularly and it's incredibly powerful, offering many optional arguments that can be used to further fine-tune the results. Check out the documentation with man convert for a full list of options. As mentioned earlier, ImageMagick is a collection of many tools; visit https://imagemagick.org for more information.

Beyond the basics: exploring advanced features

Let's dive into Bash and the magic of .bashrc on your Ubuntu system.

Unleashing the power of Bash with .bashrc

When you open a terminal in Ubuntu, you're usually greeted by the Bash shell. It's the engine that interprets your commands and makes things happen. Did you know you can customize Bash to work exactly how you want it to? That's where .bashrc comes in.

Think of .bashrc as your personal configuration file for Bash. It's a hidden file (notice the leading dot) located in your home directory (~). Every time you start a new terminal session, Bash reads this file and executes the commands and settings it contains. This means you can set up aliases for frequently used commands, define your own functions, customize your prompt, and much more – all automatically!

Finding your .bashrc file

To take a peek at your `.bashrc` file, just open a terminal and type the following:

```
ken@monster:$  ls -la ~/.bashrc
```

You should see `.bashrc` listed. To open it up and start making changes, you can use a text editor. This uses `gnome-text-editor`:

```
ken@monster:$ gnome-text-editor ~/.bashrc
```

This uses `nano`:

```
ken@monster:$ nano ~/.bashrc
```

What can you do in .bashrc?

The possibilities are pretty vast, but here are a few cool things you can do to supercharge your command-line experience:

- **Aliases**: Tired of typing long commands? Create shorter, easier-to-remember aliases. For example, instead of typing `sudo apt update`, you could type `apu`. Add lines like this to your `.bashrc` file:

    ```
    alias apu='sudo apt update'
    alias apg='sudo apt upgrade'
    alias ll='ls -alF'
    ```

- **Functions**: You can define your own Bash functions for more complex tasks. Here's a simple example that creates a directory and then moves into it:

    ```
    mkcd () {
      mkdir -p "$1" && cd "$1"
    }
    ```

    Now, you can type `mkcd mynewfolder` to create and enter the directory.

- **Prompt customization**: Tweak the PS1 environment variable to make your terminal prompt more informative or visually appealing. You can display your username, hostname, and current directory and even add colors! There are tons of examples online to get you started.

- **Environment variables**: Set environment variables that programs can use. For instance, add directories to PATH to run executables without specifying their full path.

Making your changes take effect

After you've made changes to your .bashrc file, you need to tell Bash to reload it. You can do this in a couple of ways:

- **Close and reopen your terminal**: This will force Bash to reread the .bashrc file when the new session starts.
- **Source the file**: In your current terminal, run the following command: source ~/.bashrc.

This will immediately apply the changes without needing to close and reopen.

A word of caution

While .bashrc is incredibly useful, be careful when editing it. Mistakes in this file can sometimes lead to your terminal not behaving as expected. If you run into issues, you can always revert to a backup of your .bashrc file (it's a good idea to make one before making significant changes!) or even delete it (Bash will usually create a default one when you open a new terminal).

Playing around with .bashrc is a fantastic way to make your Ubuntu command-line experience more efficient and tailored to your workflow. So go ahead, open it up, and start exploring the possibilities!

Taking it a step further: your own Bash scripts

So, you're getting comfy with Bash commands, and you've even tweaked your .bashrc file – awesome! Imagine being able to bundle up a sequence of these commands and run them all at once, automatically. That's the power of **Bash scripting**.

Think of a Bash script as a plain text file containing a series of commands that Bash can execute. It's like writing a mini-program for your terminal. This opens up a new level of automation, allowing you to perform complex tasks, manage files, and even create simple applications with just a few lines of code. Whether backing up your important documents, automating repetitive tasks, or deploying software, Bash scripting can be a real game-changer for your productivity on Ubuntu. It's a fantastic way to make your computer work for you!

Alternative shells

While Bash is the default shell on Ubuntu, there's a whole world of other shells out there that bring their own unique flavors and features to the command line! Think of them like different dialects of the same language – they all let you talk to your computer, but they might have different accents and ways of expressing things.

Two popular alternatives you might hear about are **Fish** and **Zsh**:

- **Fish** (*the friendly interactive shell*) lives up to its name by focusing on being user-friendly and intuitive, especially for newcomers. It boasts features such as auto-suggestions (it guesses what you're about to type!), super helpful tab completions, and a clear, web-based configuration. It often feels a bit more modern right out of the box.

- **Zsh** (*the Z shell*), on the other hand, is known for its incredible power and customizability. It's like Bash but turned up to 11, offering tons of advanced features, powerful tab completion, extensive theming options, and a plugin system that lets you add all sorts of extra functionality. Many developers and power users swear by Zsh for its flexibility and the ability to tailor it to their needs.

While Bash is almost universally available, exploring Fish or Zsh can offer a fresh perspective and convenient tools that make your command-line adventures more enjoyable and efficient. It's all about finding the shell that clicks best with your workflow!

Summary

In this chapter, you took your first steps into the command-line world. You learned how to navigate the filesystem, manage files and directories, understand permissions, and use powerful text manipulation tools. You also explored more advanced concepts such as shell scripting and aliases. The command line proved to be a deep and rewarding tool; what you have learned here was just the beginning. Don't be afraid to continue experimenting and exploring further.

The next chapter will introduce the essentials of network security, from understanding what's running on your system that could expose you to threats to using a firewall to block potential attackers.

Further reading

- The manual page for any command (very helpful!): `man command_name`
- ImageMagick: `https://imagemagick.org/index.php`
- Bash: `https://www.gnu.org/software/bash/`
- Fish shell: `https://fishshell.com/`
- Oh My Zsh: `https://ohmyz.sh/`

Part 3

Security and Privacy

In this part of the book, you'll learn how to fortify your Ubuntu experience with solid security practices, including firewall configuration and data encryption.

This part of the book includes the following chapters:

- *Chapter 11, Introduction to Network Security*
- *Chapter 12, Understanding Firewalls*
- *Chapter 13, Safeguarding Information with Data Encryption*

11

Introduction to Network Security

With its user-friendly interface and powerful and flexible capabilities, Ubuntu Desktop is a popular choice for desktop users. Navigating the digital world requires a proactive approach to security, not an afterthought. This chapter delves deep into the intricacies of securing your Ubuntu Desktop, empowering you with the knowledge and tools to protect your digital life.

Network security has many aspects in modern computing. Many of these concepts also apply to server and cloud workloads; however, there are many other considerations that we won't cover here.

In this chapter, we will cover the following topics:

- Understanding potential threats
- Essential security practices
- Continued vigilance

The connected world: a landscape of potential threats

The good news is that Ubuntu's out-of-the-box security posture has no open ports by default. What does this mean? Some software, when installed, will allow external access to a system, such as a web server. For a desktop use case, this isn't necessary, so none of the software installed by default can be accessed from another computer.

While this provides a great starting point, it's important to understand the implications of any other software you may install.

Understanding the threat landscape

Protecting yourself from threats involves routinely updating your system, carefully considering any software you install, following best practice configurations, and a healthy dose of common sense.

Let's learn about the three key categories of threats:

- **Software vulnerabilities**: Bugs that expose vulnerabilities in software that can be exploited.
- **Malware**: Malicious software, including viruses, worms, and ransomware, can compromise your system, steal data, or disrupt operations.
- **Network attacks**: Remote access that exploits software vulnerabilities or misconfiguration.

Follow the essential security practices outlined next to protect your system from software vulnerabilities, malware, and network attacks.

Building a secure foundation: essential security practices

Like your home, your Ubuntu system needs a solid and secure foundation. Ubuntu already provides a robust foundation, but it's important to understand it to ensure your system stays safe.

Protecting your system: essential software updates

Ensuring essential security updates are installed promptly is the easiest way to protect your system from malicious attackers.

Ubuntu offers a robust system for automatic updates, ensuring your system stays current with the latest security patches and software improvements.

Snap packages are automatically updated as new versions are published, so you do not need to take additional steps to ensure that applications you've installed from the Snap Store are updated.

For the rest of your system, you need to ensure that the automatic installation of security updates is enabled. To do this, search for **Software & Updates** in your applications and navigate to the **Updates** tab.

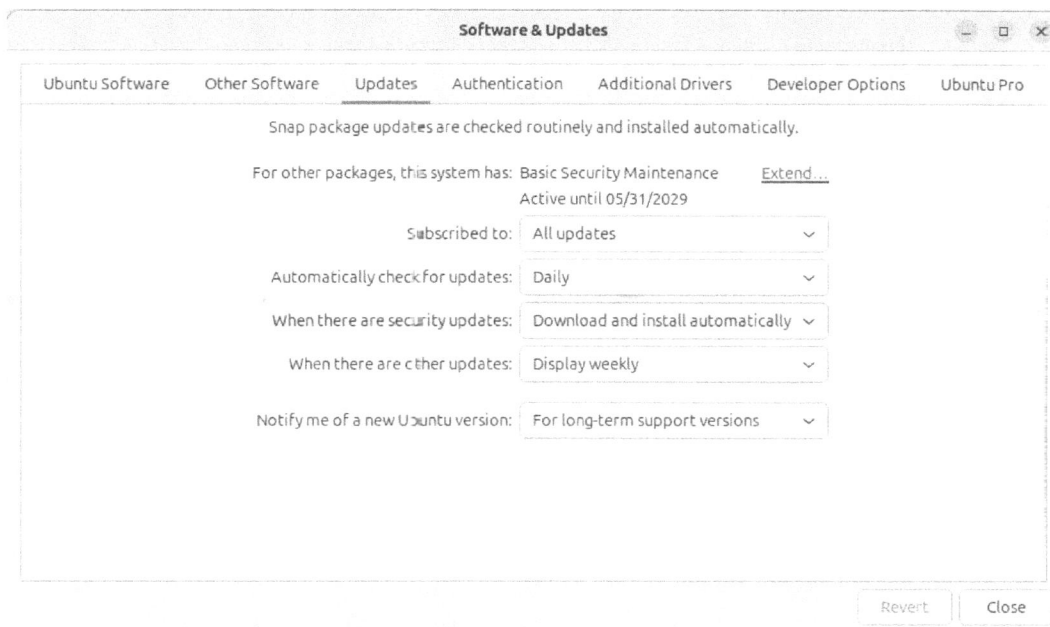

Figure 11.1 – Software & Updates

As shown in *Figure 11.1*, the **Updates** tab shows how long your system will receive security updates and the current state of when to install them. To ensure security updates are installed promptly, ensure **Download and install automatically** is selected in the dropdown next to **When there are security updates**.

> **Note**
>
> More on software updates can be found in *Chapter 7, Software Updates: Enhancing Security and Stability*.

Securing your system with UFW: a user-friendly firewall

Ubuntu comes equipped with a powerful firewall called **Uncomplicated Firewall (UFW)**. While UFW can be managed through the command line, the **Graphical Uncomplicated Firewall (GUFW)** provides an intuitive interface. This section will guide you through using GUFW to enhance your system's security.

> **Note**
>
> More advanced firewall concepts and configurations are covered in *Chapter 12, Understanding Firewalls.*

GUFW isn't included in Ubuntu's default installation, so we'll need to install the `gufw` package with `apt`:

```
ken@monster:~$ sudo apt install gufw
```

You can open GUFW by searching for **Firewall** in your applications.

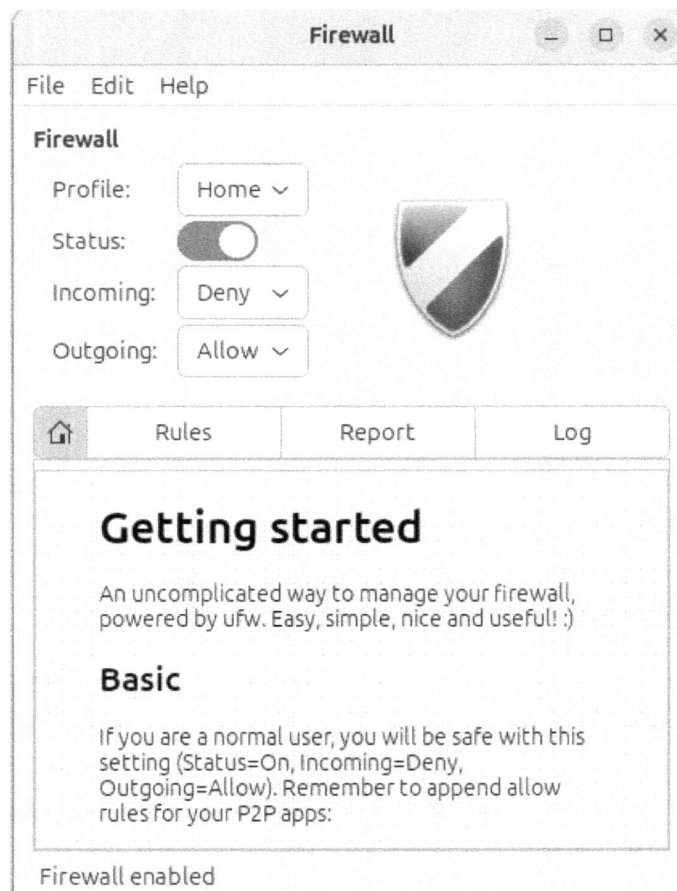

Figure 11.2 – GUFW

Understanding the interface

GUFW provides an intuitive user interface, as seen in *Figure 11.2*, with the following key elements:

- **Status**: Displays whether the firewall is active or inactive.
- **Predefined Rules**: Offer quick access to common firewall profiles (**Home**, **Public**, **Office**).
- **Incoming/Outgoing**: Separate tabs to manage incoming and outgoing network connection rules.
- **Add/Edit/Delete**: Buttons to manage your custom firewall rules.

Basic firewall operations

The intuitive interface of GUFW places the most common operations that provide the protection necessary for most users front and center:

- **Enabling/disabling the firewall**: Use the status switch to activate or deactivate the firewall. It's generally recommended that it be kept active.
- **Choosing a predefined profile**: Select a profile that best suits your network environment. Each profile comes with a set of pre-configured rules:
    - **Home**: Provides a moderate level of security for home networks.
    - **Public**: Offers a higher level of security for public Wi-Fi hotspots.
    - **Office**: Tailored for office network environments.

Creating custom rules

GUFW allows you to create custom rules to fine-tune your firewall configuration. Here's how:

- **Choose a direction**: Depending on the type of connection you want to control, select either the **Incoming** or **Outgoing** tab.
- **Add**: This opens the rule creation window.
- **Specify the protocol**: Choose the protocol (TCP, UDP, or any) for the rule.
- **Choose a port or application**: You can specify a specific port number or select an application from the predefined list.
- **Set the action**: Determine whether to allow or deny the connection.
- Click **Add** to save the rule.

Advanced features

GUFW offers additional features for advanced users, including:

- **Logging**: Enable logging to monitor firewall activity.
- **Advanced settings**: Configure options like the default policy for incoming and outgoing connections.
- **Report**: Generate a report of the current firewall configuration.

Important considerations:

- **Start simple**: Begin with a predefined profile and gradually add custom rules as needed.
- **Test your rules**: After adding new rules, test your network connectivity to ensure you haven't inadvertently blocked legitimate traffic.

By following these guidelines, you can effectively utilize GUFW to strengthen your system's security and protect it from unauthorized network access.

Network security with ss: a powerful tool in your arsenal

The ss command in Linux is a versatile utility for displaying network connections, sockets, and routing tables. It's a modern replacement for the older netstat command, offering more detailed information and improved performance. For network security, ss is invaluable for monitoring and troubleshooting your system's network activity, helping you identify suspicious connections and potential vulnerabilities.

Here's how you can leverage ss for enhanced network security:

Identifying listening ports and applications

Unnecessary open ports increase your system's attack surface. Use ss to identify all listening ports and the associated processes:

```
ken@monster:~$ ss -lntu
```

This command breaks down as follows:

- -l: Displays listening sockets (servers).
- -n: Shows numerical addresses instead of resolving hostnames.
- -t: Filters for TCP sockets.
- -u: Filters for UDP sockets.

Examine the output carefully. Any unfamiliar or unexpected listening ports should be investigated further. You can identify the process associated with a port using the **PID/ Program name** column.

Detecting established connections

To see active network connections, use:

```
ken@monster:~$ ss -s
```

This provides a summary of various connection states. For a detailed list of established TCP connections, use the following:

```
ken@monster:~$ ss -t state established
```

Pay attention to connections from unknown or suspicious IP addresses. You can use grep to filter the output and focus on specific connections:

```
ken@monster:~$ ss -t state established | grep "192.168.1.100"
```

This command will show all established TCP connections to or from the IP address 192.168.1.100.

Uncovering hidden connections

Some malicious software might attempt to hide connections. The ss command can help you uncover these:

```
ken@monster:~$ ss -a
```

This will display all sockets, including those in a TIME-WAIT state, which might reveal recently closed connections.

Filtering by specific processes

If you suspect a particular process is engaging in malicious network activity, you can filter connections related to it using the -p option:

```
ken@monster:~$ ss -tp | grep 'pid=1234'
```

This command will show all TCP sockets associated with the process ID 1234.

Integrating ss with other tools

Combine ss with other command-line tools for robust analysis. For example, use awk to extract specific information from the ss output or pipe it to grep for advanced filtering.

> **Note**
>
> To learn more about commands such as awk and grep, see *Chapter 10, Command-Line Tricks and Shortcuts: Boosting Your Efficiency.*

Security best practices with ss

- Regularly monitor your system's network connections using ss.
- Investigate any unusual listening ports or established connections.
- Keep your system updated to patch vulnerabilities that could be exploited through network connections.
- Use firewalls to restrict incoming and outgoing traffic and limit your system's exposure.

Mastering the ss command gives you a robust network security monitoring and analysis tool. It allows you to identify potential threats and maintain a secure network environment proactively.

Hunting rootkits with chkrootkit: A network security essential

Rootkits are the stealth fighters of the malware world. They burrow deep into your system, often operating at the kernel level, making them incredibly difficult to detect with traditional security tools. This is where **chkrootkit** comes in. It's a powerful open source toolkit designed to scan your Ubuntu system for signs of rootkit infections.

Why chkrootkit matters for network security

There are several reasons why you would want to use chkrootkit:

- **Early detection**: Rootkits can open backdoors for attackers, steal sensitive data, and even hijack your entire system for malicious purposes like launching DDoS attacks. chkrootkit helps you detect these threats before they wreak havoc on your network.
- **Proactive security**: Regularly scanning your systems with chkrootkit is a proactive security measure. It allows you to identify and address potential vulnerabilities before attackers exploit them.
- **Incident response**: If you suspect a rootkit infection, chkrootkit can help you confirm your suspicions and gather information about the type of rootkit you're dealing with. This is crucial for effective incident response.

Installing chkrootkit

It's simple to get chkrootkit up and running on your Ubuntu system:

```
ken@monster:~$ sudo apt install chkrootkit
```

Running chkrootkit

The most basic way to use chkrootkit is to run it without any arguments. This will initiate a default scan of your system:

```
ken@monster:~$ sudo chkrootkit
```

chkrootkit will analyze system files and directories and look for known rootkit signatures. Any suspicious findings will be displayed in the terminal.

Important chkrootkit options

While the default scan is a good starting point, chkrootkit offers several options to customize your scans:

- -q: Quiet mode – only displays warnings.
- -v: Verbose mode – provides more detailed output during the scan.
- -d: Debug mode – outputs even more information, useful for advanced troubleshooting.
- -l: Lists all the tests that chkrootkit performs.
- -x: Expert mode – performs more in-depth checks.

Interpreting the results

chkrootkit will report its findings with one of the following messages:

- **Infected**: This indicates a strong suspicion of a rootkit infection.
- **Not infected**: The test did not find anything suspicious.
- **Not tested**: The test was not performed, possibly due to missing files.

Important notes

There are several important things to consider when using chkrootkit:

- **False positives**: chkrootkit can sometimes flag legitimate files as suspicious. Always investigate further before taking action.
- **Staying updated**: New rootkits are constantly emerging. Keep chkrootkit updated to ensure it has the latest signatures.
- **Root privileges**: chkrootkit needs root privileges to perform its scans effectively.

Beyond chkrootkit

While chkrootkit is a valuable tool, it's not a silver bullet. Combine it with other security measures like:

- **Firewall**: A properly configured firewall (such as UFW) can block unauthorized network access.

- **Intrusion Detection System (IDS)**: An IDS (such as Snort) can monitor your network for suspicious activity.

- **Regular system updates**: Keep your Ubuntu system updated with the latest security patches.

Incorporating chkrootkit into your network security strategy adds a powerful layer of defense against rootkits' stealthy threat. Regular scans, coupled with other security best practices, will significantly enhance the security posture of your Ubuntu systems.

Understanding the foundation provided by Ubuntu and how to leverage the tools provided is just the first step in the ongoing journey to keep your system and your data safe. We must remain vigilant, consider the potential threats for all software we install, and routinely ensure the system is updated and malware-free.

Summary

In this chapter, we learned about potential threats to our system security, essential protection techniques, and the importance of staying vigilant about potential threats.

Next, we'll dive deeper into firewall configuration and cover more advanced uses and configurations.

Further reading

- chkrootkit: https://www.chkrootkit.org
- Snort: https://www.snort.org

Join the CloudPro Newsletter with 44000+ Subscribers

Want to know what's happening in cloud computing, DevOps, IT administration, networking, and more? Scan the QR code to subscribe to **CloudPro**, our weekly newsletter for 44,000+ tech professionals who want to stay informed and ahead of the curve.

https://packt.link/cloudpro

12

Understanding Firewalls

This chapter delves into the critical world of network security and advanced routing on your Ubuntu system. We'll explore firewalls, their importance, and how to configure them using both **Uncomplicated Firewall** (**UFW**) and **iptables**.

In this chapter, we will cover the following topics:

- Firewalls
- Advanced filtering with iptables
- Advanced routing with iptables
- Best practices

Why you need a firewall?

Imagine your computer as a house with doors and windows. A firewall acts like the locks and security system, controlling who and what can come in and out. It's a barrier between your system and the network (such as the internet), examining incoming and outgoing network traffic and blocking anything suspicious or unauthorized.

Firewalls work by analyzing network packets against a set of rules. These rules define what types of traffic are allowed or denied based on criteria such as the following:

- Source and destination IP addresses: Where the traffic is coming from and going to
- Ports: Specific communication channels applications use (for example, port 80 for web traffic)
- Protocols: Rules for communication (for example, TCP, UDP)

Ubuntu comes with a firewall pre-installed, but it's disabled by default. Enabling and configuring it is crucial to secure your system.

UFW: your friendly firewall

UFW is Ubuntu's default firewall management tool. It simplifies configuring iptables, making it user-friendly even for beginners. In *Chapter 11, Introduction to Network Security*, we discussed GUFW, the graphical interface for UFW. Now, let's look at how to use UFW without GUFW's convenience.

These are the basic UFW commands:

- **Check the status:** `sudo ufw status`
- **Enable:** `sudo ufw enable`
- **Disable:** `sudo ufw disable`
- **Allow traffic:** `sudo ufw allow 80/tcp`
    - Allows web traffic on port 80
- **Deny traffic:** `sudo ufw deny 22/tcp`
    - Blocks SSH connections on port 22
- **Allow from specific IP:** `sudo ufw allow from 192.168.1.100 to any port 22`

For example, this code allows SSH and HTTP traffic:

```
ken@monster:~$ sudo ufw allow 22/tcp
ken@monster:~$ sudo ufw allow 80/tcp
ken@monster:~$ sudo ufw enable
ken@monster:~$ sudo ufw status
Status: active


To                         Action       From
--                         ------       ----
22/tcp                     ALLOW        Anywhere
80/tcp                     ALLOW        Anywhere
22/tcp (v6)                ALLOW        Anywhere (v6)
80/tcp (v6)                ALLOW        Anywhere (v6)
```

- As you can see in the preceding example, we allowed TCP traffic to port 22 (SSH) and port 80 (HTTP) and enabled the firewall. The output of the `sudo ufw status` command lets us view the firewall's current state and the rules that are in place.

UFW can be used for much more than protecting your system as a firewall. It can also be used for rate limiting and more advanced routing features provided in the Linux kernel. Rate limiting helps protect you from Denial of Service (DoS) attacks, which occur when a malicious party attempts to make your network or system unusable by flooding it with network requests.

UFW can also set up more advanced routing features, such as port forwarding.

Diving deeper with iptables

While UFW is great for firewall management, iptables provides granular control over network traffic. In fact, UFW is a tool that simplifies the configuration of the kernel's package filter, iptables. It filters packets using chains (INPUT, OUTPUT, FORWARD) and rules.

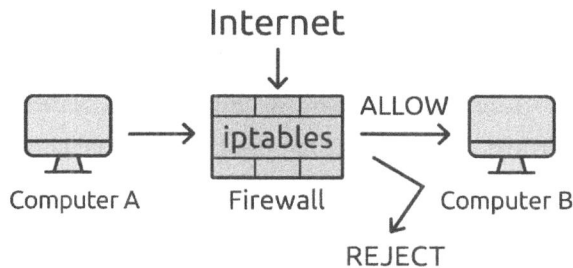

Figure 12.1 – iptables

Here is the basic iptables structure:

- **Tables**: Contain chains related to specific functions (for example, filter table for general packet filtering).
- **Chains**: Contain rules that are applied sequentially to packets.
- **Rules**: Define criteria for matching packets and actions to take (ACCEPT, DROP, REJECT).

For example, this code blocks traffic from a specific IP address:

```
ken@monster:~$ sudo iptables -A INPUT -s 192.168.1.100 -j DROP
```

This command appends (-A) a rule to the INPUT chain that drops (-j DROP) all packets from the source (-s) IP address 192.168.1.100.

Advanced routing with iptables

iptables isn't just for firewalling; it can also be used for advanced routing techniques:

- Network Address Translation (NAT): Allows multiple devices on a private network to share a single public IP address
- Port forwarding: Redirects traffic from one port to another, often used for making services on your local network accessible from the internet
- Traffic shaping: Controls the flow of network traffic to prioritize certain types of data or prevent network congestion

For example, this code shows port forwarding SSH to a different port:

```
ken@monster:~$ sudo iptables -t nat -A PREROUTING -p tcp --dport 2222 -j
DNAT --to-destination 192.168.1.100:22
ken@monster:~$ sudo iptables -t nat -A POSTROUTING -d 192.168.1.100 -p tcp
--dport 22 -j SNAT --to-source :2222
```

This redirects incoming traffic on port 2222 to port 22 on the machine with IP 192.168.1.100.

Best practices

There are a few best practices to consider when dealing with network security:

- Start with UFW: It's more straightforward and sufficient for everyday firewall needs
- Understand the default policies: UFW denies incoming and allows outgoing connections by default
- Document your rules: Keep track of the rules you add for easier troubleshooting
- Use iptables when more control is needed: Explore its capabilities for NAT, port forwarding, and more

From basic principles to practical application, you now understand the tools necessary to build a robust firewall. Securing your network ensures you can sleep soundly knowing your digital fortress is standing strong.

Summary

This chapter provided a foundation for understanding and configuring firewalls and advanced routing in Ubuntu. The Linux kernel offers very sophisticated network filtering capabilities. Consult the official documentation for more in-depth information and specific use cases.

The next chapter will teach us more about keeping your data safe, covering everything from encryption to best password management practices and remote access policies.

Further reading

- UFW: https://wiki.ubuntu.com/UncomplicatedFirewall
- IptablesHowTo: https://help.ubuntu.com/community/IptablesHowTo

13

Safeguarding Information with Data Encryption

Safeguarding your data is paramount in today's digital landscape. Imagine your laptop gets stolen during your commute to work. With physical access to the stolen device, the thief has numerous ways to attempt to access sensitive information you may have stored on the laptop.

They could attempt a brute-force attack to log in to your computer, or maybe they looked over your shoulder when you logged in and noted that you used an easy-to-remember password. Being able to log in to the physical computer is the easiest, but let's assume you did use a complex password and were cautious not to allow someone to see your password while you typed. The thief could easily remove the hard drive from the computer and attach it to another computer, bypassing the password protection your computer provides. Disk encryption can protect you from this scenario.

This chapter explores essential data protection strategies in Ubuntu, ranging from robust disk encryption methods to secure authentication practices.

In this chapter, we will cover the following topics:

- The importance of data encryption
- Options for full-disk encryption
- How to encrypt just your home directory
- Encrypting a removable drive

Why encrypt your entire disk?

Full disk encryption, typically implemented with **Linux Unified Key Setup** (**LUKS**) in Ubuntu, offers a powerful layer of protection for all your computer's data. It encrypts everything from your operating system and applications to your personal files and documents, making them unreadable without the correct decryption key.

Key benefits of full disk encryption

Let's explore the key benefits that make full disk encryption such an effective security measure:

- **Comprehensive data protection**: Unlike encrypting individual files or folders, full disk encryption protects everything on your drive. This includes sensitive data that you might not have considered encrypting separately, such as temporary files, swap space, and even deleted files that haven't been overwritten yet.
- **Protection against physical theft**: Full disk encryption prevents thieves from accessing your data if your laptop or computer is lost or stolen. The data will remain encrypted and unreadable, even if they remove the hard drive and try to access it from another device.
- **Defense against unauthorized access**: Full disk encryption helps prevent unauthorized access to your data, even if someone gains physical access to your computer. This is especially important in shared environments or if you're concerned about malicious actors trying to access your data.
- **Peace of mind**: Knowing that your entire disk is encrypted provides peace of mind. You can be confident that your data is protected, even in the event of loss, theft, or unauthorized access.

- **Compliance with regulations**: In some industries and organizations, full disk encryption is required to comply with data protection regulations and standards. Encrypting your disk helps ensure you meet these requirements and protect sensitive information.

- **Easy to implement**: Ubuntu makes it easy to implement full disk encryption with LUKS. You can encrypt your disk during installation or encrypt an existing system using tools such as cryptsetup.

- **Minimal performance impact**: Modern encryption algorithms and hardware acceleration minimize the performance impact of full disk encryption. You're unlikely to notice any significant slowdown in your system's performance.

Encrypting your entire disk creates a robust security barrier that protects your data from various threats. It's a simple yet powerful way to enhance the security and privacy of your Ubuntu system.

As discussed in *Chapter 4*, you are presented with three options for full disk encryption during installation: LVM with encryption, ZFS with encryption, and TPM-backed full disk encryption. ZFS with encryption and TPM-backed full disk encryption are considered experimental features in Ubuntu 24.04, but they may still suit your needs.

Securing your system with LUKS full disk encryption

LUKS is the standard for full disk encryption on Linux systems, including Ubuntu. It provides a robust and reliable way to protect your hard drive or SSD, ensuring that all your data remains confidential even if your device is lost or stolen.

How LUKS works

LUKS encrypts your disk at the block level, meaning every bit of data on the drive is transformed into unreadable ciphertext (scrambled data). You must provide the correct passphrase during system startup to access the data. This passphrase unlocks the encryption key, allowing the system to decrypt the data on the fly as you use it.

LUKS during Ubuntu installation

The easiest way to use LUKS full disk encryption is to choose it during the installation.

On the installer's **Disk setup** page, select **Advanced features**. This dialog will allow you to choose several options to encrypt the disk. Choose the **Use LVM and encryption** option for LUKS, as shown in *Figure 13.1*.

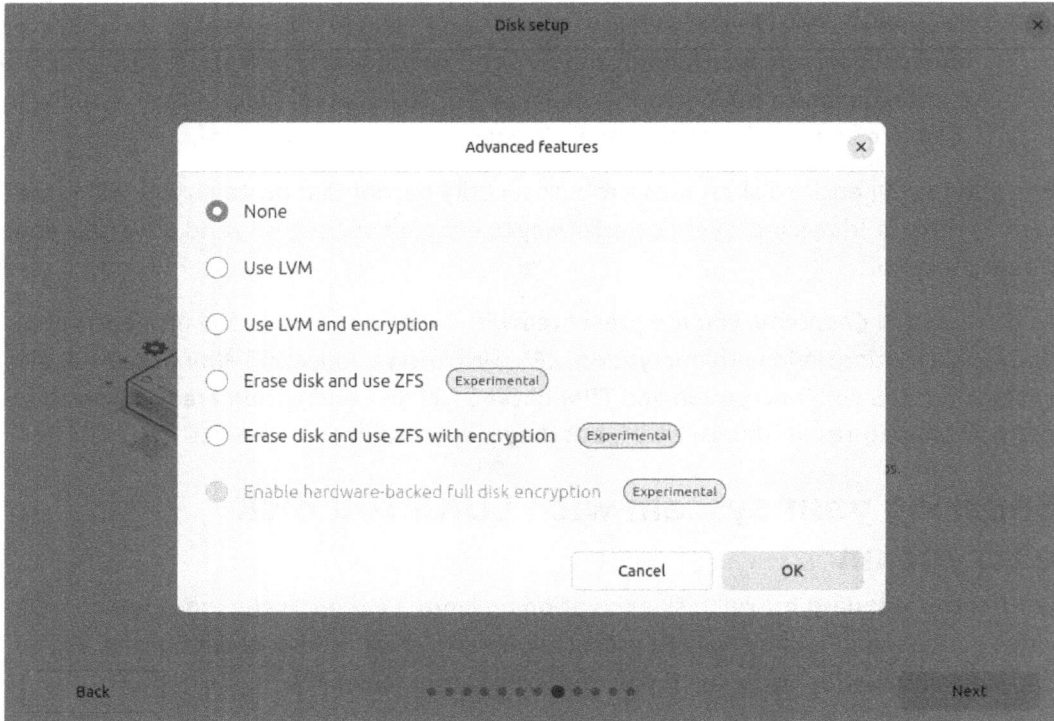

Figure 13.1 – Disk setup – Advanced features

Choose a strong passphrase, as shown in *Figure 13.2*, and complete the installation process.

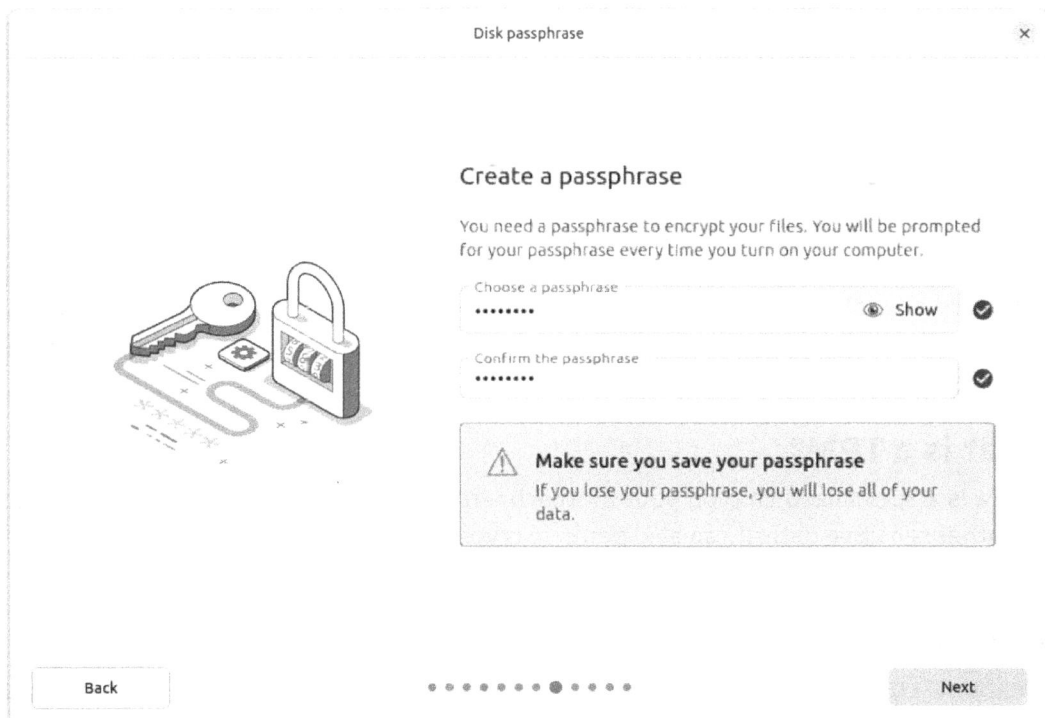

Figure 13.2 – Disk passphrase

After the installation, you'll be prompted to enter your passphrase each time you boot your computer. Once you enter the correct passphrase, your system will decrypt the disk and boot normally.

Important note

- **Recovery**: If you forget your passphrase, you will lose access to your data. The correct passphrase is necessary to recover your data. Make sure to store your passphrase in a secure location; for example, write it down and keep it with your important documents.

- **Security**: LUKS provides strong encryption, but choosing a strong passphrase and keeping it secure is essential. Avoid storing your passphrase in an insecure location

Enabling LUKS full disk encryption during installation protects your entire Ubuntu system from unauthorized access. It's a simple yet effective way to safeguard your data and enhance your privacy.

TPM-backed full disk encryption: enhanced security with hardware integration

Ubuntu now offers experimental support for TPM-backed full disk encryption, combining the robustness of LUKS with the security benefits of a **Trusted Platform Module (TPM)**. This approach enhances protection against offline attacks and provides a more seamless user experience.

What is a TPM?

A TPM is a specialized chip on your motherboard that securely stores encryption keys and other sensitive data. It can also perform cryptographic operations and verify system integrity.

Why use TPM-backed full disk encryption?

Traditional LUKS encryption relies on a passphrase to unlock the disk. While strong passphrases offer good security, they can be vulnerable to brute-force attacks or keyloggers if an attacker gains physical access to your computer.

TPM-backed LUKS addresses this vulnerability by storing the encryption key within the TPM itself. The key is released only after the TPM verifies the integrity of the boot process, ensuring that your system hasn't been tampered with.

The benefits of TPM-backed LUKS include the following:

- **Enhanced security**: Protects against offline attacks that bypass or steal the LUKS passphrase
- **Pre-boot integrity**: Ensures the system's integrity before releasing the decryption key
- **Seamless experience**: Often eliminates the need to enter a passphrase during boot manually

How to enable TPM-backed LUKS (experimental)

Important note

This feature is experimental and might not be suitable for all users. Proceed with caution and ensure you have backups of your data.``

Enabling TPM-backed encryption during installation can be done by following these simple steps:

1. **Check for TPM support**: Ensure that your computer has a TPM chip and that it is enabled in your BIOS settings.

2. **Enable Secure Boot**: Ensure that Secure Boot is enabled in your BIOS.

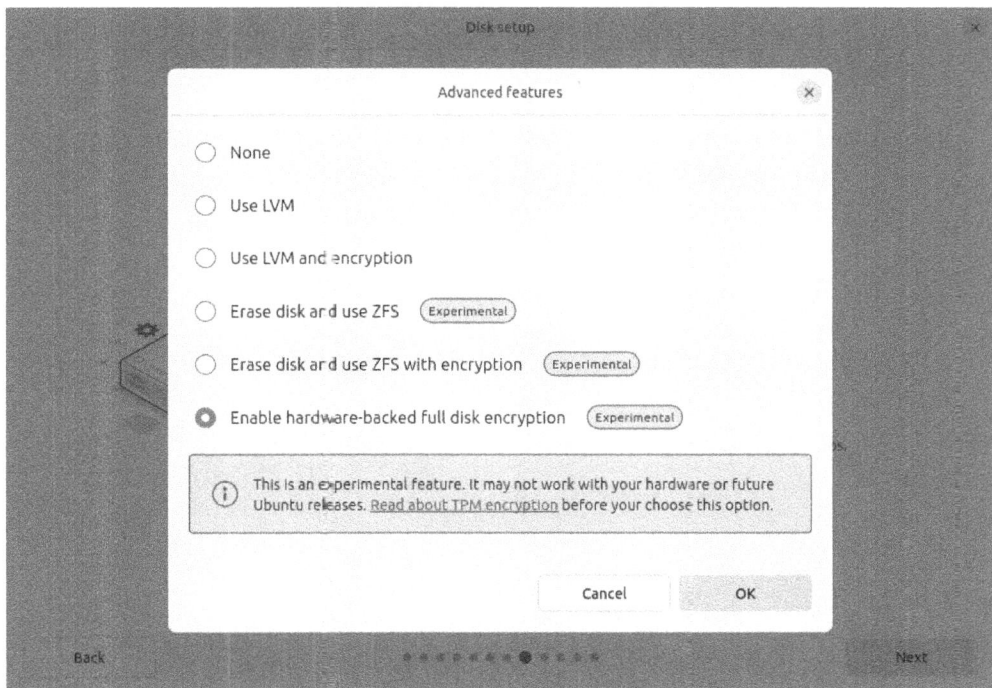

Figure 13.3 – Disk setup – Advanced features with TPM

3. **Choose hardware-backed encryption during installation**: Select the option to encrypt your disk and choose the hardware-backed encryption method, as shown in *Figure 13.3*.

> Important note
>
> The option to enable hardware-backed (TPM) full disk encryption will only be available if your device is compatible.
>
> **Requirements**:
>
> - Compatible TPM
> - Secure Boot enabled
>
> If you believe your device meets the requirements but the option is not enabled, try clearing the TPM. To do so, boot into your BIOS, find your security settings, and look for an option to clear the TPM.

4. **Follow the prompts**: The installer will guide you through setting up TPM-backed full disk encryption.

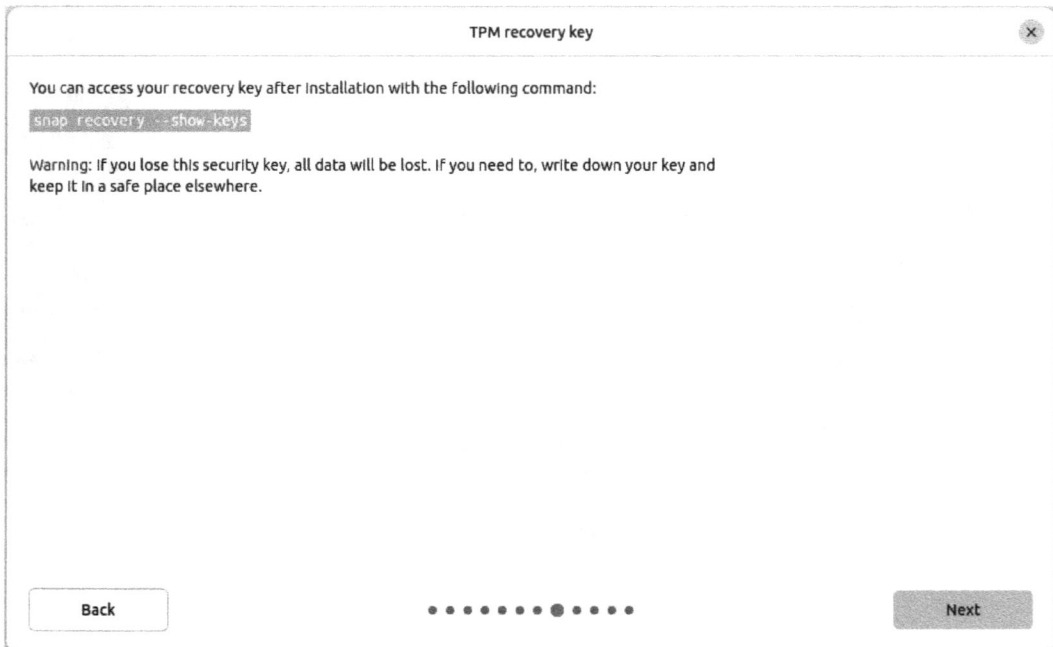

Figure 13.4 – TPM recovery key

As *Figure 13.4* shows, after booting into your installed system, you can back up your security key by writing down the output of the sudo snap recovery --show-keys command.

Considerations

A few considerstations when choosing to use TPM-backend encryption:

- **Experimental feature**: As this is an experimental feature, there are known limitations and bugs
- **TPM availability**: Not all computers have a compatible TPM chip
- **Data loss risk**: Always back up your data before experimenting with new encryption features

Future of TPM-backed encryption

TPM-backed full disk encryption is a promising development in Ubuntu's security features. As the technology matures and becomes more widely available, it's likely to become the standard for full disk encryption, offering users enhanced security and a seamless experience.

ZFS on root: a robust foundation with integrated encryption

Ubuntu includes the experimental option to install the operating system on top of the ZFS filesystem, complete with full disk encryption. This offers powerful features for advanced users seeking data integrity, snapshotting capabilities, and robust security.

Why ZFS?

ZFS is an advanced filesystem renowned for its data integrity features, including the following:

- **Checksumming**: ZFS continuously checks data for errors and automatically repairs them when possible
- **Copy-on-write**: This mechanism ensures data consistency and enables efficient snapshots
- **Pooling and RAID**: ZFS allows you to create storage pools easily and configure various RAID levels for redundancy
- **Snapshots**: Create point-in-time copies of your filesystem, allowing you to revert to previous states easily

ZFS with full disk encryption

Combining ZFS with full disk encryption provides a comprehensive data protection solution. Here's how to set it up during the Ubuntu 24.04 installation.

On the installer's **Disk setup** page, select **Advanced features**. This dialog will allow you to choose several options to encrypt the disk. Choose the **Erase disk and use ZFS with encryption** option, as shown in *Figure 13.1*.

Choose a strong passphrase, as shown in *Figure 13.2*, and complete the installation process.

After the installation, you'll be prompted to enter your passphrase each time you boot your computer. Once you enter the correct passphrase, your system will decrypt the disk and boot normally.

Considerations

A few considerstations when choosing to use ZFS with full disk encryption:

- **Experimental feature**: This is an experimental feature and may have bugs.
- **Performance**: ZFS can be more resource-intensive than traditional filesystems. Ensure your system has sufficient RAM and CPU power.
- **Complexity**: ZFS is a powerful filesystem with many advanced features. Take the time to learn its concepts and best practices.
- **Recovery**: If you forget your passphrase, you will lose access to your data. Store your passphrase securely.

Combining ZFS with full-disk encryption during installation can create a robust and secure foundation for your Ubuntu 24.04 system. This approach is ideal for users prioritizing data integrity, advanced features, and strong security.

As you can see, Ubuntu 24.04 offers several choices to protect your data. I recommend LUKS for full disk encryption, as it's a mature option that has proven reliable over time. But keep an eye on ZFS and TPM-backed options as they mature. ZFS could be appealing for advanced use cases, but TPM-backed full disk encryption will likely soon be the most desirable choice for most users.

Encrypting your home directory

While encrypting your entire disk with LUKS provides comprehensive protection, you might prefer to encrypt only your home directory containing your personal files, configurations, and other sensitive data. Ubuntu offers a way to do this using **eCryptfs**, a file-based encryption system that operates transparently in the background.

How to encrypt your home directory

You can set up home directory encryption either during the initial installation of Ubuntu or afterward, using the eCryptfs tools. The following are the steps to manually encrypt your home directory on an existing system.

Install eCryptfs utilities

Open a terminal and install the necessary packages:

```
ken@monster:~$ sudo apt install ecryptfs-utils cryptsetup
```

Create a second user account

You can't migrate your home directory data for a user account with a logged-in session. The simplest way to handle this is to create a temporary account with administrative access while migrating your home directory.

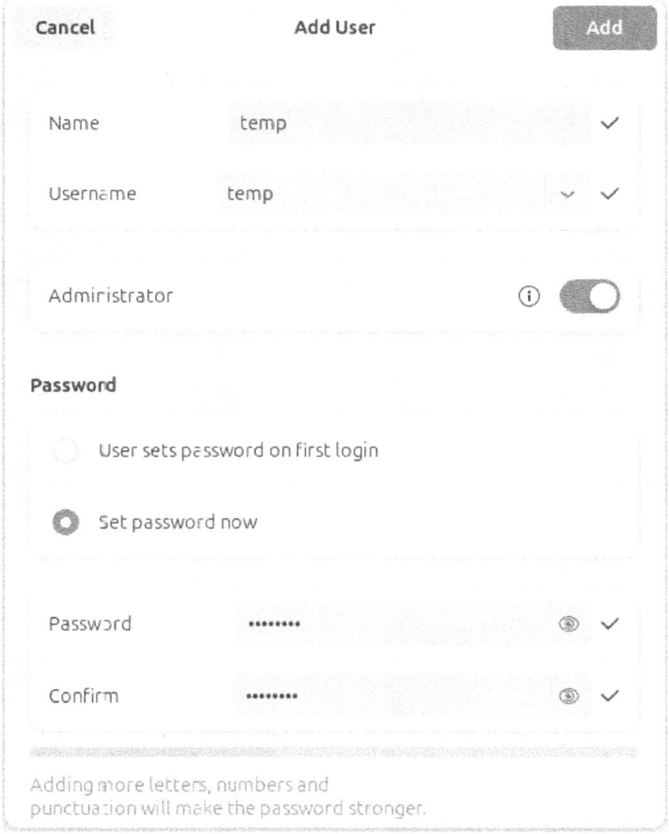

Figure 13.5 – New temp admin user

In the **Settings** app, go to the **Users** page and add a new account, as shown in *Figure 13.5.*

Log out and log in

Log out of your current session and log in with the new temp account just created.

Encrypt your home directory

Use the following command to encrypt your home directory:

```
temp@monster:~$ sudo ecryptfs-migrate-home -u USERNAME
```

Replace USERNAME with your actual username.

Enter your passphrase

You'll be prompted to enter and confirm a strong passphrase. This passphrase will be required to access your encrypted home directory each time you log in.

The encrypt-migrate-home command will output some important notes to follow to complete the migration.

Reboot your system

Reboot your computer to complete the encryption process.

Log in and verify

After rebooting, log in with your username and passphrase. You should now be able to access your home directory as usual. To confirm that encryption is active, open a terminal and run the following:

```
ken@monster:~$ mount | grep ecryptfs
```

You should see a line indicating that your home directory is mounted with eCryptfs.

Remove the temp account

Open the **Settings** app, navigate to the **Users** page, and remove the temp account previously created.

Considerations

A few considerstations when choosing to use encrypt your home directory:

- **Performance**: eCryptfs adds some overhead, so you might experience a slight performance decrease, especially with large files or frequent file access.
- **Compatibility**: eCryptfs is compatible with most applications and services, but some older or specialized programs might have issues accessing encrypted files.
- **Security**: While eCryptfs provides strong protection for your home directory, remember that other parts of your system remain unencrypted. For full disk encryption, consider using LUKS as described earlier.

Benefits of encrypting your home directory:

- **Confidentiality**: Protects your personal files and data from unauthorized access
- **Privacy**: Safeguards your sensitive information, such as browsing history, emails, and financial data
- **Security**: Adds an extra layer of defense against data breaches and theft

Encrypting your home directory can significantly enhance the security and privacy of your personal data on your Ubuntu system.

Encrypting a USB drive

Protecting sensitive data on portable storage is crucial. Thankfully, Ubuntu makes it easy to encrypt your USB stick with LUKS, ensuring your files remain confidential even if the drive is lost or stolen.

How to encrypt a USB stick

Follow these simple steps to encrypt your USB stick:

1. **Insert your USB stick**: Plug your USB stick into an available port on your Ubuntu computer.
2. **Open Disks**: Search for Disks in your applications.
3. **Identify your USB stick**: In the **Disks** utility, locate your USB stick in the list of storage devices. Double-check you've selected the correct drive to avoid accidentally erasing data from your system.

4. **Unmount the USB stick**: If the USB stick is mounted, click the *stop* button (square icon) next to its name in **Disks**.

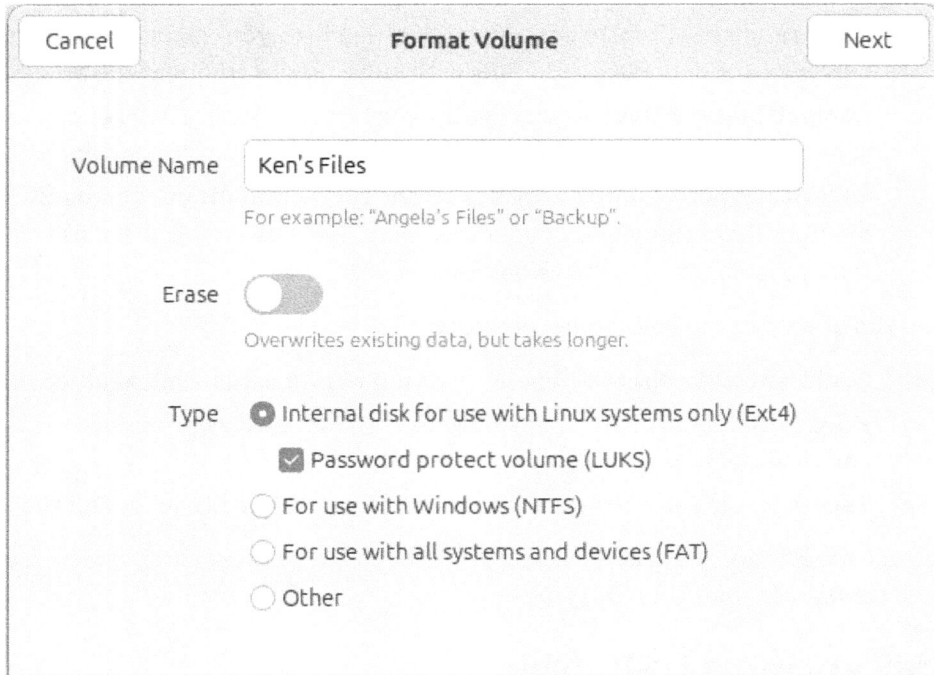

Cancel	**Format Volume**	Next

Volume Name   Ken's Files

For example: "Angela's Files" or "Backup".

Erase   ⬤◯

Overwrites existing data, but takes longer.

Type   ⦿ Internal disk for use with Linux systems only (Ext4)

     ☑ Password protect volume (LUKS)

   ◯ For use with Windows (NTFS)

   ◯ For use with all systems and devices (FAT)

   ◯ Other

Figure 13.6 – Format Volume

5. **Format and encrypt**: For a new partition or the whole drive, do the following:

   1. Click the small gear icon below the volume.
   2. Select **Format Disk**.
   3. Choose a name for the drive.
   4. Under **Type**, select **Internal disk for use with Linux systems only (Ext4)** and check the **Password protect volume (LUKS)** option, as shown in *Figure 13.6*.
   5. Click **Next**.
   6. Enter and confirm a strong passphrase, as shown in *Figure 13.7*. This passphrase is required to unlock the drive.

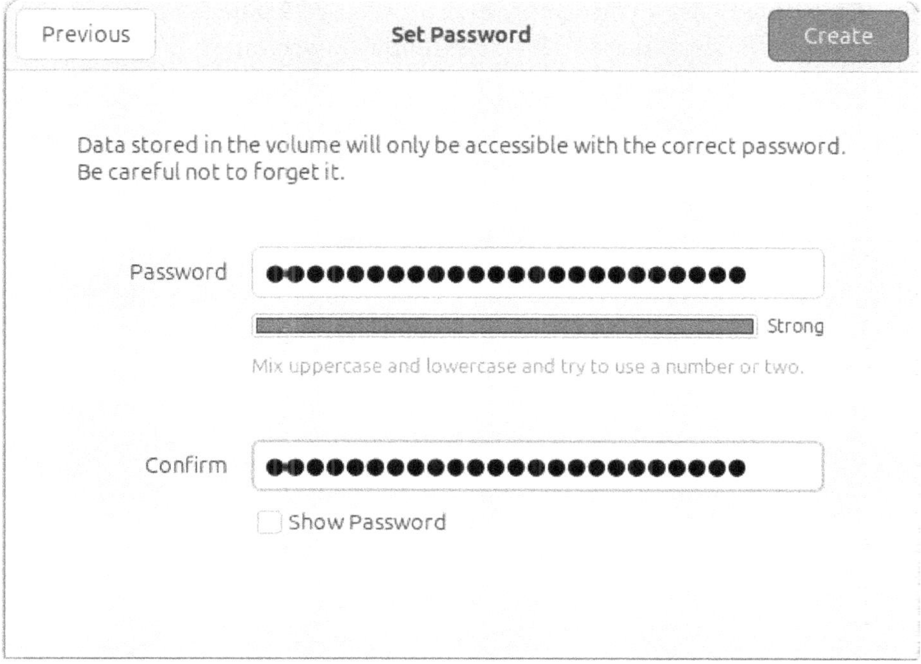

Figure 13.7 – Set Password

6. **Wait for completion**: The formatting and encryption process will take some time, depending on the size of your USB stick and the erase option you chose.

7. **Mount and access**: Once the process is complete, you can mount the encrypted USB stick by clicking on its icon in **Disks**. Enter your passphrase when prompted, and you can now use the drive as usual. You can also unplug the USB drive and plug it back in. You'll be prompted to use the passphrase to decrypt the drive when accessing it in the **Files** app.

Considerations

A few considerstations when choosing to encrypt your USB stick:

- **Backup your data**: Encrypting your USB stick will erase all existing data. Back up any important files before you begin.

- **Strong passphrase**: Choose a strong and unique passphrase that you can remember. If you forget it, you will lose access to your data. Consider using a password manager to help you generate and store secure passphrases.

- **Physical security**: While encryption protects your data from digital access, remember that physical security is also essential. Keep your USB stick in a safe place to prevent unauthorized access.

By following these steps, you can confidently secure your data on the go with a robustly encrypted USB stick.

Password: the last link in the chain

Encrypting your data is only one link in the chain of data security. Choosing secure passwords for all your accounts, including your Ubuntu system's user account, is essential. Once your hard drive is decrypted, your data will be vulnerable if your system account has an insecure password, or you leave your computer on with the screen unlocked.

There are three essential practices for physical security:

- Choose a complex password
- Ensure your screen is locked when unattended
- Require a password to unlock after suspend

Choosing a password

Strong passwords are crucial for securing your Ubuntu system. Enforce robust password policies to prevent unauthorized access.

Key password practices

A few considerstations when choosing a secure password:

- **Length**: Use passwords with at least 12 characters
- **Complexity**: Include a mix of uppercase and lowercase letters, numbers, and symbols
- **Uniqueness**: Avoid reusing passwords across different accounts
- **Regular updates**: Change passwords periodically

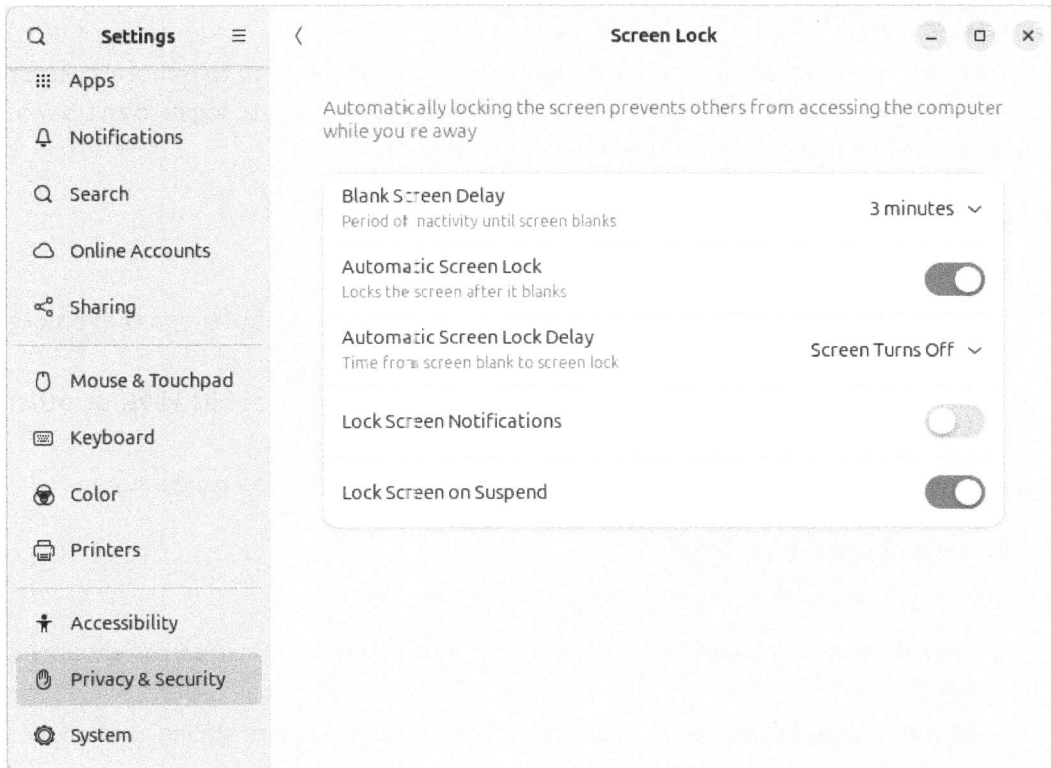

Figure 13.8 – Screen Lock settings

Screen locking

Ensuring your screen locks when you leave your computer unattended is a great idea and essential in the office or other public places. In the **Settings** app, under the **Privacy & Security** tab, you can find **Screen Lock** settings, as seen in *Figure 13.8*. Here, you can change settings for the length of inactivity before blanking the screen and enabling **Automatic Screen Lock**. With **Automatic Screen Lock** enabled, when the screen blanks due to inactivity, it will also lock, requiring a password to unlock.

You can also enable **Lock Screen on Suspend**, which will require a password to resume from suspend.

Secure remote access with SSH

Secure Shell (SSH) is a cryptographic network protocol allowing you to remotely access and manage your Ubuntu system. We generally think of SSH as a way to log in to an Ubuntu server, but in fact, your Ubuntu Desktop can also allow SSH login.

Key SSH security features

Benefits of using SSH:

- **Encryption**: Encrypts all communication between your computer and the remote server
- **Authentication**: Verifies your identity using passwords, public keys, or other methods
- **Integrity**: Ensures data integrity to prevent tampering during transmission

Best practices for SSH

A couple of considerations when configuring SSH:

- **Disable password authentication**: Use public key authentication for enhanced security
- **Use strong passphrases**: If using passwords, ensure they are strong and unique

Enabling SSH Server

To enable SSH Server on your Ubuntu Desktop system, you simply need to install the `openssh-server` package:

```
ken@monster:~$ sudo apt install openssh-server
```

Securing SSH

Installing OpenSSH Server will allow SSH login from remote machines using an SSH key or password. However, it's best to disable password login and only allow SSH key-based authentication. To do this, we simply need to create a configuration file for the SSH service and restart it:

```
ken@monster:~$ echo "PasswordAuthentication no" | sudo tee -a /etc/ssh/
sshd_config.d/disable-passwd.conf
ken@monster:~$ sudo systemctl restart ssh
```

Your Ubuntu Desktop system is now accessible for remote login with SSH, but only with SSH key-based authentication.

To learn more about SSH keys, see https://www.ssh.com/academy/ssh/keygen.

Summary

This chapter has provided a comprehensive overview of essential data protection strategies in Ubuntu. Utilizing these measures can significantly enhance your system's security and safeguard your valuable information. Encrypting the full disk at installation time is ideal. However, as an afterthought, you can still encrypt your home directory, which is quite effective.

In the next chapter, we'll learn how to best use our Ubuntu system for development.

Further reading

- *TPM-Backed Full Disk Encryption*: https://ubuntu.com/blog/tpm-backed-full-disk-encryption-is-coming-to-ubuntu
- *SSH Key*: https://www.ssh.com/academy/ssh/keygen

Part 4

Ubuntu, the Ultimate Development Platform

In this final part of the book, we will delve into advanced topics, including virtualization, containers, and Kubernetes, catering to the needs of professional developers, data scientists, and enthusiasts.

This part of the book includes the following chapters:

- *Chapter 14, Ubuntu for Developers*
- *Chapter 15, Leveraging Containers for Development*
- *Chapter 16, Cloud-Style VMs on Your Desktop*
- *Chapter 17, Kubernetes Development on Your Desktop*
- *Chapter 18, Building Your Data Science Toolkit*
- *Chapter 19, Embracing the Spirit of Ubuntu*

14

Ubuntu for Developers

Ubuntu is an excellent platform for many uses, and we've discussed many reasons for using it, how to install and configure it to meet your needs, and how to keep it secure.

Ubuntu has earned a reputation as a leading platform for developers, and for good reason. It stands out as the ideal development platform for software development.

We have a great deal of choice when it comes to how we use our desktop for development. Let's dig into some best practices and learn how to really leverage the tools at our disposal.

In this chapter, we will cover the following topics:

- Why choose Ubuntu?
- Essential development tools
- Contributing to open source

Why choose Ubuntu?

Here's a breakdown of the advantages Ubuntu offers for developers and why it's a compelling choice for your development endeavors.

It's free (as in freedom and beer)

Ubuntu is open source, meaning it's completely free to use, distribute, and modify. This eliminates licensing costs and allows for unparalleled flexibility in your development process. You can freely experiment, deploy, and scale your applications without worrying about proprietary restrictions.

It has a robust and stable foundation

Ubuntu is built on the rock-solid Linux kernel, providing a stable and reliable operating system for your development environment. Say goodbye to unexpected crashes and frustrating system instability. Ubuntu's **Long-Term Support (LTS)** releases offer extended support cycles, ensuring your development platform remains secure and maintained for years.

It has a vast software ecosystem

Ubuntu boasts an extensive software repository, providing access to a vast collection of development tools, libraries, and frameworks. With just a few commands, you can install essential tools, such as the following:

- **Programming languages**: Python, Java, C/C++, Ruby, Rust, Go, and many more
- **IDEs and editors**: Visual Studio Code, IntelliJ IDEA, Eclipse, Sublime Text, Vim, Emacs, and many more
- **Databases**: MySQL, PostgreSQL, and MongoDB
- **Version control systems**: Git and Mercurial
- **DevOps tools**: Docker, Kubernetes, and Ansible

This rich ecosystem streamlines your workflow and allows you to focus on building great software.

It has a vibrant and supportive community

Ubuntu has a large and active community of developers, users, and enthusiasts. This community provides readily available support, extensive documentation, and a wealth of online resources. Whether you're facing a technical challenge or seeking advice, you can find assistance through forums, mailing lists, and online communities.

Security is at its core

Ubuntu prioritizes security with regular updates and security patches, safeguarding your system from vulnerabilities and threats. This focus on security is crucial for developers, especially when working on sensitive projects or handling user data.

It is customizable and flexible

Ubuntu is highly customizable, allowing you to tailor your development environment to your needs and preferences. You can choose from different desktop environments, install custom themes, and configure your system to optimize your workflow.

It allows cloud-native development

Major cloud providers, such as **Amazon Web Services (AWS)**, **Azure**, and **Google Cloud Platform (GCP)**, strongly support Ubuntu. This makes it ideal for cloud-native development, allowing seamless deployment and integration with cloud services.

Essential development tools on Ubuntu

Ubuntu is a developer's dream come true. It offers a robust and versatile environment and a vast collection of tools to streamline workflow. This section explores some of the essential tools that will empower you on your Ubuntu development journey.

The foundation: build-essential

At the heart of Ubuntu's development prowess lies the `build-essential` package. This meta-package encompasses a collection of crucial tools for compiling and building software from source code. It includes the following:

- **GNU Compiler Collection (GCC)**: The cornerstone for C, C++, and other language compilation
- **GNU Make**: A powerful build automation tool to manage and simplify complex projects
- **libc6-dev**: Essential libraries and header files for C development
- **dpkg-dev**: Tools for building Debian packages, enabling you to create and distribute your own software
- **GNU Binutils**: A suite of binary utilities, including the linker and assembler, vital for working with object files

Installing `build-essential` is your first step:

```
ken@monster:~$ sudo apt install build-essential
```

Version control with Git

Git is the undisputed champion of version control systems, and Ubuntu makes it a breeze to get started. Install Git and embrace collaborative development, effortless tracking of changes, and seamless branching and merging:

```
ken@monster:~$ sudo apt install git
```

Configure your Git identity with your name and email:

```
ken@monster:~$ git config --global user.name "Your Name"
ken@monster:~$ git config --global user.email "your.email@example.com"
```

To learn more about Git, see `https://docs.github.com/en/get-started/using-git`.

Debugging with GDB

Encountering bugs is an inevitable part of the development process. **GDB**, the **GNU Debugger**, is your trusted companion for identifying and resolving issues within your code. You can use it to step through your code, inspect variables, and pinpoint the root cause of errors:

```
ken@monster:~$ sudo apt install gdb
```

To learn more about GDB, see `https://www.geeksforgeeks.org/gdb-step-by-step-introduction`.

Powerful text editors and IDEs

Ubuntu offers a rich selection of text editors and **Integrated Development Environments** (**IDEs**) to suit your preferences and project needs.

- **Vim**: A highly configurable and efficient command-line text editor favored by many experienced developers
- **VS Code**: A versatile and feature-rich code editor with extensive customization options and extensions for various languages
- **Sublime Text**: A proprietary, cross-platform editor known for its speed and responsiveness
- **Emacs**: A free, extensible, and customizable text editor designed for programmers
- **Eclipse**: A powerful IDE popular for Java development that supports other languages through plugins
- **IntelliJ IDEA**: A robust IDE from JetBrains that is well suited for Java and Android development

Explore these options and choose the one that best aligns with your workflow and project requirements.

Building GUIs with Flutter, GTK, Qt, and Electron

Ubuntu provides excellent frameworks, such as Flutter, GTK, Qt, and Electron, for crafting graphical UIs:

- **Flutter**: A free, open source framework from Google that allows developers to build applications using the same code base for multiple platforms. It supports Android, iOS, Windows, macOS, and Linux.
- **GTK**: A popular choice for GNOME applications, primarily using C, with support for Python, JavaScript, C++, and Vala.
- **Qt**: A cross-platform framework for C++, offering rich tools and libraries.
- **Electron**: A framework to build cross-platform desktop applications using web technologies such as JavaScript, HTML, and CSS.

Other useful tools

Beyond the essentials, Ubuntu offers a plethora of other valuable tools:

- **tmux**: A terminal multiplexer for managing multiple terminal sessions within a single window
- **zsh and fish**: Powerful shells with advanced features and customization options for a richer command-line experience
- **curl**: A command-line tool for transferring data from or to a server, ideal for interacting with web APIs
- **jq**: A command-line JSON processor for manipulating and extracting data from JSON files

Embrace the Ubuntu development ecosystem

This was just a glimpse into Ubuntu's vast landscape of development tools. As you delve deeper into your projects, you'll discover a vibrant ecosystem of resources, communities, and online support to guide you. Embrace the power of Ubuntu and unlock your full development potential.

Beyond the basics: Advanced development resources

While the essential tools provide a solid foundation, Ubuntu offers a wealth of advanced resources to elevate your development workflow. This section explores powerful tools and techniques that can significantly enhance productivity and efficiency.

Virtualized development with virtual machines and containers

As discussed in previous chapters, it's best to be thoughtful when choosing what software to install and run on your computer. In that spirit, Ubuntu is ideally suited for development using virtual machines and containers.

> Note
>
> We will explore containers to isolate development in *Chapter 15* and discuss virtualization and when it's best to use virtual machines for development in *Chapter 16*.

Virtual Python environments with venv

Python's venv module allows you to create isolated virtual environments for your Python projects. This prevents dependency conflicts and ensures a clean and organized development environment:

```
ken@monster:~$ python3 -m venv .venv
```

Activate the environment:

```
ken@monster:~$ source .venv/bin/activate
```

To learn more about venv, see https://python.readthedocs.io/en/latest/library/venv.html.

Advanced debugging with Valgrind

Valgrind is a powerful memory debugging and profiling tool that can help you identify memory leaks, invalid memory access, and other memory-related issues.

Install Valgrind:

```
ken@monster:~$ sudo apt install valgrind
```

Run your program with Valgrind to analyze its memory usage and detect potential problems. To learn more about how to use Valgrind, see https://valgrind.org.

Static code analysis

Static code analysis tools can help you identify potential code issues before runtime. Tools such as cppcheck (for C/C++) and pylint (for Python) can analyze your code for style violations, potential bugs, and security vulnerabilities.

Install cppcheck:

```
ken@monster:~$ sudo apt install cppcheck
```

To learn more about cppcheck, see https://cppcheck.sourceforge.io/.

Install pylint:

```
ken@monster:~$ sudo apt install pylint
```

To learn more about pylint, see https://pylint.readthedocs.io.

Profiling and performance optimization

Tools such as gprof and perf can help you analyze your code's performance and identify bottlenecks to optimize your code for speed and efficiency.

Specialized development tools

Ubuntu offers a wide range of specialized tools for specific development needs:

- **Android Studio**: The official IDE for Android app development.
- **Juju**: A tool for deploying and managing applications on various cloud platforms and on-premises servers.
- **Arduino IDE**: For developing applications for Arduino microcontrollers.
- **ROS**: The **Robotics Operating System** (**ROS**) is an open source framework that enables developers to build and program robots. ROS is based on Ubuntu making Ubuntu a great development platform for ROS developers.

Continuous Integration/Continuous Deployment (CI/CD)

CI/CD pipelines automate the build, testing, and deployment process, ensuring rapid and reliable software delivery. Explore popular CI/CD platforms such as Jenkins, GitLab CI/CD, and GitHub Actions to streamline your development workflow.

The runtime containers used by these platforms are commonly based on Ubuntu, making Ubuntu the ideal platform for creating these pipelines.

Cloud computing with AWS, Azure, and GCP

Ubuntu integrates seamlessly with major cloud providers, such as AWS, Microsoft Azure, and GCP. These platforms offer scalable infrastructure, managed services, and powerful development tools.

Because so much of the world's cloud infrastructure runs on Ubuntu, your Ubuntu Desktop provides an ideal development platform for workloads intended for public or private clouds.

Continuous learning and exploration

The world of development tools is constantly evolving. To stay at the forefront of innovation, embrace continuous learning and explore new tools and technologies. Ubuntu provides a fertile ground for experimentation and growth, empowering you to push the boundaries of your development capabilities.

Contributing to the open source community

Ubuntu, and much of the software you use on it, wouldn't exist without the collaborative spirit of the open source community. Now, it's your turn to join this global movement and contribute! Whether you're a seasoned developer or just starting out, there are countless ways to give back.

Find your project

The first step is finding a project that excites you. Here are some resources to help you discover projects that align with your interests and skills:

- **GitHub Explore**: Discover trending repositories and projects: `https://github.com/explore`

- **Open Source Friday**: A curated list of open source projects seeking contributions: `https://opensourcefriday.com`

- **First Timers Only**: Find projects with beginner-friendly issues: `https://www.firsttimersonly.com`

- **CodeTriage**: Get a daily digest of issues that need attention: `https://www.codetriage.com`

- **24 Pull Requests**: Contribute to open source during the holiday season: `https://24pullrequests.com`

- **Up For Grabs**: Find projects with clearly defined tasks ready for contributions: https://up-for-grabs.net

- **firstcontributions**: A beginner-friendly guide and repository to make your first contribution: https://firstcontributions.github.io

Start small

You don't have to write complex code to contribute. Here are some beginner-friendly ways to get involved:

- **Improve documentation**: Fix typos, clarify instructions, or translate documentation

- **Report bugs**: If you encounter a bug, report it with detailed information to help developers fix it

- **Test software**: Try out beta versions and provide feedback on usability and functionality

- **Answer questions**: Help others in forums, mailing lists, or online communities

- **Write tutorials or blog posts**: Share your knowledge and help others learn

Contribute code

Ready to write code? Here's a typical workflow:

1. **Fork the repository**: Create your own copy of the project's code on GitHub.
2. **Clone the repository**: Download the code to your local machine.
3. **Create a branch**: Create a new branch for your changes to keep them separate from the main code base.
4. **Make your changes**: Write your code, fix bugs, or add new features.
5. **Commit your changes**: Save your changes with a clear and descriptive message.
6. **Push your changes**: Upload your changes to your forked repository.
7. **Submit a pull request**: Request the project maintainers to review and merge your changes into the main code base.

Be a good community member

When engaging with the community, you are part of the community, and consider the following tips:

- **Communicate effectively**: Use clear and concise language when reporting issues or submitting pull requests

- **Be respectful**: Treat other contributors with kindness and respect

- **Be patient**: It may take time for your contributions to be reviewed and accepted.
- **Learn and grow**: Embrace feedback and use it to improve your skills
- **Mentor others**: As your skills grow, look for opportunities to mentor other new contributors to encourage others to pay it forward

Contributing to open source is a rewarding experience. You'll learn new skills, connect with other developers, and make a real impact on the software you use every day. By giving back to the community, you'll help ensure a vibrant and sustainable future for open source software.

Summary

In conclusion, Ubuntu provides a powerful, versatile, and developer-friendly environment for building innovative software solutions. Whether you're a seasoned developer or just starting your journey, Ubuntu offers the tools, stability, and community support you need to succeed.

15

Leveraging Containers for Development

The need for agile, reproducible, and isolated environments has become paramount in the ever-evolving software development landscape. LXD, the Linux container daemon, emerges as a powerful ally for developers on Ubuntu, offering a lightweight and flexible solution to these challenges. This chapter provides an in-depth exploration of LXD containers, encompassing their advantages, intricacies of setup and usage, advanced features tailored for diverse development workflows, and a glimpse into the future of LXD in the development domain.

In this chapter, we will cover the following topics:

*   Why LXD?
*   Creating development containers
*   Getting the most from your containers

The LXD advantage: Redefining development workflows

LXD containers offer a compelling alternative to traditional **virtual machines** (**VMs**) and other containerization technologies. They present a unique blend of features specifically designed to cater to developers' needs.

Lightweight and efficient

Unlike resource-intensive VMs requiring full operating system installation, LXD containers share the host kernel, minimizing overhead and maximizing efficiency. This translates to significantly faster boot times, a reduced memory footprint, and improved overall performance, making them ideal for resource-constrained development environments or when running multiple containers concurrently. This efficiency allows developers to iterate quickly and test their code in various environments without significant performance penalties.

Image-based management

LXD's utilization of images for container creation revolutionizes environment management. It allows for the effortless sharing, versioning, and reproducibility of development environments, ensuring consistency across different machines and simplifying collaboration among developers. This image-based approach fosters a robust and streamlined workflow, enabling developers to quickly spin up new environments with specific configurations and dependencies, eliminating the tedious task of manual setup and configuration.

Security fortified

Security is a non-negotiable aspect of development, and LXD addresses this with robust isolation through kernel namespaces and advanced security features. This safeguards the host system and other containers from potential vulnerabilities or malicious code that might exist within a development environment, ensuring a secure and protected workspace. LXD's security features give developers peace of mind, allowing them to focus on their code without worrying about compromising their system or data.

Scalability and flexibility

LXD excels in scalability, allowing developers to create multiple isolated environments for different projects, branches, or feature implementations effortlessly. This enables rapid switching between environments without impacting other projects, fostering a highly organized and efficient development process. This flexibility allows developers to experiment with new technologies, libraries, or frameworks without affecting their primary development environment.

Seamless Ubuntu integration

LXD's tight integration with Ubuntu leverages the operating system's robust package management system and provides access to a vast repository of pre-built images and tools. This streamlines the development process and ensures compatibility with various software and libraries. Developers can leverage the familiar apt package manager to install dependencies and manage software within their LXD containers.

LXD on Ubuntu: A step-by-step guide

Installing and configuring LXD on Ubuntu is simple; it's available in the Snap Store.

Simply install the LXD package as a snap and initialize LXD:

```
ken@monster:~$ sudo snap install lxd
ken@monster:~$ sudo usermod -aG lxd "$USER"
ken@monster:~$ newgrp lxd
ken@monster:~$ lxd init --auto
```

Installing LXD will create a system group named lxd on your system. Adding your user account to the lxd group will allow access to run the lxd and lxc commands without administrative permissions.

This will initialize LXD with the recommended settings. You can also leave out --auto, which will guide you through an interactive process of essential configuration steps, including the following:

- **Storage backend selection**: Consider factors such as performance, data management, and available disk space to choose the most suitable storage backend for your needs. ZFS offers advanced features such as data compression, snapshots, and checksumming, while **Logical Volume Manager** (**LVM**) provides flexibility in managing logical volumes.

- **Network configuration**: Configure network settings to allow your containers to communicate with the host system and the outside world, including bridge interfaces and network address allocation. You can use a bridge network to assign containers IP addresses or **Network Address Translation** (**NAT**) to share the host's network connection.

- **Image remote setup**: Connect to a remote image server, such as the official Ubuntu image server, to access various pre-built images for different operating systems and applications. This allows you to create containers with pre-configured operating systems and software quickly.

Now that we've set up LXD on our system, we're ready to start creating and using containers.

LXD container management

LXD provides a comprehensive and intuitive **command-line interface (CLI)** and a REST API for managing containers, offering a range of commands to control every aspect of their life cycle. Key commands include the following:

- `lxc launch`: This command creates a new container from an image, allowing you to specify the image source, container name, and other configuration options, such as resource limits, network configuration, and storage volumes.
- `lxc list`: This displays a list of all running containers on your system, providing information about their status, IP addresses, and resource usage. This command also allows you to filter and sort containers based on various criteria.
- `lxc start/stop/restart`: These manage the container life cycle, allowing you to start, stop, and restart containers as needed. You can also use these commands to pause and resume containers.
- `lxc exec`: This executes commands within a running container, allowing interaction with the container's operating system and applications. This allows you to install software, configure services, and run your applications within the container.
- `lxc file push/pull`: This transfers files between the host system and a container, enabling the seamless exchange of code, data, and configuration files. This is useful for transferring your code base, data, or configuration files to and from the container.
- `lxc image list/import/export`: This manages container images, including listing available images, importing images from various sources, and exporting images for sharing or backup. You can import images from remote servers and local files or create custom images.
- `lxc move`: This moves container instances within or between LXD servers.

While we were discussing LXD, you probably noticed that the command for interacting with the containers is 1xc. **LXC** stands for **Linux containers**, and **LXD** refers to the **Linux container daemon**, which provides the management infrastructure for managing Linux containers. Therefore, when we work with the individual containers, the command is 1xc.

Crafting development environments with LXD

LXD empowers developers to create highly customized and tailored development environments for various programming languages and frameworks.

Leveraging pre-built images

Take advantage of readily available pre-built images from the Ubuntu image server for popular languages such as Python, Node.js, Ruby, and Go. These images provide a solid foundation for your projects, pre-configured with essential tools and libraries, allowing you to jumpstart your development process without spending time on the initial setup.

Fine-grained customization

Customize images further to meet specific project requirements. Use 1xc config edit to modify container configurations, install additional packages and libraries, and fine-tune settings such as environment variables, resource limits, and security policies. You can also execute commands within the container to install software, configure services, and set up your development environment precisely as needed, ensuring that your environment perfectly matches your project's requirements.

Snapshots and rollbacks

LXD's snapshot feature allows you to capture the state of your development environment at any point in time. This enables you to quickly revert to a previous state, providing a safety net for experimentation and ensuring you can always return to a known working configuration. This is particularly useful when trying out new libraries, frameworks, or configurations, as you can quickly revert to a previous state if something goes wrong.

Sharing and collaboration

Export container images to share complete development environments with colleagues, ensuring consistency and reproducibility across the team. This facilitates collaboration and eliminates the "works on my machine" problem, ensuring everyone is working in the same environment. This simplifies onboarding new team members and reduces the time spent troubleshooting environment-related issues.

Creating and using your first LXD container

To create your first basic LXD container, run the following:

```
ken@monster:~$ lxc launch ubuntu:24.04 first-ubuntu-noble
```

The lxc launch command requires at least two arguments: which image to base the container on and a name for the container you create.

In the previous example, we created a new container named first-ubuntu-noble based on **Ubuntu 24.04**.

The lxc launch command creates and starts a new container instance. To access the instance, you will need to open a shell in the instance in your terminal:

```
ken@monster:~$ lxc exec first-ubuntu-noble -- bash
root@first-ubuntu-noble:~#
```

The lxc exec command will execute any command specified in the container. We must execute a shell of our choice to get a shell in the container, run commands, and install software. In the last example, we executed bash, a popular Linux shell, as the root user. This is fine for installing software and configuring and running system services within the container.

> **Important note**
>
> After entering the container with the lxc exec command, any commands run are executed inside the container. Use the exit command or the *Ctrl + D* keyboard combination to exit the container.

Running as an ordinary user with your home directory in the container is more convenient and safer for development:

```
ken@monster:~$ lxc launch ubuntu:24.10 oracular-devel -c raw.idmap="both
$UID 1000"
ken@monster:~$ lxc config device add oracular-devel homedir disk
source=$HOME path=/home/ubuntu
ken@monster:~$ lxc exec oracular-devel -- su -l ubuntu
ubuntu@oracular-devel:~$
```

In this example, we launched a new LXD container named oracular-devel based on Ubuntu 24.10 and mapped our UID through to the UID of the default ubuntu user in the new container.

Important note

A **user identifier (UID)** is a unique number assigned to each user account in Ubuntu. The UID controls your system's read or write access to files and directories.

Your newly created LXD container has a default user account named ubuntu with a UID of 1000. The preceding example configures your LXD to map your UID from your computer to UID 1000 in the container. This is important for providing access to files and folders on your system to the container instance.

After launching the container, we configured LXD to allow access to the home directory on our computer in the container at /home/ubuntu, which is the ubuntu user account's home directory.

Finally, we used the lxc exec command to run a login shell in the container. We logged in as the default ubuntu user account, which has access to the entire home directory on the host system.

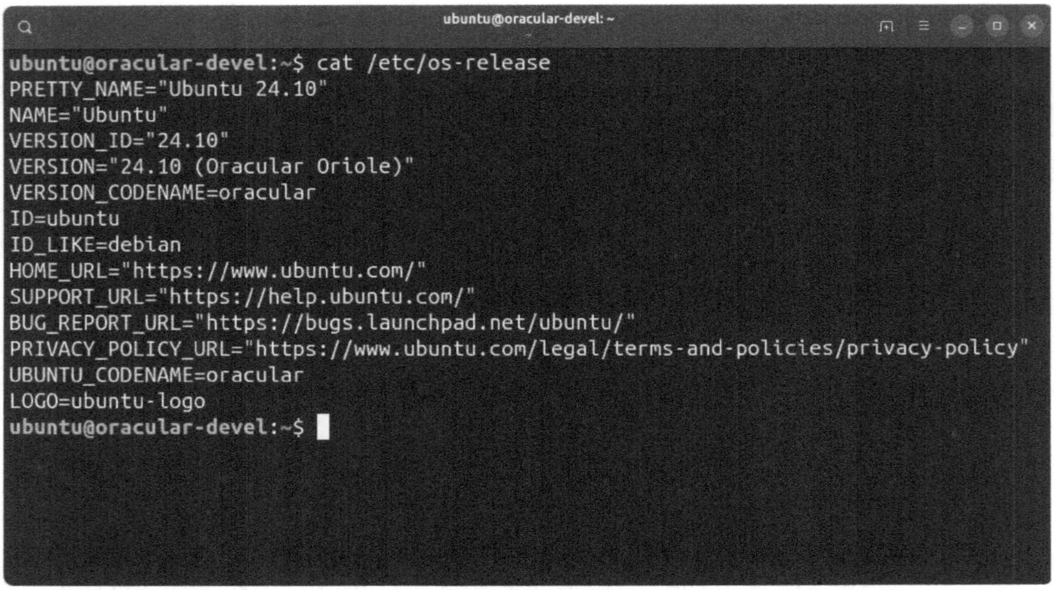

Figure 15.1 – Ubuntu 24.10 container

Figure 15.1 shows a container based on Ubuntu 24.10 (Oracular Oriole) with our home directory mounted in the container.

A development workflow like this is convenient. You can use your favorite editor on your computer while testing and executing in the container, which is isolated from your system.

Unlocking advanced LXD features for developers

LXD offers a range of advanced features that further enhance development workflows and provide greater control over containerized environments.

Remote access

Access and manage your LXD containers remotely through the secure REST API. This lets you control your development environments from anywhere, providing flexibility and convenience. You can use tools such as curl or dedicated LXD clients to interact with the API and manage your containers remotely. You can also configure a proxy device for secure connections, ensuring your communication with the LXD daemon is protected, especially when managing containers over untrusted networks.

Networking mastery

LXD allows you to configure virtual networks to isolate containers and simulate different network topologies. This is invaluable for testing and development, as it allows you to create complex network scenarios and evaluate your application's behavior in various environments. You can also create isolated networks for different projects or simulate different network conditions to test your application's resilience.

Storage management

Using different storage backends, such as ZFS or LVM, can optimize storage performance and data management. These backends offer features such as data compression, snapshots, and thin provisioning, providing flexibility and efficiency in managing container storage. You can choose the storage backend that best suits your needs, considering factors such as performance, data integrity, and storage capacity.

Profiles for reusability

Define reusable profiles with specific configurations and devices to simplify container creation and management. Profiles allow you to encapsulate common settings, such as network configuration, storage volumes, and security policies, making creating new containers with consistent configurations easy. This eliminates the need to repeatedly specify the same configuration options when creating new containers.

Moving and migrating containers

LXD allows you to move or migrate running containers between LXD hosts with minimal downtime. This feature offers flexibility in managing your development environments, allowing you to move containers to different machines for testing, scaling, or resource optimization. You can even migrate containers to various cloud providers, enabling hybrid cloud development workflows.

LXD in action: Real-world development use cases

LXD's versatility makes it suitable for a wide range of development scenarios, including the following.

Microservices development

Isolate individual microservices in separate LXD containers, fostering independent development, testing, and deployment. This approach promotes modularity, simplifies dependency management, and improves fault isolation. Each microservice can have its dedicated environment with specific dependencies and configurations, preventing conflicts and ensuring consistent behavior.

Continuous Integration/Continuous Deployment (CI/CD)

Integrate LXD into your CI/CD pipelines to create consistent build and test environments, ensuring reliable and reproducible results. LXD's ability to quickly create and destroy containers makes it ideal for automating build processes and running tests in isolated environments. This ensures that your builds and tests are not affected by inconsistencies in the host environment and provides a clean slate for each build or test run.

Reproducible research

Use LXD containers to capture and share complete research environments with all dependencies and configurations. This facilitates reproducibility and collaboration in scientific research, allowing researchers to easily recreate experiments and share their work with others. Researchers can distribute their LXD containers, ensuring that others can replicate their experiments in the same environment and with the same dependencies.

Training and education

Provide students with pre-configured development environments in LXD containers, eliminating setup complexities and ensuring a consistent learning experience. This allows students to focus on learning the core concepts without getting bogged down in environment configuration. Educators can create and distribute LXD containers with all the necessary software and tools, ensuring all students have the same learning environment.

LXD versus Docker: Choosing the right containerization tool

While Docker is a popular containerization technology, LXD offers distinct advantages for specific development scenarios and optimized integration with Ubuntu.

System containers

LXD provides system containers encompassing a complete operating system environment, including the `init` system and system services. This offers greater flexibility and compatibility for complex applications that require a complete system environment, such as those that rely on systemd or other `init` systems.

Statefulness

LXD containers can maintain state across restarts, preserving data and configurations. This benefits development environments where changes and configurations, such as databases, configuration files, and user data, must persist between sessions.

Security

LXD's strong focus on security and isolation makes it well suited for sensitive development projects or environments with strict security requirements. Using unprivileged containers and secure image management enhances the overall security posture, providing additional protection against potential vulnerabilities.

Unprivileged containers

LXD allows you to run containers with unprivileged user accounts, further enhancing security by limiting the container's access to the host system. This prevents containers from escalating privileges and accessing sensitive resources on the host.

Best practices for LXD development

To maximize the benefits of LXD for development, consider the follows best practices.

Use descriptive names

Employ clear and descriptive names for containers and images to improve organization and clarity. This will help you easily identify and manage your containers, especially when working with multiple containers or projects.

Organize with labels and tags

Use labels and tags to categorize and manage containers effectively. This lets you easily filter and search for containers based on project, environment, or other criteria, improving organization and efficiency.

Regular updates

Update container images regularly to take advantage of the latest security patches, bug fixes, and performance improvements. This will ensure your development environment is secure and up to date with the latest software.

Leverage profiles

Utilize profiles to encapsulate common configurations and devices, simplifying container creation and management. This promotes consistency and reduces duplication of effort, making it easier to create new containers with predefined settings.

Monitor resource usage

Monitor container resource usage, such as CPU, memory, and disk I/O, to identify potential performance bottlenecks and optimize resource allocation. This helps ensure your containers have sufficient resources to run efficiently and prevents resource contention issues.

Backups and disaster recovery

Implement robust backup and disaster recovery strategies to protect your valuable development work. Regularly back up container images and data to ensure you can recover from unexpected events, such as hardware failures or data corruption.

Optimize for performance

Fine-tune container settings to optimize performance for your specific development needs. This includes adjusting resource limits, configuring storage volumes for optimal performance, and using appropriate network settings.

The future of LXD in development

LXD continues to evolve with new features and enhancements, further solidifying its position as a powerful tool for developers.

Integration with Kubernetes

Ongoing efforts to integrate LXD with Kubernetes will enable developers to leverage Kubernetes' orchestration capabilities for managing containerized applications. This will provide a seamless transition from development to production, using the same containerization technology across the entire application life cycle. Developers can use LXD for local development and then seamlessly deploy their containers to Kubernetes clusters in production.

Improved virtualization support

LXD is expanding its support for virtualization technologies, offering greater flexibility and performance for demanding development workloads. This includes support for nested virtualization, allowing you to run VMs within LXD containers. This opens up new possibilities for developers working with virtualized environments within their containers.

Enhanced security features

LXD continuously improves its security features, providing robust protection for sensitive development environments. This includes enhancements to container isolation and secure boot capabilities, which further strengthen LXD's security posture, making it a secure platform for developing and testing applications.

GUI enhancements

LXD is developing a web-based user interface to provide a more user-friendly container management experience. This will make LXD more accessible to developers who prefer a visual interface over the command line, further expanding its adoption and usability.

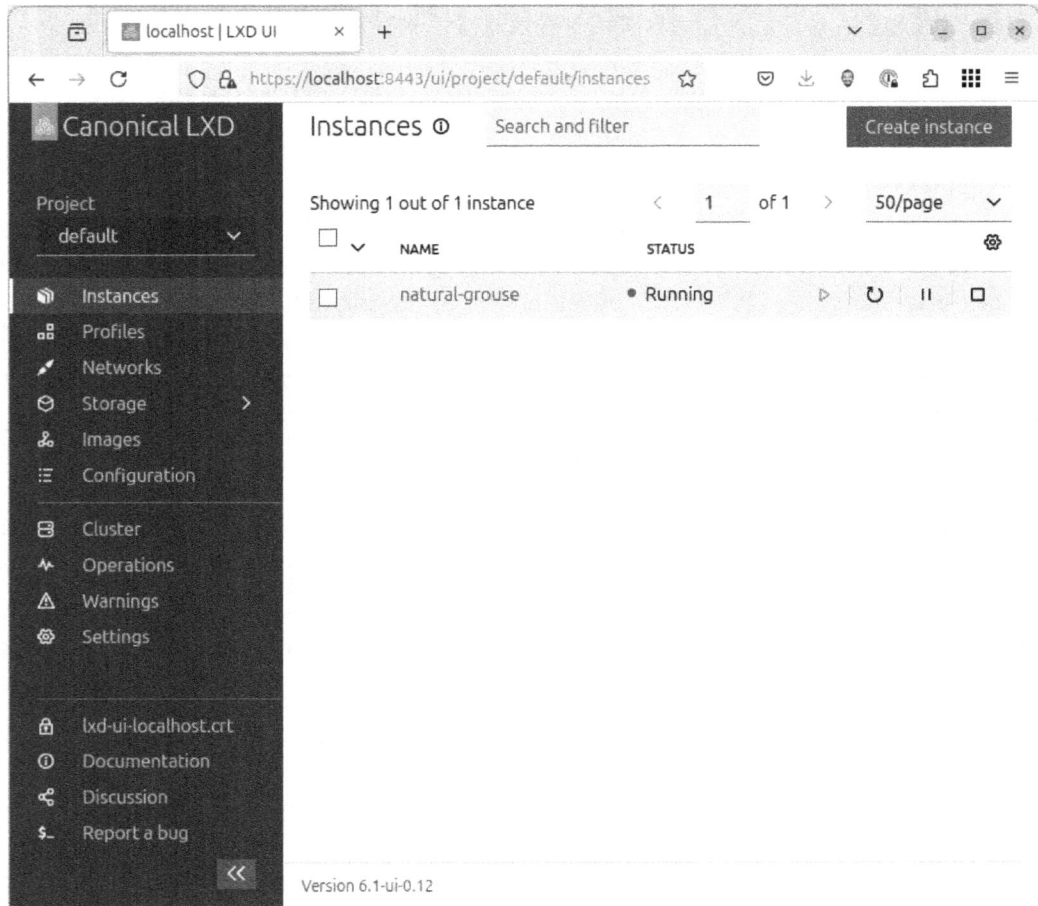

Figure 15.2 – LXD web-based user interface

The LXD web-based user interface is included in LXD but is not enabled by default. To enable the feature, run the following:

```
ken@monster:~$ sudo snap set lxd ui.enable=true
ken@monster:~$ sudo snap restart lxd
```

The feature is now enabled, but after restarting the LXD service, we still need to configure it further:

```
ken@monster:~$ lxc config set core.https_address :8443
```

Accessing the web user interface

Open your web browser and navigate to `https://localhost:8443`. If you're running LXD on a remote server, replace `localhost` with the server's IP address.

Setting up authentication

Since LXD uses a self-signed certificate by default, your browser will likely display a security warning. Proceed through the warning, then you'll be prompted to create a client certificate for secure access:

1. Click **Create a new certificate**.
2. Follow the on-screen instructions to generate and download the certificate files.
3. You'll need to add the public key to the server's trust store using the `lxc config trust add <certificate-path>` command.
4. Import the private key into your browser.

To learn more about using the LXD web-based user interface, see `https://documentation.ubuntu.com/lxd/en/latest/howto/access_ui`.

Summary

LXD has emerged as a game-changer for developers on Ubuntu, offering a compelling blend of lightweight virtualization, image-based management, robust security, and seamless integration with the Ubuntu ecosystem. By leveraging LXD's features and adhering to best practices, developers can create efficient, reproducible, and secure development environments that streamline workflows, enhance collaboration, and accelerate innovation. As LXD continues to evolve with new features and enhancements, it promises to remain a vital tool for developers in the coming years, empowering them to build cutting-edge applications confidently and efficiently. In the next chapter, we'll learn about using cloud-style virtual machines on your desktop.

Further reading

*   LXD documentation: `https://documentation.ubuntu.com/lxd/`
*   LXD user interface: `https://documentation.ubuntu.com/lxd/en/latest/howto/access_ui/`

Join the CloudPro Newsletter with 44000+ Subscribers

Want to know what's happening in cloud computing, DevOps, IT administration, networking, and more? Scan the QR code to subscribe to **CloudPro**, our weekly newsletter for 44,000+ tech professionals who want to stay informed and ahead of the curve.

https://packt.link/cloudpro

16

Cloud-Style VMs on Your Desktop

In the ever-evolving world of software development, having a clean, secure, reproducible environment is paramount. Enter Multipass, a tool that leverages Ubuntu's robust virtualization capabilities to create lightweight Ubuntu **virtual machines** (**VMs**) on your local machine. This chapter delves into how Multipass can revolutionize your development workflow and offers a deeper look at its features and benefits.

In this chapter, we will cover the following topics:

- Why choose Multipass?
- Utilizing Multipass for development
- Getting the most of Multipass

Why Multipass?

Multipass acts as your personal *developer sandbox*, providing numerous advantages:

- **Isolation of projects**: Each VM provides a pristine environment, preventing dependency conflicts between projects and ensuring consistent behavior regardless of your host machine's setup. This is crucial when working with varying versions of languages, libraries, or frameworks.
- **Testing across Ubuntu releases**: Seamlessly switch between different Ubuntu versions (including LTS and interim releases) to test your application's compatibility and identify potential issues early on. This eliminates the need for complex dual-booting or cumbersome VM managers.

- **Replicating production environments**: Accurately mirror your production server setup locally, allowing you to debug and test your application in a realistic environment. This reduces the risk of unexpected behavior when deploying to production.

- **Simplified onboarding**: Create pre-configured development environments with all the necessary tools and dependencies pre-installed. This significantly reduces the setup time for new developers joining a project, ensuring they can hit the ground running.

- **Lightweight and efficient**: Multipass VMs are designed to be lightweight and consume minimal resources, ensuring smooth performance even on machines with limited hardware capabilities.

Now that we understand these key benefits, let's drill down into some more specific reasons why you may choose to use Multipass.

Multipass for development workflows

Let's delve deeper into how Multipass enhances specific development scenarios:

- **Web development**:

  - **Isolated environments**: Set up separate VMs for frontend and backend development, each with dependencies and configurations

  - **Database integration**: Install and configure databases such as MySQL, PostgreSQL, or MongoDB within the VM, ensuring data integrity and easy access for your application

  - **API development**: Develop and test APIs in a controlled environment, using tools such as Postman to interact with your API endpoints within the VM

  - **Frontend frameworks**: Experiment with different frontend frameworks (React, Angular, and Vue.js) without impacting your host machine's setup

- **Cross-platform development**:

  - **Multiple Ubuntu versions**: Run different Ubuntu releases simultaneously to test your application's behavior across various environments

  - **GUI applications**: Utilize X11 forwarding to run graphical applications within the VM and display them on your host machine's screen

  - **Containerization**: Combine Multipass with Docker or LXD to create containerized development environments within your VMs, further enhancing isolation and portability

- **Data science**:
  - **Resource-intensive tasks**: Allocate dedicated resources (CPU, memory, and GPU) to your VMs to handle demanding machine learning models or large datasets
  - **Data science tools**: Install popular data science libraries and frameworks such as TensorFlow, PyTorch, scikit-learn, and Jupyter Notebook within the VM
  - **Reproducible environments**: Create consistent environments for data analysis and model training, ensuring the reproducibility of your experiments

As you can see, Multipass is a very powerful tool for just about any development task. Let's take a peek at some of the more advanced features of Multipass.

Advanced Multipass uses

Multipass offers a range of advanced features:

- **Cloud-init**: Automate instance customization using cloud-init configuration files. This allows you to define user accounts, install packages, configure network settings, and more during the instance launch.
- **File sharing**: Seamlessly share directories between your host machine and VMs using the mount feature of Multipass. This provides convenient access to your project files without the need for constant file transfers.
- **Snapshots**: Create snapshots of your VMs to preserve specific states. This allows you to revert to a previous state, providing a safety net for experimentation or troubleshooting.
- **Aliases**: Define aliases for frequently used Multipass commands to streamline your workflow and reduce typing.
- **Networking**: Configure network settings, including static IP addresses, port forwarding, and virtual networks, to tailor your VMs to specific needs.
- **Integration with other tools**: Integrate Multipass with tools such as Vagrant, Terraform, and Ansible to automate VM management and orchestration.

Now that we understand what a powerful tool Multipass is, let's learn how we can get started to get the most out of its deep integration in the Ubuntu ecosystem.

Getting started with Multipass

Now it's time to install Multipass, and learn how to create, launch, and use VMs.

Installation

Multipass is readily available across various platforms:

- **Ubuntu**: Open your terminal and run `sudo snap install multipass`
- **macOS**: Download the installer from the official Multipass website: `https://multipass.run`
- **Windows**: Install it through the Microsoft Store or download the installer from the Multipass website

While Multipass is available on macOS and Windows, this book will focus on using it on Ubuntu.

Launching your first instance

Creating a VM is remarkably simple:

```
ken@monster:~$ multipass launch
```

This command launches an Ubuntu instance with the latest LTS release. To customize your instance, utilize these options:

- **Naming**: `--name my-dev-vm` assigns a specific name to your instance
- **Resource allocation**: `--cpus 2 --mem 4G` allocates CPU cores and memory
- **Cloud-init**: `--cloud-init config.yaml` uses a configuration file for automated setup

Accessing your instance

There are several ways to interact with your instance:

- **Shell access**: `multipass shell my-dev-vm` opens a shell session within your VM
- **Command execution**: `multipass exec my-dev-vm -- <command>` executes a command within the instance. Replace `<command>` with any command you would like to execute in the VM
- **File transfer**: `multipass transfer my-dev-vm:/home/ubuntu/myfile.txt .` copies files between the VM and the current directory of your host machine

Now, you should have a good understanding of how to use the key features of Multipass, including creating, launching, managing, and accessing VMs from a command line.

Multipass GUI

While the Multipass command-line interface is intuitive and powerful, there's also a GUI that makes managing your Multipass instances a breeze.

The Multipass GUI is also quite intuitive, including a catalog of images to choose from, a view of all your instances with details, and the ability to get a console in each instance.

Multipass catalog

Launching the Multipass GUI takes you right into the catalog of VM and appliance images to select, as seen in *Figure 16.1*.

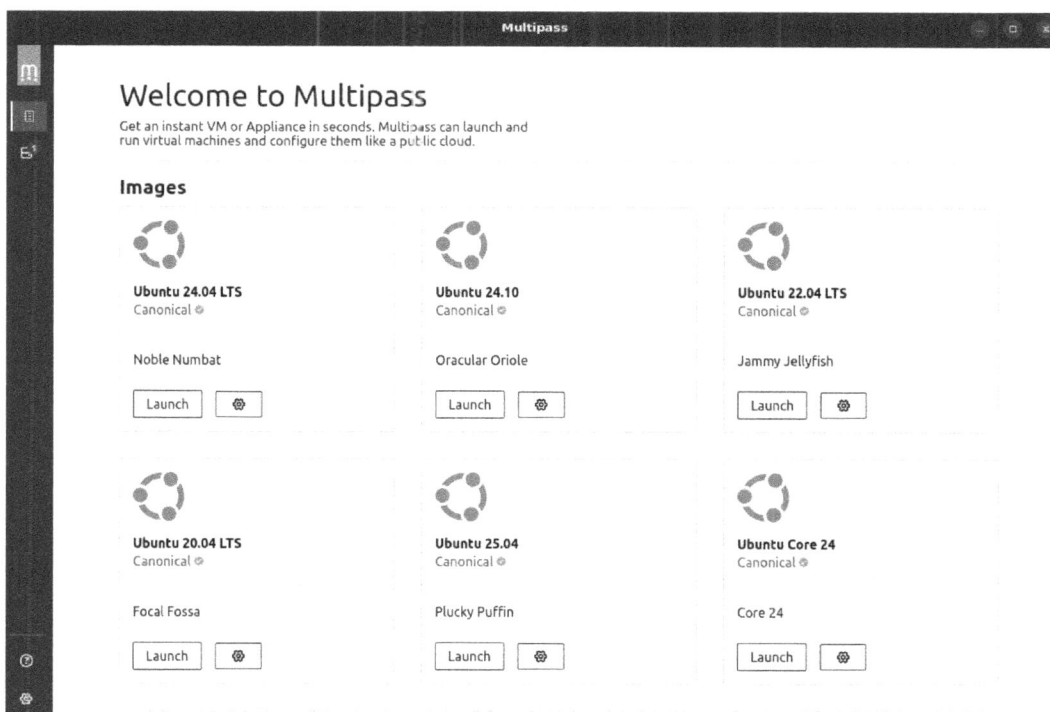

Figure 16.1 – Multipass catalog

Multipass instances

As shown in *Figure 16.2*, selecting the second button on the toolbar displays a list of available VM instances with controls to start, stop, suspend, and delete them.

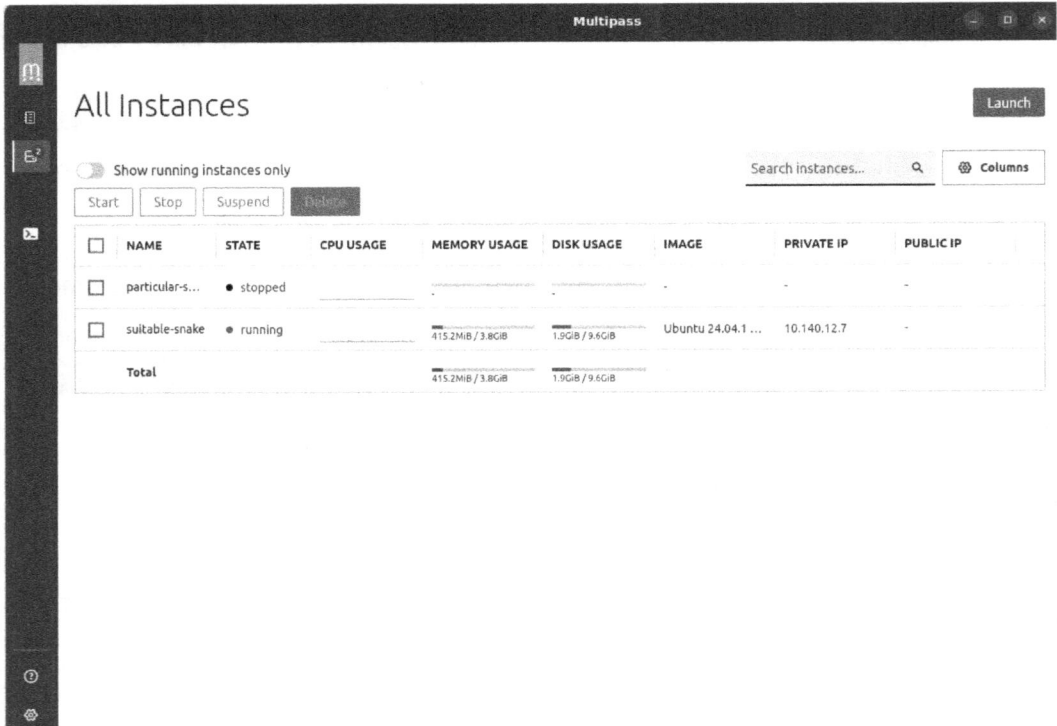

Figure 16.2 – Multipass instances

Multipass shell

Selecting an instance from the instances page or the quick list in the toolbar opens a shell in the running instance. The shell provided by the Multipass GUI will look familiar and closely match the terminal experience in the native Ubuntu Desktop.

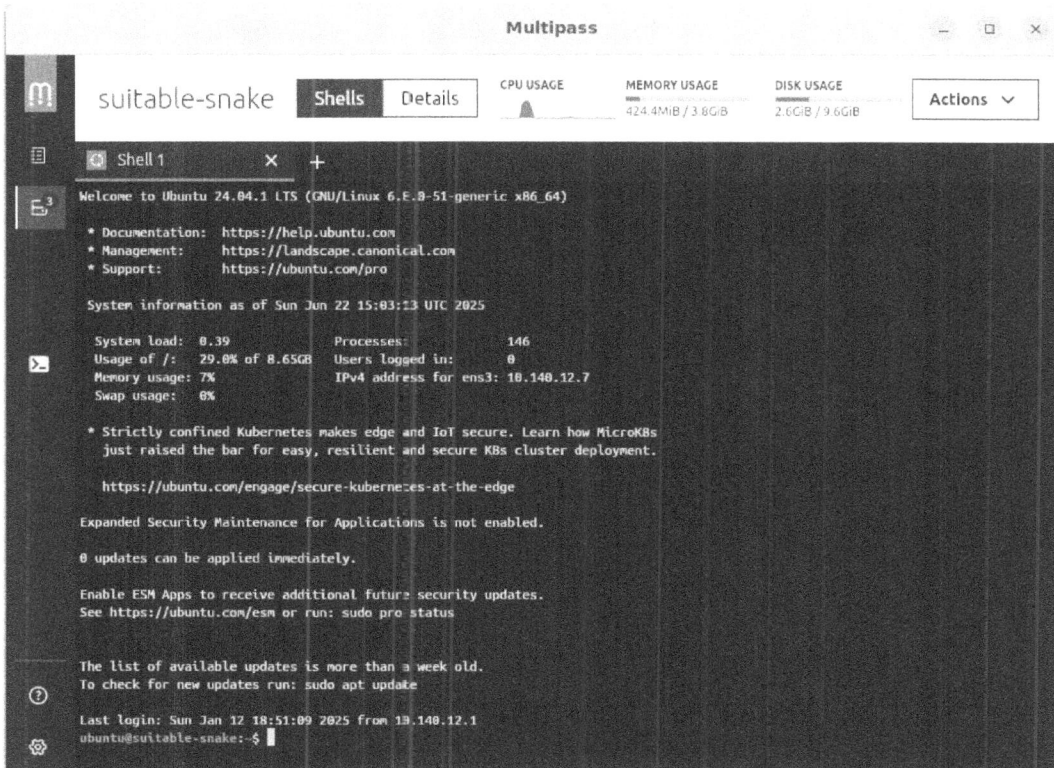

Figure 16.3 – Shell

In this shell, you can run any commands you expect on Ubuntu. For example, you can install packages, configure a database, and set up a web application you're working on.

Multipass details (configuration)

Switching to the **Details** view displays more information on the configured VM instance, allowing more advanced configuration. As shown in *Figure 16.4*, we can change the number of virtual CPUs, memory, or even disk size.

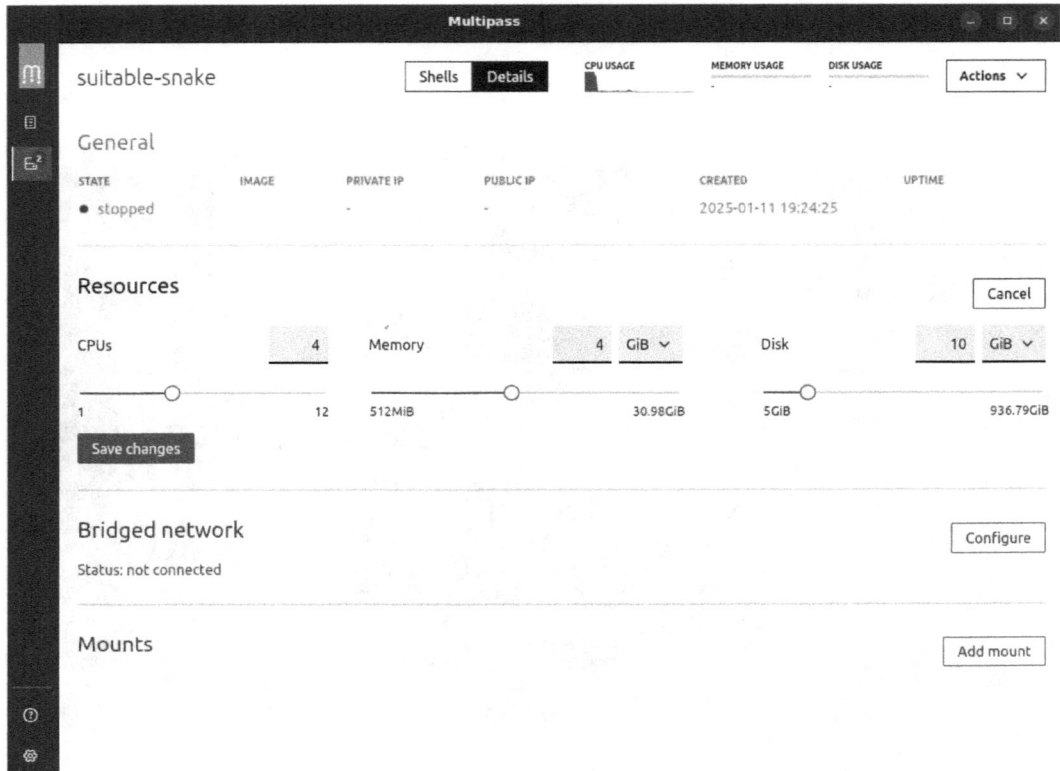

Figure 16.4 – Instance configuration: Resources

These settings can only be changed while the instance is stopped. Once it is started again, the VM will use the updated configuration.

Another helpful feature is sharing directories from your host machine with VM instances. The GUI, shown in *Figure 16.5*, makes this very intuitive: on the left, select the directory on your computer, and on the right, select the directory where it should be mounted in the VM.

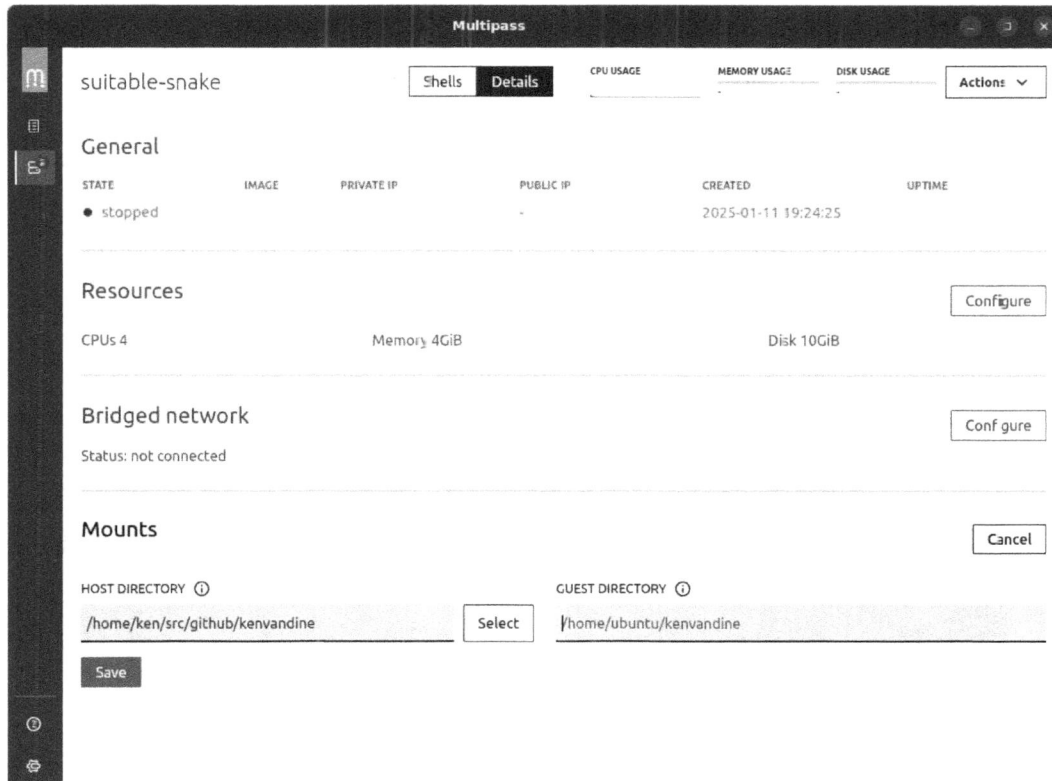

Figure 16.5 – Instance configuration: Mounts

As you can see in *Figure 16.6*, I mounted /home/ken/src/github/kenvandine on my computer at /home/ubuntu/kenvandine in the VM instance.

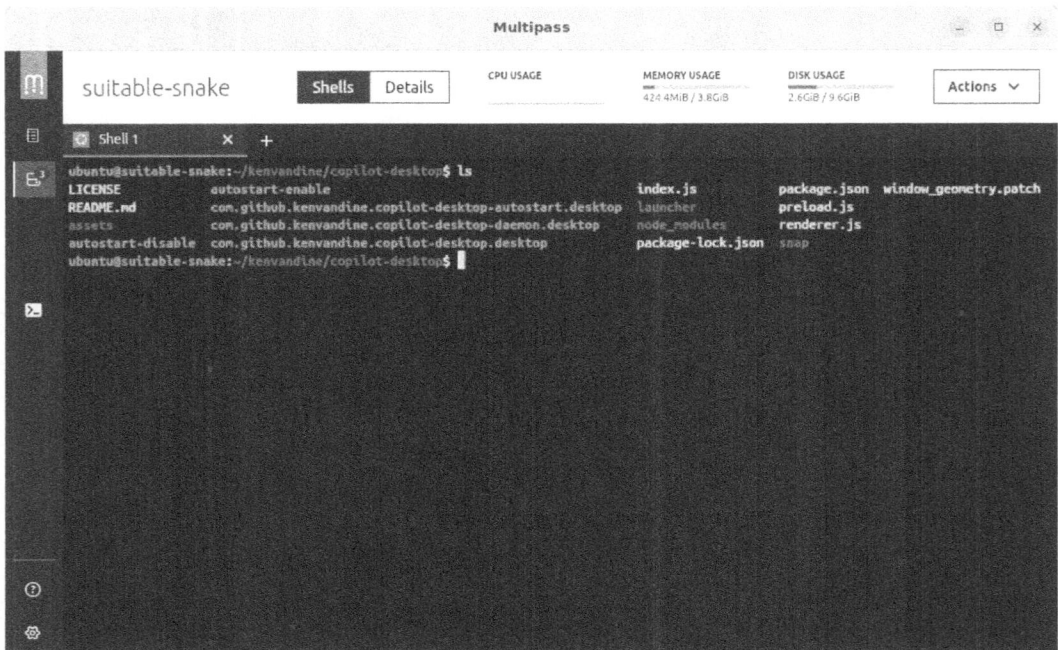

Figure 16.6 – Multipass shell with mount

As you can imagine, seamlessly exposing files from the host makes this a potent development tool. I often start pristine VM instances to quickly test code I'm working on across different versions of Ubuntu.

Summary

In this chapter, we've learned about the flexibility and security provided by leveraging VMs with Multipass. Bringing cloud-style VM capabilities to your Ubuntu Desktop system gives you unmatched parallels with application development targeting cloud deployment. In the next chapter, we'll expand on that concept, learning the basics of Kubernetes and how to run your clusters right on your Ubuntu Desktop system.

Further reading

- Multipass: https://multipass.run

17

Kubernetes Development on Your Desktop

While Multipass excels at providing isolated virtual environments for development ard LXD excels at providing well-integrated container environments, modern applications n-creasingly rely on containerization and orchestration. This is where Kubernetes shines, and MicroK8s makes it remarkably easy to set up a fully functional Kubernetes cluster directly on your Ubuntu machine. This chapter delves deep into how MicroK8s can empower your Kubernetes development workflow, exploring its extensive features and diverse use cases.

In this chapter, we will cover the following topics:

- Why MicroK8s?
- How to get started
- Developing with MicroK8s
- Advanced MicroK8s techniques

Important note

This chapter will demonstrate a local Kubernetes cluster used for development on your Ubuntu Desktop system, and it assumes prior experience with Kubernetes. To learn more, see https://kubernetes.io.

Why MicroK8s?

MicroK8s is a lightweight, single-package Kubernetes distribution specifically designed to simplify development.

MicroK8s is ideally suited for the local development of Kubernetes workflows on your desktop or workstation. Some key benefits of MicroK8s include the following:

- **Simplicity**: Install a complete and conformant Kubernetes cluster with a single command, abstracting the complexities of setting up individual Kubernetes components. This lets you focus on developing your applications, rather than wrestling with infrastructure.

- **Efficiency**: With its minimal footprint, MicroK8s is ideal for laptops and re-source-constrained environments. It enables you to run a full-fledged Kubernetes cluster without significant overhead, ensuring smooth performance even on less powerful machines.

- **Up to date**: MicroK8s closely tracks upstream Kubernetes releases, providing access to the latest features, security updates, and bug fixes. This ensures you always work with Kubernetes' most current and secure version.

- **Extensible**: Easily expand the functionality of your cluster by adding a wide range of services with simple commands. Integrate Istio for service mesh capabilities, Knative for serverless workloads, Prometheus for monitoring, and many more.

- **Consistent**: MicroK8s provides a Kubernetes environment consistent with production deployments, allowing you to develop and test applications in a realistic setting. This minimizes the risk of encountering unexpected behavior when deploying to production.

- **Secure by default**: Security is a top priority in MicroK8s. It comes with secure defaults, minimizing potential vulnerabilities and protecting your development environment.

- **Strict conformance**: MicroK8s passes the same conformance tests as upstream Kubernetes, guaranteeing that your applications will behave consistently across different Kubernetes environments.

As you can see, MicroK8s is a powerful yet lightweight Kubernetes distribution that is nicely integrated with the Ubuntu ecosystem.

Getting started with MicroK8s

Getting started with MicroK8s is straightforward. Let's learn how to install and access your MicroK8s cluster.

Installation

Installing MicroK8s on Ubuntu is incredibly straightforward:

```
ken@monster:~$ sudo snap install microk8s --classic
ken@monster:~$ sudo usermod -a -G microk8s $USER
ken@monster:~$ newgrp microk8s
```

This command installs the latest stable version of MicroK8s from the Snap Store.

Verification

After installation, check the status of your MicroK8s cluster and wait for it to be fully operational:

```
ken@monster:~$ microk8s status --wait-ready
```

This command ensures all Kubernetes components are running correctly and the cluster is ready.

Accessing the cluster

MicroK8s conveniently bundles **kubectl**, the Kubernetes command-line tool. However, you need to configure it to interact with your MicroK8s cluster:

```
ken@monster:~$ microk8s kubectl config view --raw > $HOME/.kube/config
```

These commands set up your kubectl configuration to point to the MicroK8s cluster, allowing you to manage and interact with it.

Developing with MicroK8s

With MicroK8s installed and configured, let's dig into how we might deploy applications and services on our cluster. If you have prior experience with Kubernetes, you will find the process very familiar.

Deploying applications

Deploying applications to your MicroK8s cluster is seamless, whether using YAML manifests or Helm charts. For instance, to deploy a simple Nginx web server, run the following:

```
ken@monster:~$ microk8s kubectl apply -f https://k8s.io/examples/
application/deployment.yaml
```

This command creates a deployment and service for Nginx, making it accessible within your cluster.

Accessing services

MicroK8s offers several ways to access services running within your cluster:

- **Port forwarding**: `kubectl port-forward service/nginx 8080:80` forwards traffic from your local port `8080` to the Nginx service running in the cluster. This allows you to access the service from your host machine as if running locally.

- **ClusterIP**: Each service in Kubernetes is assigned a ClusterIP address accessible from within the cluster. This enables internal communication between services within your MicroK8s environment.

- **NodePort**: This exposes services on a static port on each node in the cluster. This allows external access to your services, even from outside the cluster network.

- **Ingress**: For more sophisticated routing and external access, use an Ingress controller such as Nginx Ingress. Ingress allows you to route traffic to different services based on hostnames or paths, providing a flexible way to manage external access to your applications.

Exploring add-ons

MicroK8s provides a rich ecosystem of add-ons to enhance your development environment:

- **DNS**: Enable CoreDNS for service discovery within the cluster. This allows services to find each other by name, simplifying communication and configuration.

- **Storage**: Add persistent storage with `hostPath` for development purposes or Rook for a more production-like storage solution. This enables you to store data that persists even if Pods are restarted or rescheduled.

- **Ingress**: Install an Ingress controller such as Nginx Ingress to manage external access to your services. Ingress provides features such as load balancing, SSL termination, and path-based routing.

- **Istio**: Enable Istio to add service mesh capabilities to your cluster. Istio provides advanced features such as traffic management, security policies, and observability for your microservices.

- **Knative**: Deploy serverless workloads with Knative, enabling auto-scaling, event-driven architectures, and simplified deployments.

- **Registry**: Enable a private container registry to store and manage your container images. This lets you keep your images secure and easily accessible within your development environment.

- **Metrics server**: Collect resource usage metrics for Pods and nodes, providing insights into your applications' performance and resource consumption.

Enable these add-ons with simple commands such as `microk8s enable dns`, making it easy to customize your MicroK8s environment based on your needs.

For example, to enable the dashboard, run the following:

```
ken@monster:~$ microk8s enable dashboard
ken@monster:~$ microk8s dashboard-proxy
Checking if Dashboard is running.
Infer repository core for addon dashboard
Waiting for Dashboard to core up.
Trying to get token from microk8s-dashboard-token
Waiting for secret token (attempt 0)
Dashboard will be available at https://127.0.0.1:10443
```

This will enable the dashboard, which can be seen in *Figure 17.1*. Then, `microk8s dashboard-proxy` displays the information necessary to access the dashboard, such as the URL and a login token.

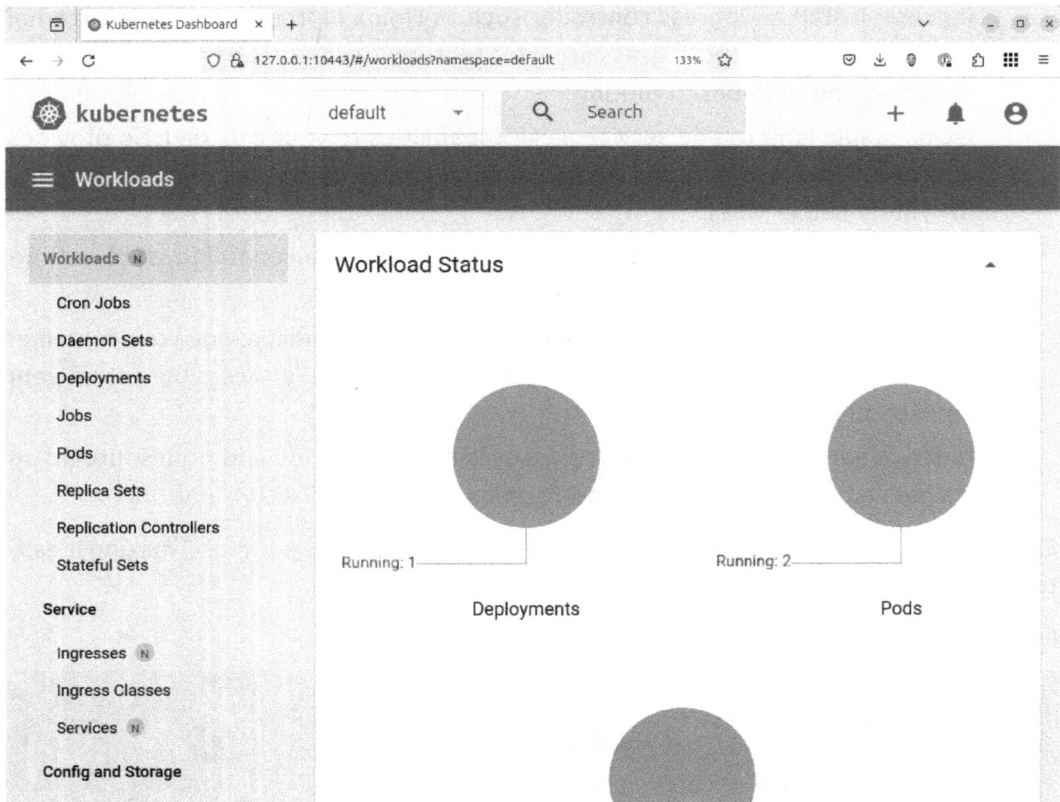

Figure 17.1 – MicroK8s dashboard

We now have our MicroK8s cluster running with our desired add-ons configured. As you can see, it's really just like any other Kubernetes distribution, but perfectly tailored for workstation or desktop use.

MicroK8s for specific workflows

As a Kubernetes distribution tailored for workstation and desktop use, let's look at some of the key workflows for MicroK8s:

- **Microservices development**:

  - **Simulate microservice architectures**: MicroK8s provides an ideal environment for developing and testing microservices locally. It simulates a real-world Kubernetes environment with service discovery, networking, and scaling capabilities.

- **Service communication**: Experiment with different service communication patterns, such as synchronous and asynchronous communication, using service discovery and various networking configurations.

- **Resilience testing**: Test resilience patterns such as circuit breaking, retries, and fault injection using Istio. This helps you build robust and fault-tolerant microservices that can handle failures gracefully.

- **Machine learning**:

  - **Deploy ML models**: Deploy and manage machine learning models as containers within your MicroK8s cluster. This lets you leverage Kubernetes' scalability and resource management capabilities for your ML workloads.

  - **GPU acceleration**: If you have GPUs available, utilize them with MicroK8s for accelerated training and inference tasks. This can significantly speed up your machine learning workflows.

  - **Model serving**: Serve your trained models using frameworks such as TensorFlow Serving or TorchServe, making them accessible to other applications or users.

- **Edge computing**:

  - **Simulate edge deployments**: Run MicroK8s on resource-constrained devices such as Raspberry Pi or other edge devices to simulate edge computing environments. This allows you to test your applications in a realistic setting.

  - **Develop edge applications**: Develop and test applications specifically designed for edge computing scenarios, such as IoT applications, data processing at the edge, and remote deployments.

- **CI/CD pipelines**:

  - **Local Kubernetes environment**: Integrate MicroK8s into your CI/CD pipelines to test deployments in a Kubernetes environment before pushing to production. This helps catch potential issues early in the development process.

  - **Reproducible builds**: Ensure consistent deployments across different stages of your pipeline by using MicroK8s as a standardized Kubernetes environment.

You can see that MicroK8s is not only lightweight but also a powerful tool with many uses.

Advanced MicroK8s techniques

Even though MicroK8s is lightweight, and designed to simplify Kubernetes workflows on a desktop or workstation, there are more advanced uses. Let's explore them:

- **Multi-node clusters**: For more advanced scenarios, create a multi-node MicroK8s cluster. This allows you to test high availability, distributed deployments, and more complex Kubernetes configurations.
- **Custom configuration**: Fine-tune MicroK8s using configuration files to customize its behavior and settings. This gives you greater control over your Kubernetes environment.
- **Snapshots**: Create snapshots of your MicroK8s cluster to preserve specific states. This allows you to quickly revert to a previous state if needed, providing a safety net for experimentation or troubleshooting.
- **Integration with other tools**: Seamlessly integrate MicroK8s with other tools in your development workflow, such as kubectl for managing the cluster, Helm for package management, and Kustomize for configuration customization.

MicroK8s is a powerful tool in a small package. You should now be familiar enough with MicroK8s to start your own adventures with Kubernetes.

Summary

MicroK8s provides a streamlined and efficient pathway to develop and test Kubernetes applications directly on your Ubuntu machine. Its user-friendly nature, extensive feature set, and strict conformance with upstream Kubernetes make it an ideal choice for local development, experimentation, and learning. By embracing MicroK8s, you can harness the power of Kubernetes and confidently build cloud-native applications. In the next chapter, we will learn how to leverage MicroK8s for data science workloads.

Further reading

- MicroK8s: `https://microk8s.io/`
- Kubernetes: `https://kubernetes.io/`

18

Building Your Data Science Toolkit

Ubuntu, renowned for its open source foundation, stability, and extensive software ecosystem, has long been the preferred platform for data scientists. Canonical, the driving force behind Ubuntu, elevates this experience with **Data Science Stack** (**DSS**) – a meticulously curated collection of tools designed to streamline the entire data science workflow. This chapter delves deep into how Canonical's DSS empowers you to effortlessly develop, train, and deploy machine learning models, unlocking new levels of efficiency and productivity.

In this chapter, we will cover the following topics:

- The components of Data Science Stack
- The importance of reproducibility
- Getting started through model deployment

Why Canonical's Data Science Stack?

DSS offers a compelling array of advantages for data scientists:

- **Simplified setup** It eliminates manually installing and configuring various data science tools and their dependencies. DSS provides a pre-packaged environment with popular libraries and frameworks, allowing you to jumpstart your projects without the hassle of complex setup procedures.

- **Optimized performance**: DSS is meticulously tuned for optimal performance on Ubuntu, leveraging hardware acceleration (especially for GPUs) and efficient resource management to accelerate your data science workflows. This translates to faster training times, quicker experimentation, and improved efficiency.

- **Streamlined workflow**: DSS integrates with popular tools such as Jupyter Notebook and MLflow, creating a cohesive environment for experimentation, model tracking, and collaboration. This integration simplifies your workflow and allows you to focus on your data and models, rather than managing disparate tools.

- **Open source and free**: Built on a foundation of open source technologies, DSS is free to use, making it accessible to everyone, from individual data scientists to large organizations. This fosters a collaborative and inclusive environment for data science innovation.

- **Enterprise support**: For production deployments and mission-critical workloads, Canonical offers enterprise-grade support for DSS, ensuring stability, reliability, and expert assistance when needed.

- **Reproducibility**: DSS promotes reproducibility by providing a consistent environment with predefined versions of libraries and frameworks. This ensures that your experiments and models can be easily recreated and shared with others.

> Important note
>
> This chapter will demonstrate leveraging Canonical DSS to ease the setup for your data science workflow on your Ubuntu Desktop system, and it assumes prior experience with standard data science tools.

The components of Data Science Stack

DSS comprises several key components that work together harmoniously to create a powerful and efficient data science environment:

- **MicroK8s**: As we learned in *Chapter 17*, MicroK8s is a lightweight Kubernetes distribution that is the foundation for deploying and managing your containerized data science workloads. MicroK8s simplifies the deployment and scaling of your applications, providing a robust and reliable platform for your data science projects.

- **Jupyter Notebook**: This is a web-based interactive environment that has become a staple for data scientists. Jupyter Notebook allows you to write code, visualize data, and document your work in a single, interactive document. DSS provides a pre-configured Jupyter Notebook server that is ready to use with popular data science libraries.

- **MLflow**: This is an open source platform designed to manage the entire machine learning life cycle. MLflow enables you to track experiments, log parameters and metrics, compare different model versions, and package and deploy models. DSS integrates MLflow seamlessly, making managing and reproducing your machine learning experiments easy.

- **TensorFlow and PyTorch**: Two popular deep learning frameworks are readily available for use with DSS. These frameworks are optimized for GPU acceleration, allowing you to train complex models efficiently.

- **Other essential libraries**: DSS includes a curated selection of essential data science libraries, including NumPy for numerical computing, pandas for data manipulation and analysis, and scikit-learn for machine learning algorithms. This provides a comprehensive toolkit for your data science tasks.

Getting started with Data Science Stack

DSS provides an integrated environment for deploying and managing machine learning workloads on Ubuntu. This section will guide you through installing, configuring, and launching essential components such as Jupyter Notebook and MLflow to streamline your data science workflows.

Installing DSS

Installing DSS on Ubuntu is remarkably simple:

```
ken@monster:~$ sudo snap install --classic microk8s
microk8s (1.31/stable) v1.31.5 from Canonical√ installed
ken@monster:~$ sudo microk8s enable hostpath-storage
ken@monster:~$ sudo microk8s enable dns
ken@monster:~$ sudo microk8s enable rbac
ken@monster:~$ sudo snap install data-science-stack
data-science-stack (1/stable) 0.1-8742e6d3c0a5450c6dbc4ea3788a from
Canonical√ installed
```

This command installs the DSS snap package, which encapsulates all the necessary components and their dependencies.

Optional configuration

If you have an NVIDIA GPU, you should enable the GPU operator in MicroK8s to utilize the hardware best:

```
ken@monster:~$ sudo microk8s enable nvidia
Infer repository core for addon nvidia
Enabling DNS
Using host configuration from /run/systemd/resolve/resolv.conf
Applying manifest
serviceaccount/coredns created
configmap/coredns created
deployment.apps/coredns created
service/kube-dns created
clusterrole.rbac.authorization.k8s.io/coredns created
clusterrolebinding.rbac.authorization.k8s.io/coredns created
CoreDNS service deployed with IP address 10.152.183.10
DNS is enabled
Addon core/helm3 is already enabled
Checking if NVIDIA driver is already installed
GPU 0: Quadro T2000 (UUID: GPU-b66bbd7c-eeae-485f-1578-0f60d29e4119)
"nvidia" already exists with the same configuration, skipping
Hang tight while we grab the latest from your chart repositories...
...Successfully got an update from the "nvidia" chart repository
Update Complete. ⎈Happy Helming!⎈
Deploy NVIDIA GPU operator
Using host GPU driver
W0216 13:06:50.956881 3666226 warnings.go:70] spec.template.spec.
affinity.nodeAffinity.preferredDuringSchedulingIgnoredDuringExecution[0].
preference.matchExpressions[0].key: node-role.kubernetes.io/master is use
"node-role.kubernetes.io/control-plane" instead
W0216 13:06:50.962865 3666226 warnings.go:70] spec.template.spec.
affinity.nodeAffinity.preferredDuringSchedulingIgnoredDuringExecution[0].
preference.matchExpressions[0].key: node-role.kubernetes.io/master is use
"node-role.kubernetes.io/control-plane" instead
NAME: gpu-operator
LAST DEPLOYED: Sun Feb 16 13:06:50 2025
NAMESPACE: gpu-operator-resources
STATUS: deployed
```

```
REVISION: 1
TEST SUITE: None
Deployed NVIDIA GPU operator
```

Initializing DSS

To configure DSS to utilize your MicroK8s deployment, we need to initialize DSS with the local MicroK8s configuration:

```
ken@monster:~$ dss initialize --kubeconfig "$(sudo microk8s config)"
Executing initialize command
Storing provided kubeconfig to /home/ken/snap/data-science-stack/36/.dss/
config
Waiting for deployment mlflow in namespace dss to be ready...
Deployment mlflow in namespace dss is ready
DSS initialized. To create your first notebook run the command:

dss create

Examples:
  dss create my-notebook --image=pytorch
  dss create my-notebook --image=kubeflownotebookswg/jupyter-scipy:v1.8.0

ken@monster:~$
```

Initialization will take some time, depending on the network bandwidth constraints.

Launching Jupyter Notebook

Once installed, you can launch a Jupyter Notebook server with a single command:

```
ken@monster:~$ dss create pytorch-cuda --image=kubeflownotebookswg/
jupyter-pytorch-cuda-full
Executing create command
Waiting for deployment pytorch-cuda in namespace dss to be ready...
Deployment pytorch-cuda in namespace dss is ready
Success: Notebook pytorch-cuda created successfully.
Access the notebook at http://10.152.183.201:80.
```

This command fetches a container with everything necessary for Jupyter Notebook with PyTorch and CUDA, starts the Jupyter Notebook server, and provides a link to open the notebook in your web browser, providing a familiar and user-friendly interface for your data science work.

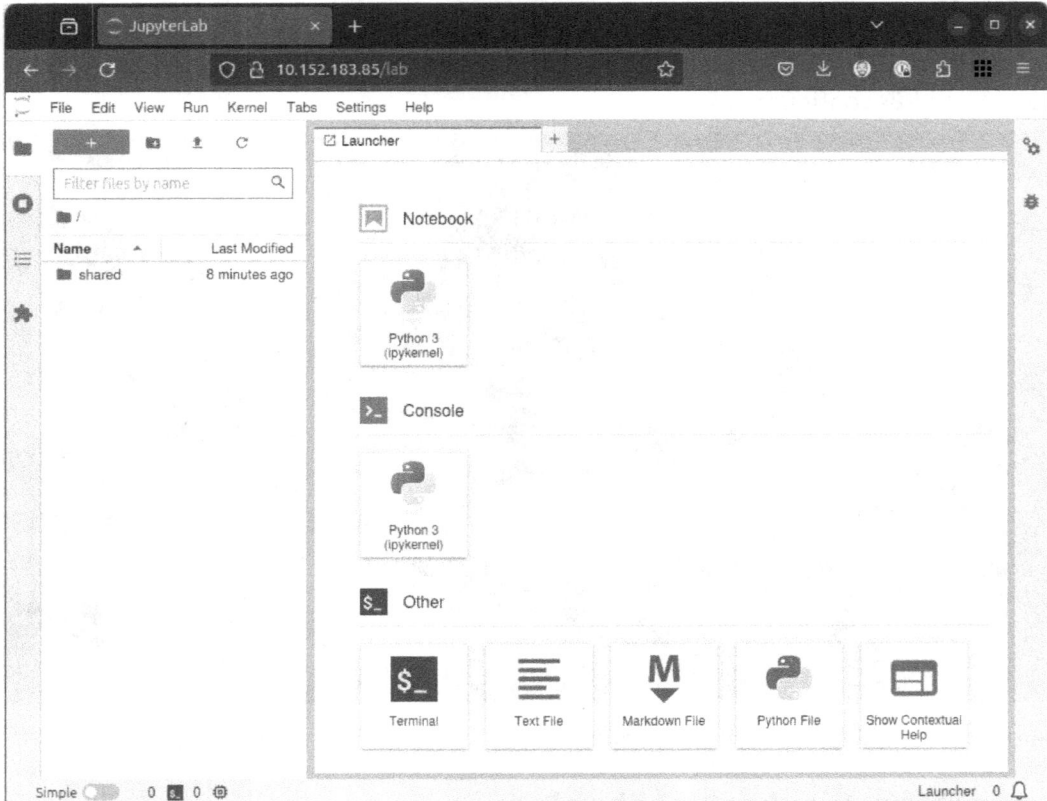

Figure 18.1 – Jupyter Notebook

If you have an NVIDIA GPU, you can easily verify that it's working with the included NVIDIA CUDA drivers in Jupyter Notebook by running the following Python code:

```
import torch
torch.cuda.is_available()
```

This will return true if CUDA is set up correctly and a compatible GPU is present.

Accessing MLflow

Similarly, you can launch the MLflow user interface with the following:

```
ken@monster:~$ dss status
MLflow deployment: Ready
MLflow URL: http://10.152.183.230:5000
NVIDIA GPU acceleration: Enabled (Quadro-T2000)
Intel GPU acceleration: Disabled
```

This command provides the current status of DSS, including the URL to the MLflow web-based interface, which allows you to manage your machine learning experiments, track metrics, and compare models.

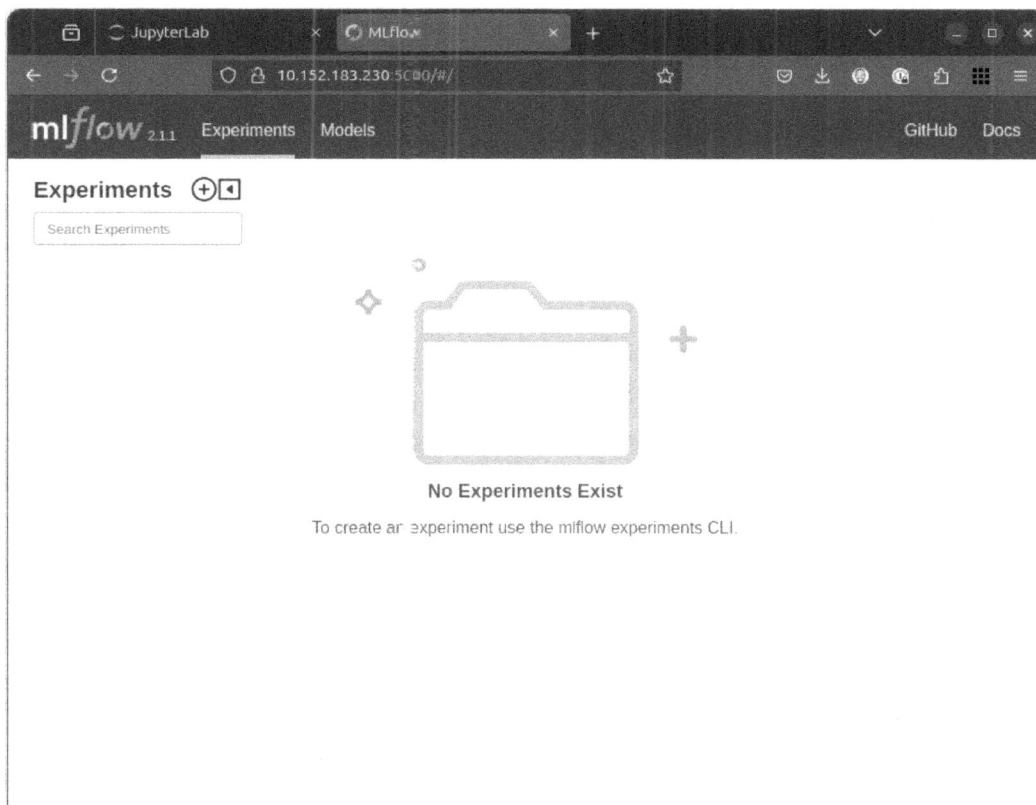

Figure 18.2 – MLflow for tracking experiments and models

Leveraging Data Science Stack

Canonical's DSS streamlines managing the entire life cycle of your machine learning journey, from model development through model deployment.

Developing models

DSS provides a ready-to-use environment for developing machine learning models. You can leverage the power of Jupyter Notebook to write code, experiment with different algorithms, visualize your data, and document your findings in a single, interactive document.

Training models

DSS harnesses MicroK8s' capabilities to distribute training workloads across multiple nodes. This enables faster and more efficient model training, especially when dealing with large datasets or complex models.

Tracking experiments

Mlflow's integration with DSS lets you track your experiments, log parameters and metrics, and compare different model versions. This helps you gain a deep understanding of your models' performance, identify areas for improvement, and make informed decisions throughout the development process.

Deploying models

DSS simplifies the deployment of your trained models, allowing you to package and deploy them as containerized applications. This makes it easy to deploy your models to various environments, from local machines to cloud platforms, ensuring consistency and reproducibility.

Advanced usage

While Canonical DSS streamlines the entire life cycle, making it easy to create reliable and reproducible machine learning development environments, it does not limit your capabilities. You can easily scale up your workflow to meet your needs:

- **Customizing environments**: Tailor your DSS environment to your needs by adding new libraries, frameworks, and tools. This flexibility allows you to create a personalized data science workspace that caters to your unique requirements.

- **Integrating with other tools**: Seamlessly integrate DSS with other data science tools and platforms, such as cloud-based services, data pipelines, and specialized libraries. This expands the capabilities of DSS and allows you to build comprehensive data science workflows.

- **Scaling for production**: You can quickly scale your DSS environment by adding more nodes to your MicroK8s cluster for production deployments. This ensures that your data science applications can handle increasing workloads and demands.

- **GPU management**: DSS simplifies the management of CPUs, allowing you to allocate resources to specific workloads and optimize performance for GPU-accelerated tasks.

- **Security**: DSS inherits the security features of MicroK8s, providing a secure environment for your data science projects. You can further enhance security by configuring network policies, access controls, and other security measures.

Canonical's DSS is a comprehensive and user-friendly platform for accelerating data science workflows on Ubuntu. With its simplified setup, optimized performance, and integrated tools, DSS empowers you to focus on what truly matters—extracting valuable insights from your data and building innovative machine learning solutions. Whether you're a seasoned data scientist or just starting your journey, DSS provides the tools and environment you need to succeed in the exciting world of data science.

Summary

In this chapter, we've learned how Canonical provides innovative tooling to streamline your data science workflow—leveraging modern Kubernetes tooling to deploy the tools you need to get your job done.

Further reading

- Canonical's Data Science Stack: https://documentation.ubuntu.com/data-science-stack/en/latest/
- MLflow: https://ubuntu.com/blog/what-is-mlflow

19

Embracing the Spirit of Ubuntu

As we conclude this exploration of Ubuntu, the ultimate distribution of the Linux operating system, we're not just closing a book; we're opening a door to a vast and dynamic ecosystem. Learning Ubuntu isn't just about mastering commands or navigating a desktop; it's about engaging with a powerful, flexible platform built on the principles of open source and community collaboration. The name *Ubuntu* itself, though rooted in a philosophy of interconnectedness, aptly describes the spirit of the operating system project: a shared effort for the benefit of all users. This final chapter reflects on the journey through Ubuntu's capabilities and invites you to continue exploring its ever-evolving landscape.

A retrospective: exploring the potential of Ubuntu

Throughout this book, we've journeyed from the fundamentals of installation and desktop navigation to the power of the command line, software management, server administration, and the vibrant community that supports it all. We've seen Ubuntu's versatility – how it capably serves as a user-friendly desktop for newcomers, a robust platform for developers, a reliable server platform, and a foundation for cutting-edge cloud, AI/ML, and IoT technologies.

We've explored the elegance and ease of use of the GNOME desktop (and touched upon other flavors), the efficiency of the APT package manager, the security features that underpin the system, and the flexibility offered by tools such as Snaps. We've seen how Ubuntu lowers the barrier to entry for Linux while simultaneously offering the depth and control that experienced users and administrators demand. Its potential lies in its adaptability, vast software repositories, strong security posture, and collective knowledge of its global community. Ubuntu offers a compelling solution, whether you're writing code, managing infrastructure, conducting research, or simply seeking a dependable and free operating system.

Beyond the book: the open road of exploration

Mastering the concepts in this book is just the beginning. The true power of Ubuntu unfolds as you integrate it into your workflow, customize it to your needs, and engage with the broader ecosystem. The road ahead is wide open for exploration:

- **Dive deeper**: Explore advanced command-line techniques, delve into system configuration files, or learn shell scripting to automate tasks.

- **Customize your experience**: Try different desktop environments (KDE Plasma, XFCE, MATE, etc.) available through official Ubuntu flavors or install them yourself. Experiment with themes, icons, and extensions.

- **Explore the software**: Beyond the default installation, discover new software available in the vast universe repository and the extensive Snap Store with the App Center.

- **Contribute**: Ubuntu's spirit thrives on community contribution. Engage in the Ubuntu Discourse or AskUbuntu to help others and learn yourself. Join the Ubuntu Matrix Server or the Ubuntu Hideout on Discord. Report bugs you encounter. If you have development skills, consider contributing code, documentation, or translations.

- **Stay updated**: Understand the difference between **Long-Term Support** (**LTS**) releases for stability and interim releases for the latest features. Keep your system updated for security and performance.

- **Specialized fields**: Explore how Ubuntu is used in specific domains, such as data science, AI/ML development, robotics (ROS), and cloud orchestration (Kubernetes).

Your Ubuntu system is a canvas. Don't hesitate to experiment (perhaps in a virtual machine first!), learn, and make it truly your own.

Figure 19.1 – Ubuntu Developer Summit, Natty Narwhal, Orlando, Florida, USA October 2010 (photo by Sean Sosik-Hamor cc by-sa 2010)

Conclusion: the spirit of Ubuntu

The spirit of the Ubuntu operating system mirrors the open source movement itself: collaboration, transparency, freedom, and shared progress. It's a testament to what can be achieved when a global community works together toward a common goal – creating secure, high-quality, accessible software for everyone.

You become part of this spirit by choosing Ubuntu, using it, learning it, and perhaps even contributing back. You are leveraging the work of thousands, and your feedback and usage help shape its future. It's an operating system built *by* the community, *for* the community.

As you move forward, carry the curiosity and willingness to learn that brought you through this book. Embrace the power and flexibility at your fingertips. Let the spirit of collaboration and continuous improvement that defines the Ubuntu project inspire your own journey in the world of technology. The command line awaits, the desktop is yours to shape, and a world of open source potential is ready to be explored. Happy computing!

Stay Sharp in Cloud and DevOps – Join 44,000+ Subscribers of CloudPro

CloudPro is a weekly newsletter for cloud professionals who want to stay current on the fast-evolving world of cloud computing, DevOps, and infrastructure engineering.

Every issue delivers focused, high-signal content on topics like:

- AWS, GCP & multi-cloud architecture
- Containers, Kubernetes & orchestration
- Infrastructure as Code (IaC) with Terraform, Pulumi, etc.
- Platform engineering & automation workflows
- Observability, performance tuning, and reliability best practices

Whether you're a cloud engineer, SRE, DevOps practitioner, or platform lead, CloudPro helps you stay on top of what matters, without the noise.

Scan the QR code to join for free and get weekly insights straight to your inbox:

https://packt.link/cloudpro

<packt>

packtpub.com

Subscribe to our online digital library for full access to over 7,000 books and videos, as well as industry leading tools to help you plan your personal development and advance your career. For more information, please visit our website.

Why subscribe?

- Spend less time learning and more time coding with practical eBooks and Videos from over 4,000 industry professionals
- Improve your learning with Skill Plans built especially for you
- Get a free eBook or video every month
- Fully searchable for easy access to vital information
- Copy and paste, print, and bookmark content

Did you know that Packt offers eBook versions of every book published, with PDF and ePub files available? You can upgrade to the eBook version at packtpub.com and as a print book customer, you are entitled to a discount on the eBook copy. Get in touch with us at customercare@packtpub.com for more details.

At www.packtpub.com, you can also read a collection of free technical articles, sign up for a range of free newsletters, and receive exclusive discounts and offers on Packt books and eBooks.

Other Books You May Enjoy

If you enjoyed this book, you may be interested in these other books by Packt:

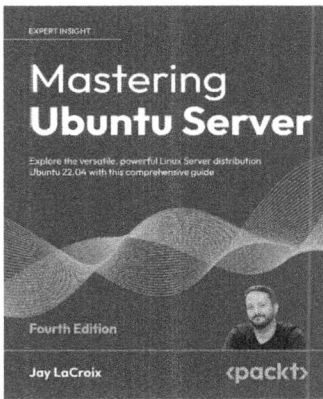

Mastering Ubuntu Server, Fourth Edition

Jay LaCroix

ISBN: 978-1-80323-424-3

- Install Ubuntu Server on physical servers and on the Raspberry Pi
- Deploy Ubuntu Server in the cloud and host websites on your own server
- Deploy your applications to their own containers and scale your infrastructure
- Set up popular applications such as Nextcloud
- Automate deployments and configuration with Ansible to save time
- Containerize applications via LXD to maximize efficiency
- Discover best practices and troubleshooting techniques

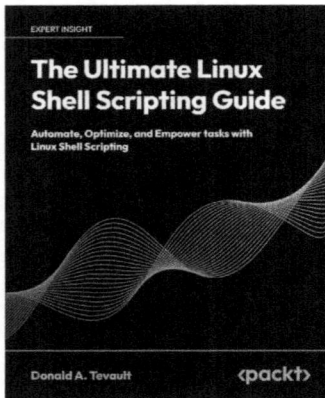

The Ultimate Linux Shell Scripting Guide

Donald A. Tevault

ISBN: 978-1-83546-357-4

- Grasp the concept of shells and explore their diverse types for varied system interactions
- Master redirection, pipes, and compound commands for efficient shell operations
- Leverage text stream filters within scripts for dynamic data manipulation
- Harness functions and build libraries to create modular and reusable shell scripts
- Explore the basic programming constructs that apply to all programming languages
- Engineer portable shell scripts, ensuring compatibility across diverse platforms beyond Linux

Packt is searching for authors like you

If you're interested in becoming an author for Packt, please visit authors.packtpub.com and apply today. We have worked with thousands of developers and tech professionals, just like you, to help them share their insight with the global tech community. You can make a general application, apply for a specific hot topic that we are recruiting an author for, or submit your own idea.

Share your thoughts

Now you've finished *The Ultimate Ubuntu Handbook*, we'd love to hear your thoughts! Scan the QR code below to go straight to the Amazon review page for this book and share your feedback or leave a review on the site that you purchased it from.

https://packt.link/r/183546520X

Your review is important to us and the tech community and will help us make sure we're delivering excellent quality content.

Index

Z

Download a free PDF copy of this book

Thanks for purchasing this book!

Do you like to read on the go but are unable to carry your print books everywhere?

Is your eBook purchase not compatible with the device of your choice?

Don't worry, now with every Packt book you get a DRM-free PDF version of that book at no cost.

Read anywhere, any place, on any device. Search, copy, and paste code from your favorite technical books directly into your application.

The perks don't stop there, you can get exclusive access to discounts, newsletters, and great free content in your inbox daily.

Follow these simple steps to get the benefits:

1. Scan the QR code or visit the link below:

https://packt.link/free-ebook/9781835465202

2. Submit your proof of purchase.
3. That's it! We'll send your free PDF and other benefits to your email directly.

www.ingramcontent.com/pod-product-compliance
Lightning Source LLC
Chambersburg PA
CBHW081048220326
41598CB00038B/7020

* 9 7 8 1 8 3 5 4 6 5 2 0 2 *